Y0-DVA-075

Issues in Psychotherapy

Volume I

Cover design: Robert C. Pryor
Revised index: Leah Kramer

Issues in Psychotherapy

Volume I

WILLIAM G. HERRON
St. John's University

and

SHEILA ROUSLIN
Rutgers, The State University of New Jersey

Oryn Publications, Inc.
Washington, D.C.

Issues in Psychotherapy, Volume I

Library of Congress Cataloging in Publication Data

Herron, William G.
Issues in psychotherapy. Volume I

Includes index.
1. Psychotherapy. 2. Psychotherapists. 3. Psychotherapist and patient. I. Rouslin, Sheila. II. Title.
[DNLM: 1. Psychotherapy. WM 420 H568i]
RC480.H444 1984 616.89'14 84-10408
ISBN 0-916207-00-5

(Formerly ISBN 0-89303-025-2)

Printed in the United States of America

84 85 86 87 88 89 90 10 9 8 7 6 5 4 3 2 1

To

Jane and Aaron

CONTENTS

Introduction

This book evolved through the years from many discussions among the authors and other psychotherapists. While the content varied, the themes of these discussions remained essentially the same. In the practice of psychotherapy, issues are encountered for which the therapist is largely unprepared; the issues are subsequently evaded. This lack of true solution troubles the therapist, because the consequences are potentially far-reaching and deleterious to the therapist and to the patient. Why are some issues in therapy not more completely resolved? There are a number of interrelated reasons.

There are realities in the field of psychotherapy which impede clear solutions. The most obvious and general is the nature of the subject matter, namely human behavior; but, interwoven with the realities is the fact that these issues touch upon the self-involvement, or narcissism, of the therapist—and this often arouses strong reactions.

Many problems have low visibility. When they do come into view, there is a personal, problematic, and controversial quality about them which the therapist might suppress or repress. Unfortunately, the issues themselves are often suppressed or repressed as well. While there are articles and books to some degree concerned with these matters, the issues we will discuss are not the customary and frequently encountered ones of technique, process, and theory addressed in most books on psychotherapy.

We are concerned with ongoing issues that are potential and actual hazards for every practitioner but which are generally ignored. Such a reaction is a hallmark of some disruption in the therapist's self-image.

Any patient problem that is threatening to the therapist is crucial in many ways. They are encountered by most therapists, whether in training, practice, or teaching. They are disturbing and personally discomforting and so are usually avoided. Yet they require as complete a resolution as possible, so that psychotherapy may continue effectively. So far, however, the resolutions are much too idiosyncratic, and too often hardly meet a criterion of really solving the issue. Such a situation provides little or no assistance to the general field of psychotherapy or to most psychotherapists. It also results in a great deal of ineffective, even damaging "therapeutic" encounters because the therapist really does not want to consider what may be happening.

While one can be sympathetic to the results of having an issue arise between the therapist and the client, no purpose is served, and much harm may be done by simultaneously wishing the problem did not exist, and then making the wish come true by going on with the therapy as though there were no issue. Many issues are unconsciously ignored and so do not come into the therapist's awareness, while others are treated with far less significance than they deserve. Most therapists *intend* to be effective, but the burying of personally distressing issues, of which the patient may be aware in varying degrees, is not doing the job well. The therapist retains his or her narcissistic composure while the therapy suffers or collapses.

Therapists learn to expect that patients will be difficult from time to time. They also realize that, depending on a variety of factors, such behavior can be a sign of progress or a problem for the therapy. What therapists do not expect are their own difficulties connected with being psychotherapists, and they are reluctant to look at these openly. We are not suggesting that therapists do not engage in self-examination. Quite the contrary; and if the therapist's orientation is psychoanalytic, many of the issues would involve countertransference, which is certainly supposed to be resolved by the therapist. Other orientations have different ways of conceptualizing the therapist's reactions. Of course all have considerable latitude with regard to determining just what is and is not a "therapeutic reaction." But more important, the issues, in whole or in part, can go unrecognized, or the self-examination process, whatever it may be called, can be merely descriptive rather than an explanation leading to constructive action. The point is that there is serious neglect, and therapists are reluctant to do enough about it. So, while narcissism is a prominent topic in the literature on psychopathology and treatment, it is the *patient's* narcissism and self-absorption that get most of the attention, not the *therapist's*.

We are by no means removed from the natural reluctance to engage in self-examination. Writing this book involved a considerable and continual struggle with that reluctance. Yet we are convinced that frank and open discussion of troublesome issues is essential to the effectiveness of the psychotherapies. As practicing psychotherapists for more than the past 20 years, we are increasingly attuned to the problems all therapists face. They may be ashamed, perplexed, disturbed, lonely, angry, and a host of other unpleasant states. These problems need to be solved for, or by, the therapists, yet their training has not really prepared them to do this, regardless of their parent disciplines or orientations. The thrust of the field of psychotherapy has been that such problems ought not to arise. If they do, which of course is the case, it is the therapist's responsibility largely on her or his own, to somehow get rid of them.

"Somehow" is very vague. For example, supervisors often point out problems to their supervisees, and then offer as the potential solution, "Work that out in your own analysis." Well, what if the "working out" takes a long time, or is only partial or does not occur at all? What happens to the therapist, the patient, and the therapy during this attempted "working out?" As another example, a well known analyst has stated that in regard to therapist behavior, "rudeness has no place in psychoanalytic therapy." But what if the analyst is indeed rude, and not just once, and has repeated difficulties in changing such behavior?

These examples are indicative of the issues we explore in this book, namely the insecurities, misunderstandings, and perplexing motivations coexisting with such positive and welcomed therapist qualities as empathy, dedication, and well-timed interventions. We focus on behaviors and events that are "not supposed to happen" in psychotherapy, yet do, and we talk about what therapists can do when such painful things occur.

Our presentation is an intermingling of personal experience and clinical and research literature, and has at its core the conception of narcissism in the personality of every therapist, and how that may be misused, or it is hoped, made effective. In broad terms, the *self* of the therapist appears to be the issue that could spawn all the issues, and could resolve them.

As the book was conceived we felt its impact would be greatest if we limited ourselves to a certain number of issues that struck us as particularly in need of attention. They are not thought of as the only issues of significance, nor do we believe that all therapists would select them as the most important issues to be discussed. What we do believe, however, is that they are indeed important issues for *all* therapists, and that most therapists have had, or will have, their struggles with them. These are also issues for therapists of all disciplines and persuasions, but not all therapists will agree with our statements. In that sense the book is designed to be provocative. We hope all therapists will read this and think more about how they use themselves, and wonder if indeed they could become more effective, even if their way is not ours. We also welcome the responses of therapists to our contentions.

The issues discussed are definition of psychotherapy, aims of psychotherapy, behavior of the therapist, occupational hazards, therapists' narcissism, contracts, therapists' termination motives, therapists' fantasies, personal meanings of being in private practice, and what is personally involved in being a "good" psychotherapist. The presentation changes as the book proceeds, in accord with the content covered and the discussion of the appropriate use of the therapist's self. The first three chapters are deliberately more formal, with considerable use made of empirical research, because it is available and appropriate to the subject matter. A balanced presentation is preferred over a primarily subjective conception. In these areas there is considerable material upon which to draw, and we combine empirical and clinical data to make inferences. It is clear in these first three chapters that there are problems appearing to be outside the therapist's obvious control. These problems make definition, goal description, and patient-therapist interaction difficult. The patient is one of these "outside" factors that can prohibit or prevent solution, and this deserves appropriate recognition. It suits certain therapist needs to "not be that concerned," and to take as inevitable reality what they could have a more prominent role in changing.

The fourth chapter is more personalized and informal, making greater use of clinical opinion and experience, yet maintaining a continuity with the evidence as compiled in the preceding chapters.

At this point we will describe what is covered in the book, thus illustrating the particulars of our total conception. This should enable the reader to understand why we began where we did, where we are going in the development of the book, and our hoped-for conclusion, stimulating a definite improvement in the quality of psychotherapy through the medium of changing therapists' perceptions and actions.

Our starting point is that the field in its very essence, its definition, is tentative. Our concern is that many therapists do not like to face this inexactitude, so that efforts to alter it are inhibited. Some feel it has a universal definition, and therefore there is no problem, while others embrace the vagueness as a method of protecting themselves from responsibilities to their clients. Therapists must learn to define what they do.

Another concern is that definitions of psychotherapy, particulary if they find their way into legislation and/or insurance contracts, tend to designate *who* are the psychotherapists more precisely than what is involved in the process of psychotherapy. The control aspect of such designation is enormous, and all the disciplines have become embroiled in struggling to be designated as a provider of psychotherapy. With people coming out of the woodwork to call themselves psychotherapists, it is obvious that standards of competence are essential. But psychotherapy is not the fiefdom of a single discipline and there is no value in chauvinism by profession in this field. The solution is in the creation of an independent profession of psychotherapy.

Of course that lies in the future, and we are in the present. Although the problems of defining psychotherapy are quite visible, psychotherapists *must* define it. Our thrust is to recognize the problems of definition, yet also show that some definition is necessary. All therapists must be prepared to understand and to explain to their clients what it is they actually do. In turn therapists then need to integrate the probable narcissistic injury such explanation can bring, rather than hiding with dexterity when it comes to the very basic issues.

The next issue, which clients often voice as their major concern, is whether therapy will help them? Therapists have to be more exact in regard to what the patient can expect by entering into psychotherapy, which is also a problem inextricably linked to definition. We first discuss in general terms the categories of the psychotherapies and their goals, and we move from that to the very large body of research on the effects of psychotherapy. We synthesize the results of the research efforts, while repeatedly making the point that all psychotherapists ought to pay more attention to research results. Our conclusion is that indeed psychotherapies affect clients, but not always positively, or the way the clients thought when they started, and certainly not all of the time. Many therapists find such a conclusion unappealing, and so will ignore the research results or seize on certain aspects to get rid of particular clients in the name of "good therapy." We stress the need for therapists to allow research results to appropriately influence their work, which generally they seem not to do, and the need for relative specificity of treatment, which is also often ignored unless the therapist is looking for a way to avoid treating a patient.

We raise the question of what makes therapy effective, and consider what a number of the major schools of therapy claim they can and will do for patients.

Stress is placed on society's growing demand for accountability and the therapist's need to be as specific as possible with the particular client about what may or may not happen as the result of any designated course of psychotherapy. We conclude with our own explanations to our clients of the aims of our type of psychotherapy. In the process of discussions about goals, we make repeated notice of the role of the therapist, which becomes the subject matter for Chapter III.

Here the relative degree of importance of various therapist behaviors is discussed, based on synthesizing the empirical research on therapist variables. These include personality factors and demographic factors, such as race, sex, and social class, as well as the matching of patients and therapists. In particular we discern the positive effect of the good psychological health of the therapist. We then consider ways in which some therapists exploit their clients, and we muse about the fit, or lack of it, between the therapist's professed theory and actual practice. Thus foundations are established for the discussion of therapist behavior, and a number of interrelated occupational hazards can be considered.

In so doing one operates more out of an experiential base than a research one. There is a central narcissistic dynamic underlying the image of the therapist as a person, an expression of his or her selfhood as the therapist wishes it to be felt and perceived. For all psychotherapists, the "doing" of psychotherapy always involves certain problems, most of which have certainly received very limited attention, in research or otherwise. First we look at what the therapist brings to the therapy, and from this conclude that the doing of therapy affects therapists in various ways that definitely merit attention and remediation rather than the more usual varieties of resignation and accommodation to their presence. Our focus is on therapist fatigue, the therapist's relationships outside of therapy, and therapists' attitudes about money. We stress the need for a greater understanding of the "hard work" of being a therapist, using examples of our own experiences in these areas.

We have provided evidence for the confirmation of a personality constellation of most therapists that so frequently entraps them. This is the general occupational hazard of narcissism, and we focus on this in Chapter V. We particularly demonstrate its operation in the obsessional personality, which is common among psychotherapists. The concept of narcissism is a recognizable and understandable one to therapists of all orientations, but it tends to be most often used as a psychodynamic construct; and so our explanation of its operations is primarily in psychoanalytic terminology. The therapist's behaviors can be features of his or her narcissism, illustrated through such activities and feelings as control, fear, anger, ambivalence, detachment, and demanding helpfulness. After identifying the problem and considering clinical examples, we raise the possibility of a "healthy narcissism" in the therapeutic relationship.

The range of narcissism, and in a broad sense, how the therapist can relate to the patient, brings us, in Chapter VI, to the issue of how therapists and patients "contract" to have a certain relationship. Contracts do exist, with their assets and liabilities, but our particular concern is the distinction between rational and irrational contracts. Most of the material contained in the literature has been with the former, while the irrational contract, which we consider the more influential for the course of therapy, has often been overlooked. We stress the need for its recognition, giving examples, and work our way into the useful conception of a "therapist—patient" alliance operating in the service of the therapy, yet largely unconscious. We discuss the appropriate recognition and use of this alliance, as well as harmful misconceptions by therapists about contracts.

In Chapter VII we face a controversial possibility resulting from one or more of the therapist's narcissistic manifestations. When we discussed the fact of an alliance we implicitly raised the question of the ending of the therapist-patient relationship by the therapist. Of course therapists and patients both make decisions about the ending of therapy, but our interest lies in why therapists terminate the process. It is often for reasons of the therapist's that are not necessarily related to the health or improvement of the patient. Perhaps for many therapists and their patients, therapy would be best conceptualized as having an unlimited duration. Countertransferential elements, the particular brand of therapist needs filling a great part of his or her fantasy, become striking in our consideration of the therapist's motivations for termination. They then take us into the broader territory of the therapist's fantasies, which is the subject matter of Chapter VIII.

Here we connect the concepts of narcissism, fantasy, and countertransference. The last concept gets a large amount of our specific attention, though within the framework of fantasy, particularly narcissistic fantasy. First we consider the therapist's ability to be aware of personal fantasies, and then the role of fantasy in countertransference. There is a general outline of the development and definition of countertransference, illustrating its application with clinical examples, plus a useful classification of countertransference responses. Then we move into the more general use of therapist's fantasy in psychotherapy. The need for an increased recognition of this is pointed out, which leads to Chapter IX where fantasy and fact may or may not match each other, but fantasy is certainly prominent. The dynamics and pragmatics of the private practice of psychotherapy are discussed.

The main concern in Chapter IX is with the relatively neglected area of the therapist's psychodynamics in regard to practicing psychotherapy independently. Pragmatic issues are mentioned, but to illustrate personal, intrapsychic concerns of the therapist, since these are the principal issue. Such a focus is consistent with the central role played by narcissism and its derivatives. The movement into private practice by therapists can be conceptualized in developmental terms, particularly through understanding the symbiotic bond and separation-individuation phases as they originally occur, and as they are repeated throughout the therapist's life. The problems of narcissism as indicated in specific manifestations of anxiety, aggression, and guilt appearing as the therapist enters private practice are discussed. These feelings are seen as inevitable, and we stress the need for recognizing and managing them effectively, and indicate some possibilities for doing this. Such discussion leads to the necessity of a true self-accountability, which is an integral ingredient of healthy narcissism. We then move into Chapter X where views on the "good" therapist are offered.

At this point of the book, the last chapter, we briefly summarize the issues discussed. Our conceptualization of the good therapist is a relative one, namely an effective person who is "good enough," and we amplify our conception of healthy narcissism to show how that is a major element in the identity of the good therapist. The increasing concern with narcissism in the psychotherapeutic field could bode well for the improvement of the field, provided sufficient emphasis is given to the narcissism of the therapists. In this vein there are a number of ways to develop the reality of the concept of the good therapist. These propositions are the effective creation of a profession of psychotherapy, an appropriate integration of research and practice, and especially the incisive, yet expanded development of the self of the therapist. This last proposition requires significant concern with the therapist's value systems, cognitive activities, and personal/interpersonal behaviors. These matters have been addressed before, but they have been neglected, to the detriment of all concerned. Such neglect is certainly not in the best interest of therapists. Our concerns are not without precedent, though we address them in a rather unique way. Our hope is that the concerns are universal, and that numerous clinicians from all disciplines involved in psychotherapy will read this book. We then hope they will develop a new awareness leading to beneficial changes for the therapists and their patients.

Acknowledgments

While we collaborated on this book, speaking as a definite "we," the acknowledgments will be best expressed in an individual way. So, first Sheila Rouslin will express her gratitude, and then William G. Herron will express his.

After finishing the book I found myself reflecting on how it came into being. In the process it became clear that there were a number of persons involved, directly or indirectly. I am indebted to my coauthor, who knew me well enough to properly time a proposal that we write together what we had been formulating independently for a number of years. For that I am grateful, and also for the realization throughout the writing that indeed we knew and respected each other's unconscious more than we had consciously considered. It was and is an unspoken communication, and our friendship has deepened because of the experience.

I will be forever grateful to my mentor, Hildegard E. Peplau, who set the example of rigorous scholarship and clinical expertise. In so doing she influenced my entire career. She was one of the first and only persons who knew what to do with my rebelliousness and intellectual curiosity. At about the same time, I met Joseph Geller, who was to become my analyst and my friend. I have been guided by his unusual perception, his unending patience (except when it ends), and his beautifully complex, obsessional mind. Truly, without his "good enough" mothering and provision of a flexible "holding environment" I would have been unable to find and harness those qualities I brought to him. In addition, in many ways, for years he has lived through the material in this book with me.

Clearly, without patients and parents this book could not have been written. For their complex contribution to my learning and my emotional development I am indebted, sometimes in convoluted ways. I like to think they may benefit from my growing understanding of our human condition. I would especially like to thank Aaron Welt, my partner and friend, who has taught me so much about intimate relationships. He has groaned and grown with me through the writing of this book.

Sheila Rouslin, October 1980
Ridgewood and Morristown, New Jersey

Despite my conceptions, without Sheila the book would never have come into being. For her special way of accomplishing this I will always be glad, and I eagerly look forward to our next book together.

I am certainly appreciative of the support of St. John's University which provided a research leave so that I could write. I am grateful to those who have been, and continue to be, my patients, for they constantly show me what psychotherapy is really about. Also, a major influence in whatever I do and have done is my therapist and friend of many years now, Jules Barron. He knows what this is all about.

My experience in the Adelphi University postdoctoral program has had a profound effect on my views, and I thank the many people there who worked with me. I particularly single out my friends and colleagues, Julius Trubowitz, Irwin Sollinger, and Thomas Kinter, as well as William Johnson who aroused my interest in going there. I also have profound respect for my supervisors at Adelphi, namely Donald Milman, Kenneth Fisher, Alfred Berl, and Matthew Besdine.

Finally, my special and unparalleled gratitude goes to my wife, Mary Jane Herron. She taught me how to live.

William G. Herron, October 1980
Woodcliff Lake, New Jersey, and Jamaica, New York

About the Authors

WILLIAM G. HERRON received his Ph.D. degree in clinical psychology from Fordham University and is a graduate of the Adelphi University postdoctoral program in psychotherapy and psychoanalysis. He is a Professor in the Department of Psychology at St. John's University, Jamaica, New York, and in private practice in Woodcliff Lake, New Jersey. He is the coauthor of *Reactive and Process Schizophrenia* and *Contemporary School Psychology*.

SHEILA ROUSLIN earned her M.S. degree in psychiatric nursing from Rutgers University. Currently she is in private practice in New Jersey. She is a lecturer at Rutgers, The State University of New Jersey, on the Editorial Board of the *Journal of Psychosocial Nursing and Mental Health Services*, and the coauthor of *Group Psychotherapy in Nursing Practice*.

About the Authors

I

At Issue: What Is Psychotherapy?

INTRODUCTION

When conceptualizing psychotherapy, a phrase that comes to mind is "psychotherapy has it all." Unfortunately, that phrase is not an unequivocal positive. What "all" translates to is that the practice of psychotherapy has joys and sorrows, rewards and punishments, reliefs and burdens, as well as critics and adherents. Furthermore, those polarities are merely the beginning of pointing out how good and bad it all is.

Fundamental to this complex of dualities is the pointed fact that there is no satisfactory definition of psychotherapy. Existing imperfect definitions, which are the only kind available, are the genesis of numerous negative and positive aspects of psychotherapy in action.

The negative aspects are the more glaring, of course, particularly something as basic as the lack of a definition. Many people have what seems a customary belief that a definition is a given expectation for both practitioner and client. Belatedly, people discover the true state of their expectation; it can only be fulfilled in part, and often unsatisfactorily. For the real state of definition in this field is such that if practitioners and their clients, for whatever reason, have to explain in precise terms just what they are doing, they are at a bit of a loss. The limits of explanation are then something with which they must contend. This means they have to guess, grapple, and grope in an attempt to make sense of whatever is occurring under the label, psychotherapy.

Confusion is not all bad, however. Far from it. The first point is that the imprecision of the term psychotherapy is a very basic issue to be faced. Yet it has not been faced. The fact that people keep coming to us despite the murkiness surrounding us, and them, lessens our incentive to concern ourselves with definition. We sort of know what to do, since we do it, and our patients sort of know because it happens to them. That is not good enough, even when such obscurity has certain satisfactions for all parties concerned. Therapists must increase the honesty factor about what is known and what is not known. After all, many definitions of psychotherapy have been proposed. So, a look at a representative sample is certainly in order as a starting point— to illustrate the nature and scope of the task at hand.

After considering the definitions, and seeing the problems involved, we will trace the cause of the problem through the development of psychotherapy—in the main seeing its enormous, confusing expansion—and move from that to the question of whether a definition of any utility can be created. The major attempts to do this have been through exploring a possible unifying concept for psychotherapies. The difficulties inherent in this are also illustrated.

There is another common approach, that is, sticking to a particular psychotherapy, with the smallest possible deviations. Admittedly there is no purity even in this, since "deviations" do occur, but psychoanalytic and behavioral therapies are used as homogeneous cases in point. Neither gets high marks for clarity. At the same time, there are the possible advantages of faith in the specific process for both therapist and client, and the probability of making some inroads into definition via specificity.

Finally, we explore the issue of competence, suggesting the formation of a profession of psychotherapy, and offering our own imperfect explanation of psychotherapy.

DEFINITIONS

Polatin, in 1966, attempted to provide a road map for treating psychiatric disorders, in which specific disorders were to be matched with specific therapies. In the process he offered the following definition: "Psychotherapy is a form of treatment in psychiatry relying essentially on the verbal communication between therapist and patient and on the interaction between the personalities of therapist and patient in a dynamic interpersonal relationship, whereby maladaptive behavior is altered toward a more effective adaptation, relief of symptoms occurs, and insights are developed" (p. 41).

What is unsatisfactory about this definition? First, there is marked disagreement in the field as to whether the techniques in psychotherapy should be considered "treatment," or "education." Then, "in psychiatry" is a restrictive phrase implying at the least that psychiatrists are the vast majority of the stockholders in the psychotherapy corporation. At the most, this highlights the controversy about who indeed is a psychotherapist (as opposed, some would say, to who should be a psychotherapist). By law in New York state, as one illustration, a number of major groups of professionals are licensed to do psychotherapy, independently, which is the key word. Psychiatry is only one of these groups.

The emphasis on verbal communication could be disputed because it excludes nonverbal procedures. Also, words such as "interaction," "dynamic," and "maladaptive" are subject to a number of interpretations of their meanings. Finally, the goals of adaptation, symptom relief, and insight could be argued as to both meaning and scope.

Admittedly this definition was proposed in 1966 and we are looking at it from the perspective of another fourteen years of the ongoing development of the field. These years have not made the definition unrecognizable, yet it certainly would not now get anything approaching universal acceptance, nor would it have even in the sixties. In a recent attempt at tracing the history of psychotherapy, Ehrenwald (1976) broadly depicts it as mental healing. In historical order this includes magic, philosophy, religion, and science, with overlaps in approximations in the time frame, and, currently, psychosocial components that mitigate the emphasis in a scientific approach aimed at rational insight. The problem of definition is painfully evident in the preface of Ehrenwald's extensive book. He states: "Psychotherapy on the contemporary scene seems headed in all directions at once" (1976, p. 5).

If anything, it used to be easier to define because there was less knowledge and less variety. Orne recognizes this in attempting to describe psychotherapy for the *American Handbook of Psychiatry*. He even begins by asserting that, "It is fair to ask why psychotherapy (which after all is often described as old as man himself) has failed to develop a readily transmitted body of cumulative knowledge that can ensure the competence of its average practitioner" (p. 4).

He then substantiates the difficulty of having an "acceptable" definition. While citing a number of definitions, his conclusion is that all are inadequate, based either on their overinclusiveness or on their failure to make essential distinctions. In practice he sees psychotherapy as being used in a broad sense, which includes a host of "treatment" procedures, and in a more circumscribed way. The latter is considered the majority viewpoint by Orne, and "refers to a method designed to alleviate specific difficulties through the use of specific therapeutic procedures practiced by highly skilled professionals" (p. 7).

This is a relatively safe definition, imparting general information that is accurate, but the use of "highly skilled professionals" would be met with some arguments. First, there are the supporters of the peer self-help psychotherapy movement who want to eliminate professionals, and are part of a somewhat larger movement to deprofessionalize psychotherapy. Then, there is considerable disagreement among the professionals themselves as to what constitutes "highly skilled." This is a crucial concern, as illustrated by Orne's comment that "psychotherapy is defined more by *who* does it—by the role relationship and the training of the therapist" (p. 5).

Wolberg (1977), in his third edition of the comprehensive *Technique of Psychotherapy*, offers this definition, "Psychotherapy is the treatment, by psychological means, of problems of an emotional nature in which a trained person deliberately establishes a professional relationship with the patient with the object of (1) removing, modifying, or retarding existing symptoms, (2) mediating disturbed patterns of behavior, and (3) promoting positive personality growth and development" (p. 3).

As with the other definitions, this also has limitations. Wolberg admits the need for elaboration, and attempts it with regard to "treatment," "psychological means," "problems of an emotional nature," and most of the other components of the definition. Yet in so doing he espouses definite points of view that are not universally accepted, for example, the elimination of somatic modalities as forms of psychotherapy, or stressing the emotional nature of problems in contrast to emphasizing social factors.

While preferring his own definition to other ones, he nonetheless lists thirty-six other possibilities that reflect disagreement on technique, process, goals, and personnel. Thus a sampling of definitions indeed verifies the point made earlier regarding the unsatisfactory nature of any existing definition of psychotherapy. The next question: Why such a problem?

THE DEVELOPMENT OF PSYCHOTHERAPY

It seems accurate to date the beginnings of "formal" psychotherapy (or "scientific" psychotherapy, or what most professionals would call psychotherapy today) in the nineteenth century with the advent of psychoanalysis. At that time psychotherapy was a fairly circumscribed entity in terms of most of its components—treatment procedures, treatment agents, and problems to be treated. But it did not stay that way.

Instead, growth in a number of areas occurred, more or less at the same time, although they tend to be interdependent. There was a marked increase in therapeutic tactics, moving from hypnosis and free association to the addition of virtually hundreds of different procedures designed to produce behavioral changes. Along with this, the range of problems to which psychotherapy was applied increased. First the type-of symptom problems expanded from one neurosis to character problems and psychoses. Since then, there has been a trend to help the healthy be healthier, so that in a sense psychotherapy became applicable to anyone who wanted to attempt a personality change.

Accompanying these expansions was an increase in the number of disciplines producing people who were considered psychotherapists. Regardless of background, many workers in human service systems used psychotherapeutic procedures and, in differing fashions, practiced psychotherapy. Of course, the proliferation of methods, problems to be worked upon, and workers also involved theoretical differences. There have been numerous conceptions of human development, psychopathology, and the most effective treatment procedures.

The expansion continues on all fronts, with not much left behind. Along with the increase in numbers of procedures, kinds of problems, types of therapists, and theoretical conceptions, there has been a distinct rise in confusion as to what psychotherapy is, other than a code name for the psychotherapies, which in turn is another code name for a heterogeneous grouping of theories and procedures also having more code names. The current practice of psychotherapy is a diverse process, applied to a host of life issues by a legion of practitioners with varied backgrounds, theoretical rationales, and goals. What constitutes success is up for grabs in numerous instances (as is what constitutes failure).

As noted earlier, there are some advantages to all this diversity. Since living is in itself a complex process, the complexity of psychotherapy tends to have a certain complementarity to the very problems and people that are its subject. While there are indeed those who like simple solutions, there are also many people who do not. Psychotherapy as a complicated art form can have its own mysterious appeal to both practitioner and client. In essence, a reasonableness is at the same time attached to its ambiguities, for living is often like that, making less than perfect sense.

Also, there is the "cop-out" or "readiness" factor, which means that considering the state of the psychotherapeutic art right now, it is hard to establish accountability for results. What precisely does "getting better" mean? If indeed there is a behavioral change, to whom or to what is it due? At the moment it is both easy to avoid responsibility and to take credit for the therapist and the client in respect to any given event. Sometimes such a state of affairs makes life easier for all concerned.

We are not touting these advantages, but they do exist. In facing them we can include complexity, conflict, and confusion in our list of realities and still realize there is a marked need to define psychotherapy more clearly than the way many, if not most of us, have been doing. After all, the distinct probability exists of a circular effect in which the original definition deficiencies foster confusion, which increases the difficulty of arriving at a subsequent adequate explanation.

THE FIELD OF PSYCHOTHERAPY

A logical next question is: Considering all this heterogeneity, what are the possibilities of ultimately producing a unifying, comprehensible definition of psychotherapy? By now there appears to be general recognition, if not acceptance, that there are indeed the *psychotherapies,* and in this regard a number of authors attempt to define psychotherapy through a search for similarities (most psychotherapies having already pronounced their differences from each other). That this borders on a Herculean task is apparent in a recent survey citing the existence of 130 psychotherapies, with at least one more appearing on the scene each year (Parloff, 1976).

Most synthesizers narrow this approach on various grounds—as probable obsolescence, or overlap, or incompleteness of particular therapies. Nonetheless, it is a formidable undertaking. For example, Patterson (1966) divided the field into five different general approaches. These were rational, learning theory, psychoanalytic, perceptual-phenomenological, and existential, each with its own subdivisions. In so doing, the common elements he perceived are a belief in the capability of clients to change, an awareness that the patients' problems are painful, and a belief that such states should be changed, as well as the expectation that future consequences will influence present behavior. With regard to the process of therapy, there is the use of an interview situation involving verbal interaction, and certain characteristics of both therapists and clients which all appeared to share. Therapists were pictured as having genuine interest and concern for their clients, as well as strong desires to be helpful as change agents. Therapists accepted and respected the individuality of their clients, were sincere in their approaches, committed to their theories and methods, and expected their clients to change as a result of the therapy.

The patients revealed suffering, the presence of problems, and the motivation to change. Thus, the clients also believed change was possible and expected it to occur. Finally, patients were active in the process of attempting to change. Therefore, all approaches seemed to show clients needing help, recognizing the need, believing change could occur through the medium of the therapy, and participating actively in the process.

There are a number of questionable points in this collection of similarities, starting with the variability of some of the elements, such as the belief in change and the commitment to theory in terms of actual practice. It is possible to easily mitigate a number of these assumptions with a certain amount of cynicism. For example, the client's belief in her or his ability to change, and in the power of the therapy, are ideals of psychotherapy, not automatic facts. The possibility also exists that certain psychotherapists do what they do out of habit, and patients participate out of fear rather than hope. And some therapists are more interested in being perceived as helpers than actually thinking they know how to be helpful. Thus a more accurate picture of our profession must include these aspects in counterpoint to overvaluing the people and the process.

In particular, when Patterson (1966) glorifies the therapist-patient relationship as the integrative essence of psychotherapy, he is working with only part of the evidence about success and failure in psychotherapy. (This is an issue we will explore further in the next chapter.) He is also not considering the many people who must use "extratherapeutic" agents to recover, since they never had any formal psychotherapy. These ingredients, which are apparently therapeutic and can or do exist in therapy, as well as the role of theory, are given insufficient attention.

There is also the problem of what the words used to describe the similarities mean when any attempt is made to translate them into specific behaviors for specific clients. This problem of meaning continually plagues any attempt to define psychotherapy and increases with the attempts to cross from one psychotherapy to another and describe commonalities.

For example, Patterson believes that one of the unifying aspects of the goals of the psychotherapies can be described as the self-actualization of the patient, yet he admits this self-actualization could be considered subjective and vague. Nonetheless, he holds out hope for the possibility of describing the concept in terms of behavior. One would like to share both the hope in and efforts toward such a possibility, but realizing such things as self-actualization, and another of his goals—openness to experience—is extremely difficult. Personality words have neither the exactness nor the catholicity of words such as "triangle" or "square." Instead, personality words, which are the verbiage of the psychotherapies, have variable meanings, depending on individuals and on situations. Often, to be understood we are compelled to restrict our definition, to make it more of a specific than the generality we might desire.

Urban and Ford (1971) appear more realistic in their attempts, admitting the basic question of whether a definable field of psychotherapy even exists. However, they recognize the existing categorization of diverse activities under the psychotherapy rubric, and speculate that this is due to a continuing belief in the relationship of the procedures. As they say, interrelationships "ought" to exist. The problem is simply discovering them.

All the psychotherapeutic approaches are viewed as understanding aspects of humans operating within social settings. All methods want to make some modification in behavior, and most seem to have some success. Urban and Ford believe there are fundamental relationships resulting in a unity that could be identified and validated, though this has not yet been accomplished.

Furthermore, they state: "It is not too strong a statement to assert that this 'field' we are dealing with is a multifaceted, heterogeneous aggregate of conflicting, competing, segmented and unarticulated versions of theories, practices, practitioners, and researchers" (1971, p. 6).

Nonetheless, they offer one possibility for synthesis in which psychotherapy is defined in terms of problem-solving. This model involves as a first step the identification of the problem. It is categorized in behavioral concepts whose parameters—as severity, frequency, and others—are then explored. The aim is to articulate what is amiss, and that requires effective classification of human behavioral difficulties. Thus, we need a way to conceptually relate apparently discrete viewpoints and to cross disciplinary boundaries. So far we do not have such a schema. Assuming one could be developed, the next step would be to conceptualize the reasons for the problem behavior. Therapists need theories, and while many therapists do have them, what they also have are many theories. There does seem to be agreement as to the multiple determination of human behavior, but theories are often mere parts, even if very significant of the whole. Conceptual integration has not occurred, and the existing models are not sufficient.

The evidence is no more satisfying with regard to other parts of the problem-solving model as a definition for psychotherapy. Goal selection, implementation, and evaluation all involve controversy and current limitations. As a result the problem-solving definition of psychotherapy has to be classified as a possibility whose day has not yet come, and there are probably those who still might not even like the name of the model. At the same time, the desire for a conceptual synthesis appears to prevail in the "field" of psychotherapy.

Wolberg (1977) considers the psychotherapies to have more in common than is claimed by their apparent methodologies. He brings them together by conceptualizing the approaches as communications forms providing avenues for similar processes of influencing people. He is particularly interested in the unity of successful psychotherapies. Three main categories are suggested. These are the relationship, reward-punishment and cognitive restructuring approaches.

While their manifest descriptions certainly differ, their unity is pictured in the observation that they deal with basically the same processes. These involve nonspecific therapeutic elements, therapist's personality, reinforcement of certain responses, and cognitive change. The nonspecific therapeutic factors include placebo, catharsis, and suggestion, among other possibilities that are not the primary aim of the therapies in most cases, yet can and do occur. Of course their occurrence is variable as is their degree of helpfulness.

Regarding the therapist's personality, there is a more planned though nonetheless varied activity. Therapists convey to the client the possibilities for feeling liked, respected, and understood, as well as the probability of being helped. This general approach involves positive, selective response reinforcement and degrees of cognitive restructuring.

This rather broad designation places heavy emphasis on the therapist and essentially on the therapeutic relationship. In that sense it is akin to Patterson's approach, yet somewhat unique in its incorporation of extratherapeutic agents as a part of any therapeutic process. Again, the terms used pose the problem of their own uncertain definitions. Furthermore, the ingredients of the Wolberg similarities description are supposed to be the ingredients of "successful" psychotherapy. Successful therapy is even more difficult to define by consensus than psychotherapy regardless of outcome. Nonetheless, were it possible to identify successful and unsuccessful therapies with greater consistency, some useful narrowing of the concept of psychotherapy could take place. At least to be designated as psychotherapy one of the characteristics of the approach would have to be some *known* success potential (as opposed to "claimed" success potential).

Recently, Prochaska (1979) took his turn at it, with a comparative analysis of seventeen systems of therapy. The systems he addressed were psychoanalysis, ego psychology, psychoanalytically oriented psychotherapy, existential analysis, logotherapy, reality therapy, client-centered therapy, gestalt therapy, Adlerian therapy, rational-emotive therapy, transactional analysis, character analysis, vegotherapy, bioenergetics, primal therapy, implosive therapy, and behavior therapy. He proposes an integrative, eclectic theory with five basic processes of change which are viewed as emphasizing similarities across systems.

The first change factor is consciousness raising, which involves making the patient aware of experiential or environmental information of which he or she was not aware previously. Then emotional release, the making of choices, changes in conditional stimuli, and contingency control are described as the other basic processes. Actually, Prochaska points out that verbal therapies have stressed consciousness raising, catharsis, and choosing, while action or behavioral therapies have emphasized conditional stimuli and contingencies. He in turn suggests an integrative model combining the two approaches, but that is scarcely an appropriate, encompassing definition for the varieties of the psychotherapies, since they all do not do these things. His transtheoretical approach is at best a relative one in which he stresses the frequency of a process across therapies while admitting to greater divergence of content focused upon, due to the multiplicity of theoretical orientations. The presentation is not a particularly convincing case for the universal core of the therapies, nor for the possibility of a transtheoretical therapy.

What remains then are a number of attempts to define psychotherapy as an entity through its probable common elements. Unfortunately these attempts have their limitations. If we are very general, we are less prone to obvious errors, but the utility and exactness of the definition are reduced. For example, psychotherapy is a means to change behavior, administered by a professional. And so are torture, boxing, and prostitution (if you are willing to give a little on the definition of professional which psychotherapists usually have in mind). What would indeed be helpful would be a generally agreed-upon definition of psychotherapy which clearly specifies objectives, techniques to accomplish these, and methods to evaluate progress, all in a very lucid language. Lacking such a definition, which we certainly do, the question still remains. How best may we handle explaining what psychotherapy is?

One possibility, and next to be examined, is to define only one school of psychotherapy—ours (or yours)—and rule out the others as not really capable of an acceptable definition (as well as earnestly believing that this is just the beginning of what other psychotherapies lack). The question is, if we stay away from eclecticism on any grand scale, and instead adhere to a specialty, as psychoanalysis or behavior therapy, explaining ourselves and the process in that language, will we be more effective in making a realistic, comprehensible presentation?

That question is asked with two realities in mind. The fact is that only relative eclecticism is possible for most therapists anyway, because there is too much to know to be proficient at all the available forms of psychotherapy. We are forced to have at least a focus or be inept at a multitude of approaches beyond the most simplistic. So, some kind of major theoretical and technical orientation is undoubtedly the case for most therapists, and this means they will tend to define psychotherapy in terms of that orientation.

At the same time, it is hard to be a purist in this field (and the value of such is questionable). So, we will discuss relative specificity and theoretical adherence, as well as the frequent divergence of practices from what theoretical pronouncements could lead one to expect. Nonetheless, there are the stated proponents of a particular school of psychotherapy, and their relative commitment is our next possibility for exploration.

SPECIFIC PSYCHOTHERAPIES

Probably the most dominant professed orientation of psychotherapists is psychoanalytic. An appropriate description of what this means in regard to psychotherapy is provided by Langs (1973, 1974), who conceptualizes psychotherapy as aimed at alleviating emotional problems appearing in the forms of symptoms, affective disruptions, and behavioral difficulties. The psychoanalytic conception translates these into the language of intrapsychic conflict and ego dysfunction, with insight-oriented psychoanalytic psychotherapy aiming at what are termed structural alterations.

This means that intrapsychic conflicts as methods of resolution are discovered and defined, with a focus on how the methods have failed and how new solutions are developed. This is accomplished through the patient-therapist relationship and the interventions of the therapist. Psychoanalytic psychotherapy offers the possibility of a change in the totality of the person, that is, new self-experiences which can result in different integrations and forms of relatedness. The resolution of conflict is through insight and structural change, which provides new personality resources.

As in all the definitions we have looked at, there is the question of what the words mean. A particular school of psychotherapy, as psychoanalysis, has its own conceptual framework, including language. But the conceptions can be extremely complex and the translation difficult for both analyst and patient. The word "ego" is an example. Blanck and Blanck (1974) have traced the evolution of the definition of this concept from its origins in the works of Freud. What emerges is considerable divergence as to meaning, as well as the introduction of a plethora of other words connected to ego in an explanatory fashion, yet often requiring more explanation themselves. For example, describing the ego also involves describing psychosexual maturation, drive-taming processes, object relations, adaptive functions, defensive functions, anxiety level, identity formation, and processes of internalization.

Bellak (Bellak, Huryich, and Gediman, 1973) agrees that the ego is usually defined by its functions, but there is a lack of agreement as to content and number of functions, as well as methodological circularity in such definitions. Furthermore, while there is a major tendency to define the ego in terms of functions describing adaptive actions and reactions of the individual, a variety of definitions can be found.

Thus the psychoanalytic approach would describe the ego in terms of functions such as reality testing, judgment, sense of reality, drive control, object relations, defenses, and mastery. In contrast, using the same word, "ego" (which tends by its very use to create an association to psychoanalysis), Ausubel and Kirk (1977) criticize psychoanalytic theories for their stress on the unconscious and their alleged impressionistic nature. These two authors then offer what they call a "naturalistic developmental approach," in which ego is differentiated from the words self, self-concept, and personality. All of these are rather weighty terms themselves and appear in a number of theoretical conceptions, again not always having the same meaning. In this case, self is a grouping of individual perceptions and memories, such as the visual image of how one's body appears. The "self" concept is an abstraction of distinguishing characteristics of the self, while the system that develops—of interrelated attitudes, motives and values associated with self—is termed the ego. And all of that does not do a great deal toward clarifying the concept of ego, other than to illustrate that what people often think of as a psychoanalytic concept can turn out to be at least declared in someone else's psychotherapeutic province.

Switching from an emphasis on a concept to technique, we can consider the possible protection afforded therapist and client by adherence to psychoanalytic technique. Can this technique, which is supposed to be the obvious manifestation of this particular theoretical approach, be clearly explainable and explained? Agreeing on what is indeed the technique is part of the problem, but the work of Greenson (1967) is representative. The general aim of psychoanalytic technique is to increase insight. There are four major procedures to do this, namely, confrontation, clarification, interpretation, and working through. Greenson attempts what he terms "working definitions and simple illustrations" of these techniques. The first three come across in a fairly lucid manner, but "working through" is another matter.

Greenson defines it as "a complex set of procedures and processes which occur after an insight has been given . . . the repetitive, progressive and elaborate explorations of the resistances which prevent an insight from leading to change

. . . reconstructions are also of particular importance. A variety of circular processes are set in motion by working through in which insight, memory, and behavior change influence each other" (1967, p. 42).

Actually he highlights the problem of defining this important concept in another work. He states: "Although working through is one of the basic elements of psychoanalytic technique, there are few contributions to this subject. In part this seems to be due to some confusion about the meaning of the term. In addition, working through is the result of so many procedures performed simultaneously by the analyst and the patient that it is very difficult to describe systematically" (Greenson, 1978, p. 225).

Greenson indicates that working through has as its aim analysis of factors preventing insight from leading to important durable changes in the patient. The "how" of this, nonetheless, he believes is most accurately illustrated in an ongoing case presentation, which is a complex way to describe a procedure, as well as difficult to generalize.

The conceptual and explanatory limitations of a psychoanalytic orientation are still more vividly illustrated by Langs (1978) in his recent book on transitions in technique. It is both fascinating and unclear what is really meant by his adoption of "a broad adaptational-interactional approach." He too uses case illustrations, as well as a glossary to handle the host of new terms that begin with "the abstract-particularizing process" and end, alphabetically anyway, with "validation via type two derivations" and "the validating process." In this case, explanation feeds upon itself to grow more terms requiring further explanation. Accepting possible and probable limitations in our ability to grasp meaning, we are more than ever impressed with the burden given psychotherapists to make it lucid.

Perhaps the complexity of psychoanalysis makes it too apt an example, yet there are similar problems in other therapies. Behavior modification recognizes the fact that a client may want an explanation of the rationale for a behavioral model, and that requires illustration of terms such as operant behavior, primary reinforcers, conditioned reinforcers, generalized reinforcers, adventitious reinforcement, response cost, time out, discriminated operants, chaining, and respondent extinction. There are still other behavioral terms and concepts, and they do not strike us as automatically any more definitive than the previously discussed psychoanalytic concept of "working through."

Thus, each school of therapy has its language that is supposed to help both its adherents and consumers (at least in application). Yet the complexity of the processes described by the language make it vague by varying degrees, and in addition, the proponents of a school vary in their degrees of acceptance. Nonetheless, they usually have considerable faith, and ask the same of their clients. Gambrill, in her massive handbook of behavioral procedures, states: "The client's conceptualization is not accepted at face value, but must be molded to fit one that will be helpful in terms of change efforts" (1977, p. 74).

Our overall impression is that despite difficulties in conceptualizing for adherents of any detailed and extensive school of psychotherapy, it is of greater security for both patient and therapist that the latter be a relatively firm adherent to what is being practiced. While faith can certainly perpetuate error if it is blind, there is too much insecurity and confusion in blanket skepticism. There is a therapeutic advantage in inherent faith in one's own curative powers. However, being a disciple does not solve the problem, but merely orders it a bit, making it somewhat easier to know and describe what psychotherapy is. An orientation creates the possibility of greater understanding of at least that kind of psychotherapy for client and therapist. A small, specific step may be taken though the issue is hardly solved in this manner. One school of psychotherapy often debunks and/or misunderstands another, and the best of each therapeutic world is mused about but not yet discovered.

It is an interesting and disturbing fact that up to this time research on psychotherapy has had little impact on practice. If the research was not being ignored, then it was being criticized. However, as we will discuss in greater detail in the next chapter, despite methodological problems, the thrust of psychotherapy research is that psychotherapies can and have been proved to be effective—not all of them for everybody, nor are all psychotherapies equally effective, regardless of orientation. Malan (1973) has substantiated the specificity of therapies. As therapists we have to be more attuned to this issue, and more honest with ourselves and our potential clients as to what we and they may be able to do in the type of psychotherapy we offer.

The hasty need for doing this is unintentionally shown by Saccuzzo (1977), who rather blithely offers a new blueprint that uses the science of psychology as a treatment technology. Key aspects would be the use of group rather than individual procedures; relatively brief time in psychotherapy; the therapist as a consultant coupled with the use of paraprofessionals as therapists; new delivery systems; and models of therapy based on learning theory, cognitive and social psychology, and psychophysiology. His description is a selected potpourri of behaviors that have indeed occurred, but his evidence is not a comprehensive review of the field by any means, nor does he make anything other than a generalized attempt to draw it all together under the rubric of psychology.

At this point we are very skeptical of such assertions on his part that "the next 10 years will see a revolution in the practice of psychotherapy"; or, "the major ingredients in successful psychotherapy will no doubt be isolated"; or, "the application of scientific psychology to psychotherapy is providing the thread by which all systems and schools of psychotherapy can be tied" (1977, p. 303).

As previously indicated, there is not an ongoing revolution, but just *more therapies*. Nor are the basics agreed upon, and unity remains elusive. Sacuzzo appears to be writing about how he wants things to be, and ignores a lot of what exists as well as the numerous basic unanswered questions that psychotherapists live with even when they do not know it. We do not fault him for wanting, but desire is not reality, nor are certain trends occurring in 1976 representative of the major thrusts of the field of psychotherapy. His optimism is so appealing, however, that we do want to agree with something in his projection for the future. He states: "Therapists will learn how to use such principles as interpersonal attraction, reinforcement conditioning, cognitive dissonance, scientific suggestion, and placebo enhancement . . . in conjunction with psychotherapeutic hardware, such as biofeedback devices, that will enable patients to control anxiety and produce the calm, relaxed alpha state in the shortest possible time'' (p. 303).

In light of our emphasis on the great need for clarity and specificity, the obscurity and expansiveness of the preceding quoted sentences is incredible. No wonder the field is confused and confusing. But the last phrase of his article is, ''anything is possible in the last quarter of this century.'' We can agree with that.

THE COMPETENCE QUESTION: WHO CAN DO PSYCHOTHERAPY?

If indeed, as one author suggested earlier, psychotherapy is often defined by who does it, then definition poses the possibility of exclusion (or inclusion) for a field that has seen enormous growth in numbers of practitioners from diverse disciplines. To be a psychotherapist is not an explicit formula package akin to being an attorney or physician, and that fact has aroused an enormous amount of often bitter controversy. In actuality many people perform acts that could be described as psychotherapeutic techniques. These people include physicians, psychologists, social workers, nurses, clergy, educators, counselors, lawyers, and paraprofessionals. Some of these, such as teachers and lawyers, would not consider themselves (or be considered) as psychotherapists, while others definitely would. The most prominent of these are physicians, particularly psychiatrists.

Psychiatry has tended to define psychotherapy as part of the practice of medicine, and to countenance the use of psychotherapeutic techniques by others in any formal sense only under psychiatric supervision, and because of the shortage of therapeutic personnel. However, the variety of existing practitioners and their techniques indicates that psychotherapy cannot be legitimately classified solely as a medical technique.

In fact, the difficulties in defining psychotherapy highlight the issue of deciding just what is and is not involved. The tendency to exclude somatic treatments from definitions of psychotherapy further support a broader model than medicine. The model most practiced is an interdisciplinary one, with the focus by the practitioner on the patient's psychobiological problems. Psychiatrists themselves are likely to refer their patients to other nonpsychiatric physicians for any physical ailments they may have. Routine physical examinations, for which psychiatrists are trained, are not routinely given by the psychiatrists, but instead patients are referred, as they are by any other therapist from any other discipline. In essence, regardless of the therapist's orientation, if physical problems are suspected, a physician other than a psychiatrist is consulted for both diagnostic and treatment purposes.

While psychological problems involve the totality of the person, psychotherapists are specialists in treating only part of that whole. As it stands now, psychotherapy is not the province of a single health discipline, unless that is a newly created one called psychotherapy, which in turn involves appropriate competencies derived from a number of disciplines.

Why then has there been so much acrimony about the "nonmedical" psychotherapist? It appears to lie partially in a belief that emotional problems are medical problems, and therefore not successfully treatable by anyone other than a physician. Treatment sought and received from other professionals, as well as from nonprofessionals, should by now lay this contention to rest. Psychotherapeutic competence is not vested in a particular discipline, but in the ability to do well what are designated as the activities of psychotherapy.

We tend to think of diagnosis as a given in such a process, although we have already indicated that for most therapists an assessment procedure deals primarily with the recognition of psychological factors. Possible physical involvements are considered, but if suspected, the patient is customarily sent to a physician for that "diagnosis" in detail. Still, this approach implies at least the ability to "check out" or be aware of possibilities other than psychological. That model is really more of a private practice one. In an article on diagnosis and psychotherapy, the point is made that in institutions the diagnostic process and the diagnosticians are not the psychotherapists (Shectman, de la Torre, and Garza, 1979). While this procedure is depicted as having liabilities as well as assets, nonetheless, given the diagnosis by some other expert, the psychotherapists can then proceed with psychotherapy. Such a model could be applied in all psychotherapy settings, making psychodiagnosis one specialty, and psychotherapy another. Our point is that psychotherapy does not have a necessary medical connection, but just a somewhat recent historical one, and that through Freud, who happened to be a physician but did not think all psychotherapists ought to be physicians. In terms of what therapists actually do, there is no support for the position that coming from one discipline (of those customarily involved) will make a person a better psychotherapist than coming from another.

Not that we have laid that issue to rest by any means. However, we suspect that along with the fear of allowing incompetence to be fostered, which ought to be the fear of all responsible professional disciplines, there is a more penetrating shared concern about competition. As third-party payers increase, more providers want to be included as designated recipients of payment for psychotherapeutic services. Thus far psychiatry dominates this scene, but psychology has increased its status remarkably, and social work is now moving significantly toward inclusion, as is psychiatric nursing. If indeed the disciplines fear a great loss of revenue for any one of these by recognizing another as an equal, they are mistaken. There are more than enough patients, and considering the limited knowledge we have of the possible causes and prevention of emotional problems, there is little chance of a reduction in people to treat. Obviously we ought to give strong emphasis to prevention, but with the best efforts in the foreseeable future, we know the need will remain for more treatment personnel and better treatment methods.

THE FIFTH PROFESSION

Matarazzo (1979) has distinguished between psychotherapy, and psychotherapy for a fee. In both there is the suffering person, the helping person, and some kind of ritual. But in the former, the helper may be a friend, and the techniques, whatever happen to be used. He cites the example of talking with a close friend and then feeling better. This is obviously a possibility with a variety of people in many situations, and while it can be therapeutic, so far it has not proved to be sufficient to solve the world's emotional problems. Instead, the climate of our existence is such that people in general have neither the skill nor the widespread inclination to be psychologically helpful when so asked. This does not negate the therapeutic aspects of relationships, but the need existed for something other than friendship. The result has been the development of a formalized helping process, namely the psychotherapies.

To add to the list of definitions, Matarazzo describes this as "the deliberate use of psychological techniques by a legally and professionally sanctioned counselor to the end of helping a patient or client who labels himself or herself as psychologically distressed by consulting such a fee for service practioner" (1979, p. 231).

His aim is to show how similar this is to numerous daily encounters between friends. Similar it may be, but identical it is not. Instead, we have the need for a more objective and formalized helping process as a profession called psychotherapy. We envision this profession as a distinct one, with its own training programs involving multidisciplinary content. A similar proposal was made in 1947 by Kubie and reinforced by Henry, Sims, and Spray in 1971, yet little has come of it. The project founders on disagreements about training criteria, accreditation, and the essence of the curriculum.

Instead of giving such a possibility top priority, the existing professions concentrate on establishing their independence as psychotherapists, and alternate getting along with attempts to eliminate some of the exclusivity of the other professions. No doubt there is fear that a merger may destroy certain favorable status conditions, or result in less effective training and so more incompetence than already exists. However, the consumer is the one who is being poorly treated by the fears and suspicions of the professionals. We need to come together, not just in a collaborative way, but to form a profession of psychotherapy.

Nearly everyone from the disciplines that currently comprise the body of practicing psychotherapists have an awareness of parts of our training that have not proven to be relevant to the actuality of being psychotherapists. In addition, there are opinions about the kind of training, both content and type, that would indeed be relevant. No doubt there is disagreement as to the relative value of particular bodies of knowledge. Yet a consensus could and should be developed which could be more appropriate and satisfactory than the current diversity.

Rather than take the apparent next logical step of suggesting a sample program here, the more immediate requirement is getting the disciplines together to discuss and solve the problem. In fact, if at this time a program were proposed, it would probably mitigate the likelihood of the concept coming into being. One program might well be written off by other disciplines, as well as by those people who would balk at any suggested need to acquire a variety of additional skills. Many if not most current practitioners can have substantial practices without the development of a profession of psychotherapy. Furthermore, projections of the needs for the future indicate the demand will remain very much there, with things staying as they are. However, the boat should be rocked because a better job could be done for more people by the development of a distinct profession trained in the practice of the psychotherapies.

The following tentative blueprint begins with a series of official meetings of the various disciplines primarily involved in offering psychotherapeutic services. Out of these meetings might come the development of competency-based training programs that would include all the curricula deemed necessary to practice psychotherapy. Undoubtedly this would cover much of what is now taught in medical school, psychiatric nursing, clinical psychology, and psychiatric social work programs, but it would be taught to *all* psychotherapists. Arrangements would also be made for current practicing psychotherapists, as well as those in training at that time, to acquire skills they might be lacking through the proposed new program. Critera for competency would be established, and all who would be licensed as psychotherapists would have the training and legal power to practice the variety of procedures making up the psychotherapies.

Our aim is the relative standardization of practitioners and assurance of uniformly high quality services for clients. To reiterate, the first step is that those who are now involved in practice and training, come together, put aside special interests (and suspicions), and formulate an interdisciplinary plan to train and license psychotherapists. This issue is long overdue for solution, and the time for change is now.

The establishment of a profession generally involves licensing, which is incorporated as part of the proposal, but which is also restrictive to the members of the profession. Hogan (1979) believes such regulation is advisable only when the field is clearly defined and there is consensus as to the standards for competence. At the moment he does not put psychotherapy in a category this mature; however, faced with the possibility of its regulation he offers general guidelines of narrowing the definition, making standards competency-based, then defining competence and providing more than one path to certification.

Despite the fact that there is currently no profession of psychotherapy, there are nonetheless regulations of a number of the professions involved in the practice of psychotherapy. These are by no means uniform, nor is there evidence that they effectively protect the public (or the professionals) against incompetence, but regulation has become quite popular.

The reasons for what from some aspects could be considered premature regulation will be explored in the next section. The difficulty with definition is, of course, a prevailing paradoxical decrement in developing regulation. Even Hogan's proposals for regulation, which are critical of existing procedures, still need that defining base. He is compelled to use something, and his choice is derived from many of the conceptions of Frank (1973), in which psychotherapy refers to types of influence carried out by a socially approved healing person. The client is considered as suffering and looking for relief from the suffering. The healing is designated as occurring mainly through verbal methods, although somatic methods are also designated as appropriate. The influence is aimed at changing emotional states, attitudes, and behavior. In the light of what has already been said about definition, this is a broad one. Hogan increases the latitude by including healers other than those officially designated as such, and also admits to the client ranks those who are not "suffering" in the customary sense, yet are seeking help for such things as self-growth, and personal actualization.

The point is made that the realities of the field force such broad definitions, which in turn hamper the establishment of standards for appropriate professional practice. While our concern at the moment is only with part of this paradox, it is obvious that the limitations of definition weaken the possible value of regulation and its stated aim of guaranteeing competence. One is in the unfortunate position of having to define uncertainties in order to attempt regulation. As Hogan points out: "Definitions of what constitutes psychotherapeutic practice need to be carefully and precisely drawn. Most statutory definitions of practice fall seriously short in this regard" (1979, p. 369).

THE PRACTICAL QUESTION: WHAT IS PSYCHOTHERAPY?

By now the point has been made that there is no universally acceptable definition of psychotherapy. The difficulties that exist in attempting to solve this problem have also been highlighted. The emphasis has been on the disturbances this causes in the practice of psychotherapy for both practitioners and clients. A related issue is the regulation of the practice of psychotherapy. In this regard, "the initial point to be made is that psychotherapy is almost impossible to define, especially for legal purposes" (Hogan, 1979, p. 201). Yet it is being defined for just these purposes, (and numerous other reasons), with the increasing legitimization of the right to deliver psychotherapeutic services by various professionals, particularly physicians, psychologists, social workers, psychiatric nurses, and marriage counselors. The reasons for the increase appear to be need and opportunity.

The need is that mental illness remains the nation's major health problem, with devastating social and economic impact (Dohrenwend, 1975; Levine and Levine, 1975; President's Commission on Mental Health, 1978). Unfortunately, this enormous need probably tends to mitigate precision and move definition in an encompassing and therefore blurring direction. For example, the American Psychological Association had suggested the following definition of psychotherapy for state legislation: "Psychotherapy . . . means the use of learning, conditioning methods, and emotional reactions, in a professional relationship, to assist a person or persons to modify feelings, attitudes, and behavior which are intellectually, socially, or emotionally maladaptive or ineffectual" (1967, p. 1099).

The opportunity is a mixture of dedication and interest (since psychotherapy is the predominant procedure for dealing with mental illness) and financial gain. Being a psychotherapist is a financially comfortable way of making a living, with growing provision for such services by insurance carriers making it available to more people (Reed, 1975), and in turn creating opportunities for more psychotherapists to practice. However, it is not a particularly easy or simple means of livelihood, nor, for the majority of practitioners who are not psychiatrists and in turn less well paid, is it a way to get rich. *Time* magazine (1979) reports that the average annual income of psychiatrists is $47,565, which is by no means a great amount, and that the number of physicians entering the field is decreasing. The increase in allied fields will fill some of the gap if this trend continues, and at a lower cost, assuming that trend also continues. For most therapists, regardless of their particular professional orientation, there is an urge to serve and a definite, perhaps irreplaceable satisfaction in doing so.

When we work, we feel needed, and in responding to the need that is expressed between patient and therapist, a definition of what we do is necessary. As such, there are certain variations around a central core that conceptualizes psychotherapy as a health service with a marked educational component as well as a theoretical orientation. Psychotherapy is an interaction between people. The ingredients of this interaction, such as warmth, trust and understanding, can only be incompletely explained. Examples are useful, but they are limited by the frequent specificity of their application.

Furthermore, one of the participants in the interaction has one or more problems in living. Examples of such problems are feeling anxious, feeling depressed, or being unable to get along with significant people in one's life. These problems in living, even if as "healthy" as self-curiosity, motivate initiating the interaction and hopefully will be solved by having the interaction. The person having the problem is designated as the patient or client and pays a fee to the other participant. That other person is designated as a professional psychotherapist. As such, the therapist is required to have knowledge of how to bring about the solution of the client's problems through the medium of the therapist-patient interaction. The problem-solving knowledge includes theories of behavior and methods for altering behavior, as well as an awareness of limitations in the power of the interactive therapy process.

The consideration of these features, and their concurrent explanation to clients, provides a general picture of psychotherapy which is sufficient to enable both therapist and client to gain an overall view of much of what is going to happen in psychotherapy. Acknowledged are the limitations of words, the presence of some mystery and certainly uncertainty, yet change, at least in many areas of concern, is likely and worth the struggle.

The picture can then be filled in by the ongoing interactive experiences of the participants in the psychotherapeutic relationship. There a learning process occurs in which each can be touched by the pain, effort, excitement, joy, and hope that may occur. Of course, the universality of application is restricted by the variety of methods and theories used.

We do not hold out our definition of psychotherapy as "the" definition by any means. It does not have universality and it requires further explanation of its components. But *some definition* is indeed necessary. We also maintain a continuing interest in the improvement of definition. In studying definitions we look at what other therapists write and say, and our own current formulations. Mixed in with the ideas are the conceptualizations and descriptions of psychotherapy which we derive from our patients. They define it and redefine it, particularly in terms of their involvement, effort and change, or difficulties encountered, as financial cost to them and time they have spent in psychotherapy. So the reality of what happens in psychotherapy may eventually be viewed as a mutual perception, which certainly would put more emphasis on factors such as cost, time, and effort, as well as suffering and/or enjoying the process. We recognize these factors in the patient's reactions, and try to appropriately include them in our explanations and conceptions of psychotherapy. For both patient and therapist, psychotherapy is akin to life itself—what you can make out of it given certain real possibilities.

In this chapter we wanted to make a central point—that we need to define psychotherapy, for ourselves and for our clients. In the next chapter we are more specific about psychotherapy. We also suggested the development of a profession of psychotherapy as another major priority. Now we elucidate what the profession can actually offer the consumer. What can psychotherapy actually do? How well does it meet the expectations of all involved? What does it offer? How does it make the offer? Finally, does it work? These can appear simple, yet they prove to be hard questions. In addition to our responses to these questions we make suggestions about what could or ought to be to improve the state of the art and science of psychotherapy.

REFERENCES

American Psychological Association. *Casebook on ethical standards of psychologists* (Washington, D.C.: American Psychological Association, 1967)."

Ausubel, D. P., and Kirk, D. *Ego psychology and mental disorders: A developmental approach to psychopathology* (New York: Grune & Stratton, 1977).

Bellak L., Huryich, M., and Gediman, H. K. *Ego functions in schizophrenics, neurotics and normals: A systematic study of conceptual, diagnostic, and therapeutic aspects* (New York: Wiley, 1973).

Blanck, G., and Blanck, R. *Ego psychology: Theory and practice* (New York: Columbia University Press, 1974).

Dohrenwend, B. P. Sociocultural and social-psychological factors in the genesis of mental disorders. *Journal of Health and Social Behavior* (1975) **16**:365–392.

Ehrenwald, J. (Ed.) *The history of psychotherapy: From healing magic to encounter* (New York: Aronson, 1976).

Frank, J. D. *Persuasion and healing: A comparative study of psychotherapy* (Baltimore: Johns Hopkins University Press, 1973).

Gambrill, E. D. *Behavior modification: Handbook of assessment, intervention, and evaluation* (San Francisco: Jossey-Bass, 1977).

Greenson, R. R. *Explorations in psychoanalysis* (New York: International Universities Press, 1978).

Greenson, R. R. *The technique and practice of psychoanalysis* vol. I (New York: International Universities Press, 1967).

Henry, W. E., Sims, J. H., and Spray, S. L. *The fifth profession: Becoming a psychotherapist* (San Francisco: Jossey-Bass, 1971).

Hogan, D. B. *The regulation of psychotherapists. Vol. 1. A study in the philosophy and practice of professional regulation* (Cambridge, MA.: Ballinger, 1979).

Kubie, L. S. *Elements in the medical curriculum which are essential in the training for psychotherapy—Training in clinical psychology* (New York: J. Macy Foundation, 1947).

Langs, R. *Technique in transition* (New York: Aronson, 1978).

Langs, R. *The technique of psychoanalytic psychotherapy* vol. 1 (New York: Aronson, 1973).

Langs, R. *The technique of psychoanalytic psychotherapy* vol 2 (New York: Aronson, 1974).

Levine, D. S., and Levine, D. R. *The cost of mental illness*—1971 (Washington, D.C.: GPO, 1975).
Malan, D. H. The outcome problem in psychotherapy research *Archives of General Psychiatry* (1973) **29**:719, 729.
Matarazzo, J. D. A good friend: One of mankind's most effective and inexpensive psychotherapists. *Journal of Clinical Psychology* (1979) **35**:231–232.
Orne, M. T. Psychotherapy in contemporary America: Its development and context. In D. X. Freedman and J. E. Dyrud (Eds.). *American handbook of psychiatry*, vol. 5. (New York: Basic Books, 1975) 3–34.
Parloff, M. Shopping for the right therapy. *Saturday Review* (February 21, 1976) 14–16.
Patterson, C. H. *Theories of counseling and psychotherapy* (New York: Harper & Row, 1966).
Polatin, P. *A guide to treatment in psychiatry* (Philadelphia: Lippincott, 1966).
President's Commission on Mental Health. *Report to the President* (Washington, D.C.: GPO, 1978).
Prochaska, J. O. *Systems of psychotherapy: A transtheoretical analysis* (Homewood, IL.: Dorsey Press, 1979).
Reed, L. S. *Coverage and utilization of care for mental conditions under health insurance—various studies, 1973–74* (Washington, D.C.: American Psychiatric Association, 1975).
Saccuzzo, D. P. The practice of psychotherapy in America: Issues and trends. *Professional Psychology* (1977) **8**:297–304.
Shectman, F., de la Torre, J., and Garza, A. C. Diagnosis separate from psychotherapy: Pros and cons. *American Journal of Psychotherapy* (1979) **33**:291–302
Time Magazine. Psychiatry on the couch. *Time Magazine* (April 2, 1979) 74–82.
Wolberg, L. R. *The technique of psychotherapy*, 3rd edition, Parts 1 & 2. (New York: Grune & Stratton, 1977).

II

At Issue: The Aims of Psychotherapy

INTRODUCTION

If psychotherapy had the definition desired, it would of course be easier to work from that to the description of its goals. Specification of their implementation would also be simpler. But, in the previous chapter we made it clear that we are operating in relative confusion.

Akin, but not equal to "good enough mothering," we use "good enough definition," meaning, as previously indicated, that it is the best explanation available at the time. A key aspect of that explanation, which in all therapies is going to be made to the client at some point and in some way, is what psychotherapy will do for the patient's problems.

Given a particular client, problem, therapist, method, and all the hedges—legitimate and otherwise—what is it that is going to happen? There is no definitive answer to that question. There are probabilities that may occur, however, and the starting point would be the affirmed objectives of the different psychotherapies. The schema developed by Wolberg (1979) is a useful formula for doing this, with the broad divisions of supportive, reeducative, and reconstructive therapies. First we will discuss the goals of each of these categories. Then we will consider the effectiveness of the psychotherapies, with side journeys into some specifics, as the possibility of deterioration effects. This will be followed by an exploration of the applications of major therapeutic systems, the responsibilities of the psychotherapies, and finally a personal statement of the aims of psychotherapy.

Goals of Supportive Therapy

Supportive therapy includes techniques such as guidance, reassurance, and relaxation. The aims are to "support" strengths in the personality. Such support includes strengthening defenses, discovering better control mechanisms, and generally creating some kind of acceptable behavioral functioning. While these goals can be difficult to define, they are more easily specified than in many other types of psychotherapy. For example, a person who is on the verge of being discharged from their employment because of a failure to be punctual in the presentation of their work may respond favorably to a therapist's suggestions about creating an effective schedule and so may avoid a potential disaster. The goal is clear and specific, with an obvious result.

While all psychotherapies contain supportive elements, their goals are often more elaborate, and people's problems more complex than the example just given. Environmental manipulation to change difficult circumstances is sometimes definitely useful, as one possibility, but the number of people to which this applies is also fairly limited. The problems of most people are primarily demanding of other measures. In turn, specification of goals becomes more of a problem, as will be illustrated.

Goals of Reeducative Therapy

The next step up the ladder of complexity appears in reeducative psychotherapies. These include behavior therapies and nondirective therapies, but the focus is not on insight or causality. Instead, the aim is to remodel attitudes and behaviors in such a way as to increase the patient's effectiveness. Behavior is to be modified directly through reinforcement and through the therapeutic relationship. The specification of goals here involves deciding what is indeed emotionally constructive behavior. While that can be done in many instances, it is not as easy to achieve as the delineation of supportive goals. Actually, manuals exist for cognitive and behavioral therapies where both aims and procedures are clearly delineated.

For example, one way to cope with stress would be to develop a clearly prescribed program with definite steps. First the client would be educated as to the nature of a stress reaction. Then, the client would be taught coping skills and given the opportunity to work on them. Finally, the client would be offered chances to practice coping behaviors where stress and anxiety are experienced and successfully reduced. The patient learns to be resourceful and feel more confident. This is certainly helpful when it works, but it does not always do so. In addition, this kind of structured treatment applies to only some of the reeducative therapies, and also is applicable to only certain problem behaviors.

Goals of Reconstructive Therapy

It is in reconstructive therapy that the complexity of the aims becomes the most apparent. Psychoanalysis and its derivatives are the prime examples of reconstructive methods, and the goals are relatively extensive. Thus, objectives include personality growth, alteration of the character structure, awareness of important unconscious conflicts, ego strengthening, emotional and interpersonal maturation, and the creation of new enabling potentials. Reconstructive therapy wants to go beyond support and reeducation, though these methods may at times be part of the process.

In addition, it is in reconstructive therapy that the goals are the least precise, and in turn, evaluation of their achievements are difficult. By embracing ambitious though vague goals, at least in operational terms, such therapy is often seen as both having done nothing and/or everything, depending on who makes the observation. Reconstructive therapy, by nature of the word "reconstruct," holds out the most hope for change, but the defining of change concepts, such as "increased ego integration," is very difficult. Reconstructive psychotherapy offers the possibility of "making a new person," yet that is a very personalized, quite subjective construct. What does it mean to be a "new person?" We must immediately hedge, and state that it depends on the therapist, the person, the state of the world, and various other contingencies.

Moving from supportive to reeducative to reconstructive categories of the psychotherapies was done as one fairly lucid way of highlighting the problems in describing and defining goals. Actually, such categorization involves considerable overlap, as illustrated in the previous chapter. There we quoted a number of definitions, in addition to mentioning the existence of many others. Of the definitions quoted, the first had as its goals altering maladaptive behavior, which involved more effective adaptation (implying at least some current adaptation), symptom relief, and insight. The second definition aimed at alleviating specified difficulties, while a third added positive personality development. This sample indicates that defining goals as part of the definition of psychotherapy is also fraught with complexity, regardless of attempts at categorization. Of course, these samples have their goals broadly set, while, as indicated, certain psychotherapies can be more specific and lucid about their goals. Still, psychotherapy as an overall concept has to be seen as having a host of goals, many of which are hard to explain.

A case in point is a report by Herbert in the July/August 1979, issue of the American Psychological Association publication, *Monitor*. While the focus of the report is on the issue of third-party payment, in the process various therapists issued statements as to what psychotherapy can or cannot accomplish. In one instance a psychiatrist who was employed by an insurance company asserted that behavior therapy dealt effectively with symptoms, but not with emotional problems, nor with psychoses, nor did psychotherapy of any sort, "cure." However, the possibility of "improvement" was admitted. "Progress toward competence" was also offered as a distinct possibility for someone who becomes free of certain symptoms.

It may begin to sound like word games, and part of it is a type of intellectual, territorial jousting that needs to be eliminated. But words are vital tools in this field. The expectations for the patient are generally expressed in words, so that there is a definite importance attached to perceived meanings of what psychotherapists may state they can offer to the client. In the case alluded to, the therapy in question was behavioral, and according to our categorization, reeducative, with a greater possibility of goal definition than reconstructive, although still subject to question. One can speculate that had the therapy been psychoanalysis, the arguments would have been more fierce.

Since psychotherapists have struggled for years to be classified as health service providers, the conclusion has to be that at least therapists purport to offer something. And whatever it is, a large number of their clients think they are going to get it, think they are getting it during the process, and after termination, often report that they got it. In the long run, what therapists offer, in varying degrees, is this mysterious "it" in translation, which becomes the opportunity for the client to "feel better" (or function better, or some other variation on "better").

Further translation involves certain operational concepts, often of quantity as well as quality. An example would be "less anxiety," or elimination of some other obvious symptoms. Some of these concepts are more easily expressed and observed than others, and so easier to explain to all concerned. Broad concepts, such as intrapsychic change, are more challenging on all fronts, but nonetheless an integral part of many of the psychotherapies. The problem of aims and goals is not going to be solved by eliminating all concepts that are difficult to establish and explain. These concepts are simply more personalized, and we are going to have to struggle with their existence. We are going to have to learn the great variety of ways to explain what can and does happen in all the psychotherapies. As a beginning step let us look at the much-criticized, much-discussed, or much-ignored research on the effects of the psychotherapies.

THE EFFECTIVENESS OF PSYCHOTHERAPY

Strupp states: "Without attempting a formal definition, it may be said that psychotherapy is an interpersonal process designed to bring about modifications of feelings, cognitions, attitudes, and behavior which have proven troublesome to the person seeking help from a trained professional" (1978, p. 5).

Since Strupp has already implied limits to his definition by disclaiming the above as a "formal definition," we will focus only on the broad goals described, that is, changes in emotions, thought, and actions. The type of change is not specified, but the behaviors to be altered are described as subjectively "troublesome," and the client is seen as seeking aid from a psychotherapist. Thus *change* becomes the overall goal of the psychotherapies, which are learning processes and therefore need appropriate conditions for the *learning* to take place. For example, some of these conditions fall under the broad heading of the client's motivations to change, and include personal desire, effort, and tolerance of anxieties and frustrations.

Change, then, refers not only to the more obvious relief of the suffering expressed by the patient in the first place, but also to subsequent difficulties that may be expressed during the course of the therapy, and to motivational blocks that may appear, even at the beginning, and usually throughout the therapy. For example, patients who stay in therapy for some length of time often express dissatisfaction with the pace of therapy. This does not automatically or even frequently mean they consider the pace unreasonable, but it does mean they are registering a complaint which is often connected to a block in their willingness to participate in the learning process. As a result, there is a fairly constant need in therapy of any duration to alter the patient's aversion to what appears as unknown and unsafe by virtue of its being different.

While there are many difficulties in defining what the "change" is supposed to be, we at least know it is supposed to be for the better by the end of the treatment. "For the better" means broadly that the patient has increased self-worth and has altered his or her behavior in a way desired by the patient. In that sense the goals are to be the patient's, not the therapist's. However, such goals must be attuned to realities, and here the therapist, as an expert, has responsibilities. In the context of the aims of psychotherapy, the therapist must make it clear what a particular psychotherapy can or cannot do, given the particular patient.

The question of the power of the psychotherapy to effect change has to be answered in a specified fashion, patient by patient, therapist by therapist. Of course some general statements can be made. But in essence, goal achievement depends on the specific psychotherapy, change desired, and situational characteristics, especially the particular patient and therapist.

While there have been a great number of studies on the outcomes of psychotherapy, the approach has been considerably more general than the specific focus we have been stressing. There is a practical push for accountability in the general sense. So, people continue to ponder the question in that way: does psychotherapy work? Yet it is not a unitary process, which is what the pondering customarily reveals. The question ought to be asked in more specific terms, and that is starting to happen, as we will illustrate.

For the moment, however, we are going to look at what might be the fruits of research on the effectiveness of the psychotherapies. Strupp, in 1978, remarked that psychotherapy "has become the primary secular religion." Along with this popularity, and third-party payment, has come accountability. As a result, outcome research is becoming a very practical issue. Two of the most complete and lucid reviews that we could discover are those by Bergin and Lambert (1978) and by Hogan (1979). The latter will be considered first.

OVERVIEW #1

Hogan reviews the reviews, beginning with Eysenck's work in 1952 and its update in 1965. It seems that Eysenck started the still existing controversy as to the effectiveness of the psychotherapies. It was an explosive inception because he concluded that as many patients are likely to improve with psychotherapy as without it, with the exception of behavior therapies. These were demonstrated to be more successful than no therapy and so, better than other psychotherapies.

Such conclusions naturally have set off a furor, resulting in more studies of outcomes and numerous reviews and rejoinders. The most frequent refutation of Eysenck has been the demonstration of the selective nature of his reviewing, that is, using data in such a way as to support his beliefs. Kellner (1966) points it out, as have a number of subsequent reviewers.

Hogan considers Meehl (1955), Bergin (1966, 1971), Kiesler (1966), Dittman (1966), Truax and Carkhuff (1967), Cartwright (1968), Meltzoff and Kornreich (1970), Malan (1973), Bordin (1974), Luborsky, Singer, and Luborsky (1975),

Bergin and Suinn (1975), and Glass (Smith and Glass, 1977). The conclusions are that psychotherapy research has improved in quality, and that when studies are appropriately designed and adequately analyzed, the psychotherapies are certainly more effective than no psychotherapy. Furthermore, there is evidence as to the cost effectiveness of psychotherapy, though the specifics of a cost-benefit analysis need further consideration. In addition, there is evidence that psychotherapy can be harmful as well as helpful. While the extent of the harm appears to be less than the help, again specifics need to be explored. The relative efficiency of the psychotherapies is still open to dispute. Psychotherapy appears as a powerful process, with the need existing for the determination of the specifics of its operations. Hogan concludes: "Psychotherapy does appear to have value and to bring about personality changes. At the same time, the potential for negative effects has also been documented . . . " (1979, p. 29).

Hogan's coverage—the number of reviews as well as those chosen—is extensive, but the review is really a summary of conclusions from the other reviews. It is not a critical evaluation, but depends on the validity of the other reviewers' conclusions. Because of this, more weight will be attached to the work of Bergin and Lambert (1978).

Before considering their findings we are going to look at the second part of Hogan's review. In the first part he concentrated on what he termed "traditional schools" of psychotherapy, such as psychoanalysis and behavior therapy. In the second section he gives separate attention to encounter groups and various humanistic therapies. This review appears less balanced as he seems to favor these psychotherapies over the others. The evidence for such favoritism is not particularly convincing. The humanistic therapies, including encounter groups, are quite difficult to define, presenting a definite methodological problem. Many of the studies conducted also suffer from design problems. The review of outcome studies on marathon groups by Kilmann and Sotile (1976) is illustrative of these difficulties.

Hogan's conclusions are based especially on reviews by Gibb (1975) and by Smith (1975). Their impressions are favorable, and Hogan states: "With a high degree of confidence one can state that encounter groups do bring about significant changes in those who participate in them" (1979, p. 62). The effectiveness of encounter groups appears similar to the results of the traditional psychotherapies, but we do not see evidence for superiority. Also, as Hogan admits: "One may say with reasonable certainty that encounter groups do cause harm to at least some individuals in certain circumstances" (p. 69).

Thus far, based on Hogan's summaries of the reviews of psychotherapeutic effectiveness, we can conclude that as a generality, with some expected exceptions, the psychotherapies are effective in bringing about some desired personality changes. For the specific patient, however, we have to be less conclusive. Even the success rate is open to question, along with the failure and/or damage rate.

OVERVIEW #2

These reviewers conduct a more critical, evaluative survey, beginning also with Eysenck and with Rachman (1971, 1973), both of whom presented surveys designed to support the contention that psychotherapy was not effective. However, it turns out that varying improvement rates may be derived depending on the criteria and tabulation methods used. Reevaluation of the studies and the methods used to evaluate them indicates numerous difficulties in arriving at definitive conclusions. Some of the problems are the lack of comparability of cases across studies, variations in the amount and quality of therapy received, and the lack of objective equivalent outcome criteria.

Summarizing additional outcome studies that took place between 1953 and 1969, Bergin and Lambert conclude that the approach during that time was a very broad one which supported the belief that psychotherapy had "modestly positive effects." The observed effects of therapy appeared limited by the designs effects." The observed effects of therapy appeared limited by the designs of studies, but as this improved, the focus has come to rest on two other factors. These are the possibilities of spontaneous remission and/or deterioration.

Spontaneous remission, or getting better with the passage of time and without receiving psychotherapy, has been the favorite weapon used to attempt to puncture the psychotherapy success balloon. The argument is that as many people improve without therapy as with, so why bother with therapy? In addition, if psychotherapy is to be attempted it must justify its use by demonstrating an improvement rate greater than that derived from spontaneous remission (which now becomes the "baseline" for deciding the value of psychotherapy). However, in reviewing articles arguing that there is indeed a two-thirds "baseline" rate for neurotic patients, Lambert (1976) concludes such a figure is an overestimate. Taking into account the deficiencies present in the studies reviewed, it is then possible to conclude that 43 percent is a more realistic figure for "spontaneous remission" (with the implication of generosity in the estimate). Formal psychotherapy surpasses this with an estimate of 65 percent improvement. Also, it appears that the spontaneous remission rate may well be caused, to a significant degree, by therapeutic procedures. That is, the spontaneous remitters are not really therapy-free, but receive what we might call supportive psychotherapies from a variety of sources. Such a finding further highlights the thrust of our previous chapter as to the importance of clarifying what we mean by psychotherapy, or, in this case, "no psychotherapy." Thus, Bergin and Lambert conclude: "The data, with all the difficulties they present for the integration of knowledge, do lead us to the conclusion that, on the average, psychotherapy is better than no psychotherapy, that above average psychotherapy often yields excellent results, and that below average therapy may well be harmful . . ." (1978, p. 152).

Before looking at the issue of psychotherapy as harmful as well as helpful, we want to consider the more recent studies described by Bergin and Lambert, since these show considerable methodological sophistication. As a result their conclusions carry greater weight as to the value of the psychotherapies. At the same time, research on psychotherapy still retains limitations, and these have to be accounted for whatever one's bias regarding outcome studies.

The first of the "new" studies is a comparison of three treatment approaches: systematic desensitization, rational emotive therapy, and client-centered therapy (DiLoreto, 1971). The clients were 100 college student volunteers desiring treatment for reported high interpersonal anxiety. The therapists were advanced graduate students following one of the three therapy modalities. There were control groups, and evaluations involved tests as well as behavioral observations. Limitations include the type of sample, the inexperience of the subjects, and the way in which each school of therapy was observed to be "impurely" practiced. The results were that while apparently not really surpassing each other, all three psychotherapies did better than no psychotherapy.

These findings are in accord with a more elaborate study of ninety outpatients, the majority of whom were classified as neurotic, the remainder as having personality disorders (Sloane, Staples, Cristol, Yorkston, and Whipple, 1975). Patients were placed in short-term, analytically oriented psychotherapy, behavior therapy, or a waiting list minimal treatment group. Subjects were actual patients matched on important dimensions across groups, and the therapists were experienced, judged similarly competent, and committed to their approaches. Also, outcome measures were varied and appropriate. Again, the therapy groups did better than the control, but the two types of therapy appeared similar in effectiveness.

Other studies considered of particular significance by Bergin and Lambert are that of Rusk, Beck, Kovacs, and Hallon (1977), which found cognitive therapy superior to drug therapy for the relief of neurotic depression and so challenged a number of previous studies that had concluded the opposite; the work of Mitchell, Bozrath, and Krauft (1977), which raised the possibility of a very limited relationship between the supposedly therapeutic attitudes of empathy, warmth, and genuineness, and client improvement; studies by Voth and Arth (1973) and Malan (1976), which support the value of transference and psychoanalytically oriented psychotherapy in bringing about personality change; and the work of Strupp and Hadley (1978), which while partially analyzed at this time, seems to raise questions about the specificity of the therapist and client factors that determine outcome.

To the studies mentioned above we would particularly add the large scale research by Smith and Glass (1977) which surveyed 375 controlled outcome studies varying in design, treatments, therapist characteristics, and many other variables. Despite these complexities, the authors concluded that the average patient receiving therapy was better off than 75 percent of the controls who were depicted as untreated.

Another study of particular interest is that of Mintz, Luborsky, and Christoph (1979). It concerns itself with the relationships among diverse psychotherapy outcome measures, and illustrates that consensus measures of psychotherapy outcome can be defined meaningfully. Also of interest is the comparison of two different psychotherapy projects. The level of prediction of success was modest, but similar (Luborsky, Mintz, and Cristoph, 1979).

Finally, we would like to draw attention to the research by Marecek, Kravetz, and Finn (1979). While this study has shortcomings, it suggests that chances for a positive outcome in therapy may be enhanced by a more careful consideration of the client-therapist match (in this case with regard to women's political views).

As indicated earlier, we have tried to focus on two extensive reviews of outcome studies. Also, without detailing all the studies mentioned in the reviews, we have called attention to certain particular factors that are of interest in determining the aims of psychotherapy. Our main purpose in this section is to establish the *fact* of sufficient research evidence to support the contention that the psychotherapies indeed "work." In so doing we mentioned that their workings are not always positive, and at this point we return to the issue of patient debilitation during (and as a possible result of) therapy.

DETERIORATION EFFECTS

There has been a recurring finding that a certain number of patients have gotten worse after treatment. In particular, this "worseness" has included reduction of resilience, vigor, or usefulness from a previous state, a worsening of the patient's symptoms, development of unrealistic expectations, sustained dependency, and the lack of improvement where it could be reasonably expected. Bergin and Lambert conclude: "It is our view, after reviewing the empirical literature, that although there are many methodological shortcomings and ambiguities in the data, ample evidence exists that psychotherapy can and does cause harm to a portion of those that it is intended to help" (1978, p. 154).

Certainly such harm is not one of its aims, particularly when the reference is to post-therapy (some "deterioration" may occur during therapy, but is to be reversed, especially in the "you may have to get worse before you get better" types). Nonetheless, examining the possibility of negative effects further indicates their occurrence in a wide variety of patient populations, therapists, and treatment modalities. Actually the research is too sparse regarding the specific causes of the problem, although patient, client, and treatment methods have at times all been implicated. Right now the issue of the power of psychotherapy in a negative direction certainly deserves more consideration than attempting to disprove its existence. We are the dispensers and users of a very complex process, open to misuse and error. We certainly need more emphasis on proper matching of the key variables involved in psychotherapy, that is, process, patient, and therapist.

CONCLUSIONS REGARDING EFFECTIVENESS OF PSYCHOTHERAPY

Our general experience has been that practicing psychotherapists do not take research about psychotherapy seriously. That is, they do not engage in such research nor even read it very often. When confronted in some fashion with studies that depreciate psychotherapy on any universal basis, the therapists take the position that the findings are erroneous. The discovery of design errors and the admitted difficulties in psychotherapy research based on the complexity of the variables, support the position of denying what you do not believe or even like. The same theme is applicable to studies deploring the value of your kind of psychotherapy. In contrast, studies supporting what you claim you do are treated with different logic. They are thought of as appropriate studies to be integrated smugly and swiftly, as are those showing the ineffectiveness of therapies you do not like anyway.

In addition, researchers on psychotherapy have lamented that even as their designs and methods improve, practicing therapists largely ignore their findings. As a group therapists appear locked in to whatever they like in conjunction with believing in its effectiveness. The patient who "doesn't do it right" and the vagaries of human existence are powerful allies in our complacency. This situation must change.

As we continue in the act of practicing psychotherapy we do so with a conviction as to its value. Such a conviction is founded particularly in our daily experience with clients. But there are real reasons to believe that research can solve some of the many puzzles we now face, provided we pay better attention to what is happening.

Of course, Eysenck's opening salvo was disturbing, if one thought of research as possibly supportive or at least explanatory of psychotherapy's effects. Yet in the face of that pessimism we had and have our reality, namely that people continually have problems, so we have the demand and the need to do something about them. The "something" would consist of more than waiting for "spontaneous remission." Still, it is quite understandable that with all the uncertainties surrounding the psychotherapies, questions indeed would be asked about their operations. Questions ought to be asked, since the imperfections of the psychotherapies can certainly be documented (as can the successes); none of it is appropriately reported in simple fashion, however, nor apparently can it be at the moment.

Up to this time, what are the major questions asked, and answered, in some fashion? Gottman and Markman (1978), in their detailed discussion of experimental designs for research on psychotherapy, consider three major questions. The first was (and will likely continue to be), "Is psychotherapy effective?" As those authors point out, if you cannot qualify your answer, and so have to choose between yes or no, then the answer is, "yes." It should be clear by now, however, that such a general question is really no longer appropriate. Instead, questions about psychotherapy should be more specific. After all, we are now quite aware that therapies, therapists, and patients are not uniform concepts. We are also aware that consumers tend to generalize and even project universalities from these varying concepts. We must become careful delineators in educating patients about the particulars in psychotherapies, therapists, and the consumers. We have help, if we use it, in the fact that outcome research is moving in the direction of specifying the groups to be studied, the treatment strategies, and using a variety of carefully described outcome measures.

As indicated, it is not easy to achieve what we are suggesting, that is, *relative* specificity, but we believe that it is possible. An example of this kind of research is the study by McLean and Hakstian (1979) which compares the treatment efficacy of four approaches. The target population was 178 moderately clinically depressed clients who were so designated on clinical evidence and psychometric testing. The four psychotherapies were short-term psychodynamic psychotherapy, relaxation therapy, behavior therapy employing practice and modeling techniques, and drug therapy consisting of treatment by amitriptyline. All therapies are operationally described, and while it is possible to find some of the descriptions open to debate or a variety of interpretations, nonetheless, there is a definite attempt to specify treatment procedures. Finally, the clients were measured on forty outcome variables. All treatment were time-limited to ten weeks.

Our aim here is not so much to make a case for or against the findings of this study, but to underscore the potential value of studies designed with a focus on specifics. We mentioned that in the past many practicing psychotherapists had ignored research literature on the professed grounds of its procedural inadequacies, which in turn could distort results. Such reasoning now has to be called into question, since the literature is changing and deserves attention. In fact, it should be carefully scrutinized because it will soon be capable of saying definitive things about the psychotherapies, which in turn could increase the effectiveness of the therapist.

Of course an investment in a psychotherapeutic system probably overrides openness to change for many psychotherapists. They believe that what they do does work fairly well, and this belief is based on their impressions that they see it work (or believe they understand why it does not if that is the case). Considering the vagueness of the treatment possibilities, and the probability of a less than objective view, that position is a weak one. Such disregard for research, particularly the more current outcome work, is not justified. As psychotherapists we owe it to the clients and ourselves to be aware of what is happening, and that means more than what you observe in your office, or hear from your colleagues. It means reading the literature, evaluating research, and constantly reevaluating your theories and procedures in the light of research, as well as in terms of what you think you see happening to your clients.

Actually, outcome research has not thus far posed a threat to a particular psychotherapy. Gottman and Markman (1978) have also explored this second question—the issue of *the* most effective therapy. Here it appears that all psychotherapies evaluated do work some of the time, and that they are approximately equal in their effectiveness across a broad range of problems. However, hidden within such comparative sweepstakes is the probability of differential responses to various therapies, based on a variety of factors, as the different problems that are to be treated. Differential treatment effects do not, of course, mean the general ineffectiveness of psychotherapy, but rather selective effectiveness. Beutier (1978) maintains this can be demonstrated by a consideration of the interaction of patient-symptom dimensions across therapies.

The first dimension is a dichotomy between complex and noncomplex symptoms. Complex symptoms include generalized reactions to internal states, such as schizophrenia and character disorders, while the noncomplex are those symptoms having a specific chronic history, such as phobias and habit disorders. The second dimension is the patient's mode of coping with psychic conflict, polarized on defensive style, external or internal. External defenses are projection, somatization, and acting out, while internal defenses emphasize anxiety-binding mechanisms, such as intellectualization. Finally, the dimension of reactance is used. This deals with the predisposition to resist external influence. These three dimensions are depicted as reliable and functionally independent.

Psychotherapies are then conceptually categorized into five groups, with an assumed relationship between theory and practice, which may not be justified even though it is an understandable assumption. The categories were cognitive modification, as verbally mediated behavior therapies; cognitive insight treatments, as psychoanalytic procedures; behavior therapy, namely imagery-mediated, behaviorally based treatment, as systematic desensitization; behavior modification, restricted to behavioral treatment not relying on explanatory concepts, such as aversive conditioning; and, affective insight, which includes emotional awareness methods focusing on current behavior.

Beutier considered fifty-two studies to be methodologically adequate for comparing treatment procedures in terms of the three previously described symptom dimensions. He then explored certain possible hypotheses comparing treatments and considering interactions between type of treatment and patient attributes. While it is possible to disagree with the manner in which he categorized and the model used, the approach has promise. He points out that many previous comparisons have been unfair or inadequate, or both. We can support his conclusion that "more specificity is needed both in defining therapy technique and in the operationalization of patient characteristics" (1979, p. 895).

Of course this is quite hard to come by. It is being attempted, however, and it merits our continued concern. At the same time, it appears that we can conclude that psychotherapies are relatively effective (a well-hedged statement to which we hasten to add the further qualification: depending on a number of factors as yet not at all clearly discernible). This tempered conclusion leads to the third major question proposed by Gottman and Markman (1978), that is, what are the therapeutic processes of greatest effectiveness?

The comments by Frank (1979) are interesting in answer to this question. He begins by accepting the belief that psychotherapy has demonstrated effectiveness, and generally he agrees with the abilities of most psychotherapies to be effective, at least in certain circumstances. He then suggests, however, that a principal effect of psychotherapy may be to speed up improvement, in line with the possibility that the healthier clients improve the most. Of course, whether one agrees with this or not, it does highlight the need for discovering factors leading to improvement in specified samples. Frank feels that probably more of the determinants of success lie in patient-therapist interactions and their respective qualities than in the use of particular methods, while Gottman and Markman consider the therapist an overrated factor. Obviously effectiveness ingredients are very much in the exploratory stage.

Frank considers the broad possibility that determinants of therapeutic success include patient characteristics, which is not an unfamiliar conclusion. Moving from this generality, he suggests studying certain kinds of characteristics, namely the degrees of demoralization. He believes that patients with brief episodes of demoralization are prone to respond to any kind of therapy. In this respect Frank raises the interesting possibility of the patient to whom we can "guarantee" help because he or she is the type of person who will respond favorably, regardless of the type of therapy. In this category he puts "patients with fluctuating conditions who enter therapy in the trough of a cycle, those in the midst of a crisis who can be expected to regain their equilibrium when it passes, and patients possessing good ego strength who are motivated by subjective distress to seek help'' (1979, p. 332).

Returning to the issue of demoralization, he also categorizes some patients as so demoralized that they would respond poorly to any type of therapy, and for those one could conclude there is little most therapists can offer. Demoralization is estimated on such features as sadness, dread, anxiety, poor self-esteem, perceived physical health, nonspecific psychophysiological complaints, psychogenic complaints, helplessness-hopelessness, and confused thought patterns.

Further speculation includes the possibilities that verbal, psychologically minded patients will be the best candidates for insight therapies, while action-oriented clients are better suited for behavioral therapies. Also, congruence between patients' and therapists' expectations may facilitate therapeutic progress.

Regarding the therapist the current focus appears to be on therapist-patient interaction, particularly the ''goodness of fit'' on relevant dimensions. Two of the more popular conceptions in this area, which have appeared in past research, have been the ''active personal participation'' concept, described in the A-B therapists dichotomy (Razin, 1977), and the triad of empathy, genuineness, and warmth (Truax and Carkhuff, 1967). Neither has held up that well as crucial or necessary conditions for effective therapy, though they remain of interest. They are probably more restricted in application than their originators had hoped. Frank (1979) indicates the search for aspects of successful therapists is still very much alive, and he proposes a few probabilities—persuasiveness, healing ability, and patient-therapist conceptual congruence.

Thus far we have considered fairly specific treatment variables that might be used in projecting outcome and therefore depicting therapeutic goals. Wilkins (1979a) suggests that there is sufficient evidence to support the superiority of at least some forms of therapy over nonspecific treatment effects, although others have suggested these as alternative explanations for the apparent success of specific therapeutic procedures.

A problem in this controversy (and a familiar difficulty in discussing psychotherapy) is definition. ''Nonspecific'' has been used in a variety of ways, such as placebo effects, face validity of operations, and demand characteristics of the situation. Thus, there is a lack of homogeneity (and specificity) that causes confusion in sorting out therapy procedures as such from all nonspecific events that have somehow been connected to personality and behavioral changes aimed at by the psychotherapies.

Wilkins focuses on client expectancies as an example of a nonspecific factor, and asserts that there is sufficient evidence of the superiority and independence of therapeutic effects in relation to client expectancies. In contrast, Kazdin (1979) considers expectancy factors quite important. He sees the need to demonstrate that specific treatment techniques cause change beyond that generated by credibility. Kazdin admits to the vagueness associated with the term ''nonspecific'' treatment factors, and instead suggests ''common treatment factors,'' such as attendance at sessions, talking to another person (in this case, a therapist), and faith in treatment. This issue is also by no means settled, as demonstrated in additional comments (Bootzin and Lick, 1979; Wilkins, 1979b). Its importance at this juncture is that in explicating the aims of the psychotherapies, we would like to be as certain and particular as possible in describing factors necessary to bring about change. The greater the number and variety of possible contributing factors, the greater the task. From what has been described so far, the task is quite formidable.

Still, we have not been touting recent types of psychotherapy research, and the need for the practitioner to look at them, just to prove how demanding it is to attempt to be clear about the aims of psychotherapy. Certainly one aim is the increased awareness of therapists, but we are not attempting to construct and/or support complexities that could keep many of us in the all too common state of confusion so familiar to the profession. We already have some simplifiers (which does take some doing), and plenty of bypassers, which is an easier path, and a fair number of confusers. While insisting on the complexity of what is done, and indeed needs to be done in practicing psychotherapy, the main purpose is to describe what we might be able to do for the patient all things (at that time) considered.

Orlinsky and Howard propose this definition: "Psychotherapy is (1) a relation among persons engaged in by (2) one or more individuals defined as needing special assistance to (3) improve their functioning as persons, together with (4) one or more individuals defined as able to render such special help" (1978, p. 284).

The authors indicate that (1) is designed to approach therapy in encompassing terms, and that is does, for a relation is not a *relationship* as such, but could suffice for even the most tangential of therapeutic contacts. The other numbers, (2) and (4), indicate the least a person has to do in therapy to classify themselves as patient or therapist, though the word "special" requires attention. What patients need, and therapists offer, is classified as other than ordinary. It is special, therefore requiring accountability, proof of its "specialness," for both parties. Finally, (3) indicates the terms of anticipated outcome, namely *improvement* in *functioning* as *persons*, again necessitating specific elaboration.

From this bare-bones definition, it is possible to conclude that psychotherapy aims to have a relation between therapist and client, with the therapist giving unique help to improve the client's personal functioning (in ways not specified, but capable of specification, starting with broad categories, such as personality functioning, and then being demonstrated in particular life situations).

Ultimately, Orlinsky attempts to utilize the definition through the medium of empirical research, with a focus on the beneficial aspects of the process of psychotherapy. As a result the primary ingredient is considered the development of a cohesive bond between the participants. The components of this bond are first a strong and effective energy investment in the roles of what becomes a relatively defined relationship. The patient expresses emotional attachment to the therapist and the therapy, while the therapist provides collaboration through techniques that are in accord with the therapist's capabilities and confidence in the methods and theories being utilized.

Besides the productive investment of energy by the parties involved, there is an atmosphere to the contact between them that is characterized by mutual trust, openness, genuineness, and reciprocal understanding. Finally, there is a sense of affirmation that involves acceptance and encouragement of autonomy, and which is both supportive and stimulating because of concern and respect for each other's interests.

These are considered the hallmarks of positive therapy. In contrast there may be ineffective therapy and harmful therapy. Ineffectiveness probably would involve limited energy investment from either or both of the participants, reservations regarding personal contact (lack of mutual comfortableness), and conditional types of affirmation of independence. More negative would be deterioration through unpleasant contact, such as misdirected energy investments, discouragement of autonomy, and exploitation.

There is agreement then that change is the aim of the psychotherapies, but not always the outcome. Or, if it is the outcome, it may not always be positive change. This should be faced by the therapist and explained to the patient, and undoubtedly at varying intervals in the therapy.

For example, considering therapy as an interpersonal process, it is certainly possible to describe specifics of the triad suggested (Orlinsky and Howard, 1978), namely, effective investment of energy, good personal contact, and mutual affirmation. How these core characteristics are or are not working, and the possible consequences thereof, are then subjects for patient-therapist evaluation and discussion.

This is one possible framework that helps therapy make sense, since it has goals that bear examination. Of course, this is not the only way to do it, but it offers greater specificity and elaboration of what is happening in the therapy. In so doing it is important to be aware of distinctions between occurrences during the therapy, that is, the description of the process and the state of the client when therapy is completed, which is the outcome.

In attempting to specify aims it is also necessary to consider the baseline abilities of both patients and therapists to bring about changes. The degree to which different goals may be attained varies in reference to this baseline. The problem can be illustrated with the patient (Orlinsky and Howard, 1978). Some people begin at a minimal level of age-appropriate behavior, others at an average expectable functioning level, and still others at high levels. Thus some begin at points that others never achieve; the same might be said of therapists. There is a strong need for a more prescriptive cast to therapy, with patients and therapists learning to maximize their resources, considering an appropriate assessment of their initial and potential abilities.

Garfield (1978), in his review of client characteristics in psychotherapy, supports the need for determining what can be accomplished, considering the variability of patients, therapists, problems, and procedures. The idea of matching therapists and patients for maximum therapeutic success is agreed upon as a good one. But so far there is no definitive way to do it. Effective guidelines are needed for putting into action the "best fits" for all involved. We have emphasized this need, and pointed out that research explorations in this direction are beginning. They deserve notice and encouragement from practitioners. Yet while that is starting to happen, there is the practical issue of what to do at the moment in the daily routine of psychotherapy. Before making explicit suggestions, we will look at what some of the major schools of psychotherapy claim they are doing, or can do, for patients.

APPLICATIONS OF MAJOR PSYCHOTHERAPIES

Corsini (1973) edited a book on various psychotherapies, such as psychoanalysis, rational-emotive therapy, behavior therapy, and Gestalt therapy, and eight others. For illustrative purposes we will consider the four therapies just named.

Psychoanalysis is considered applicable to all disorders, but less successful with the more seriously disturbed patients usually categorized as psychotic. Major goals are clarification of feelings, interpretations to make the unconscious conscious, providing insight, working out transferences and resistances, and alteration of the patient's inner psychological structure.

Rational-emotive therapy also applies to a wide range of problems, though it is considered more successful with slightly disturbed clients or those having a single major symptom. The primary goal is the lessening of a self-defeating outlook considered the core of all problems treated, and the subsequent acquisition of a more tolerant, realistic life philosophy.

Behavior therapy concerns the treatment of nonadaptive behavior. This behavior (thought, feeling, action) is targeted for change using a variety of procedures derived from learning theories. The procedural aspects, such as systematic desensitization, are fitted to the particular client's problems, with the client's cooperation. The presentation of this kind of therapy in the Corsini book does not appear to show limitations akin to the previous two therapies mentioned, but their proponents may well be more skeptical of such unqualified success for any of the psychotherapies.

Finally, Gestalt therapy is described as a process aimed at eliminating a symptom that is broadly viewed as a signal of a distressed process. Current interaction between the client and the therapist is the focal area for making this change. In the client-therapist relationship, the aim is to view symptoms as one part of the personality refusing to accept another part. The goal is to have the parts recognize and appreciate one another so that they no longer conflict. This therapy is considered applicable to a wide range of problems since it is based on a philosophy of living which has broad applications. However, it is limited by the interests and skills of a particular Gestalt therapist in working with specific individuals.

These encapsulated descriptions obviously do not present a total picture of the complexities of these systems, but they do illustrate that each system sees itself as having explicable goals. That does not mean the reader will easily understand these goals, however. As stressed in the previous chapter, these systems illustrate the idiosyncracies of their languages. Any one system is often partially incomprehensible to practitioners who use other systems. One response, also mentioned previously, is to designate the "other" systems by simplifying them out of useful existence. Another approach to consideration of the aims of the psychotherapies is attempted unification.

For those who can do everything (or would like to be able to do it all), we point to a fascinating case history described by Naar (1979). He was able, with a little help from some of his friends, to use different treatment modalities at different times with the same patient over a seven-year span. Naar started with client-centered individual therapy in which he provided a nonjudgmental empathetic atmosphere aimed at forming a trusting, honest relationship between himself and his client. She was able to recognize and express her feelings, and after a year of this, moved into group therapy. The aim was to establish with others the kind of relationship already formed with her therapist. The group was very supportive, but during this time the patient's father died, and she became obsessed with his memory. She returned to individual therapy where the aim was to cope with this obsession. Two techniques were employed. These were psychodrama, using a "surplus reality" method which would get at her anger for her father; and the "reformed auxiliary ego" technique, to make the patient aware of repressed love and the need for love. Both approaches were apparently successful, and after a few months the solution of a new problem became the objective. The patient was a teacher, and she had a disturbing impulse to touch her pupils' genitals. The method now employed used projective and negative reinforcements under hypnosis. After this impulse disappeared, another problem—guilt about the death of a childhood friend—was worked out through age regression under hypnosis. Hypnosis was also used to explore another traumatic memory, with the patient again experiencing relief. Finally, desensitization through relaxation was used to overcome sexual inhibitions, and the patient finished therapy. A six-month followup report indicated the patient felt she was doing quite well.

Of course this apparently effective diversity of approaches is not within the realm of all of us (and many assert that it need not be; they claim that, given seven years, their technique could deal with all these problems). We use the example because it is definitely prescriptive psychotherapy, problem oriented, and with reported success. The specification of problems, goals, and the techniques used to achieve them is striking in both particulars and the many examples Naar uses to illustrate what the therapist and client actually did.

Karasu (1979) explores the aims of the psychotherapies somewhat differently, through his perception of a complementary chronological evolution. First, using the slogans that may broadly characterize (or caricature, depending on one's point of view) various psychotherapies that have gained some prominence, he inadvertently suggests what the consumer might see as the aims of these therapies. For example, there are the following: talking cure (psychoanalysis); screaming cure (primal therapy); reasoning cure (rational-emotive therapy); realism cure (reality therapy); decision cure (decision therapy); orgasm cure (orgone therapy); meaning cure (logotherapy); relaxation cure (reciprocal-inhibition); and, spiritual cure (transcendental meditation).

These "quickie labels" actually point up what different therapies aim at in some fashion, such as the expression of emotion, the use of reason, sexual satisfaction, and what could be called "peace of mind." Also indicated are the varying methods primarily used by a particular therapy, such as reasoning, meditation, and activity. Thus, it is quite possible with many psychotherapies to give a definite flavor of what their main aims are. For example, the patient's description of his behavior may lead to the conclusion that he is unrealistic. Illustrations of what is meant by "unrealistic" can be presented, and the aim can then be to enable the patient to be more realistic, again illustrating through examples of behavior the meaning for the patient of "more realistic." The scope and complexity of the problems and therapies involved makes explanations of aims and goals more or less difficult, but not impossible. Therapists' anxieties and uncertainties are significant contributors to the vagueness with which psychotherapies are often described, particularly to the consumer.

According to Karasu, the aims of the therapies are, in a way, reflective of primary human needs existing at different times. Thus, he sees three major types of therapy evolving chronologically to answer concerns of the society at that point. The first therapy, depicted as "psychodynamic," was aimed primarily at the resolution of sexual conflicts, while the second, "behavioral," focused on the alleviation of anxiety, and the third, "experiential," has as its major goal the reduction of alienation.

In the dynamic therapies, the goals of therapy focus on developing a strong ego to master instinctual aggressive and sexual drives, thus integrating the structure of the personality. This is to be established through cognition and insight, ultimately translated into action. Experiential therapies tend to reverse the process, putting emphasis on present action, the arousal of emotion, and the immediacy of experience. These examples have been cited because they support the contention that meeting the realistic, here-and-now need (that existed in the past, and also has a future) of being able to describe what the various psychotherapies are trying to do for their various clients is an achievable goal.

Psychotherapy's Responsibility

The psychotherapies, one by one, and in sum, should include as part of their self-description, statements of what they are trying to accomplish. These goals are an outgrowth of the theory of the psychotherapy and are designed to make sense of putting the theory into practice. Aims of the therapy must then be specified. This means there must be disclosure by the therapist to the client of information about the treatment. In this chapter our focus is on the aims of the treatment, which include the procedures to be employed, the probable results of using these procedures, and the client's freedom to make choices about the treatment as described (and as experienced, if under way).

It becomes apparent, then, that a major aim of psychotherapy must be the protection of the client through the inclusion of procedures that maximize clients' chances for making informed choices. There must be an integration of the conception of roles in the therapy and the outcome of the therapy so that a specification of aims embraces rights and responsibilities of all parties, as well as the delineation of the process and its possible results.

Three major areas have been described in this regard (Hare-Mustin, Marecek, Kaplan, and Liss-Levinson, 1979). The first is the outlining of procedures, goals, and possible side effects of therapy. As indicated earlier in this chapter, there are negative possibilities in therapy. This issue has been addressed at some length on an introspective basis by a number of authors, both in regard to why failures occur (Chessick, 1971; Wolman, 1972), and in terms of the particular harmful effects for the patient (Strupp, Hadley, and Gomes-Schwartz, 1977). In connection with our concerns in this chapter, Strupp et al. state that therapists at times did not discuss or acknowledge "goals" of the therapy. Other difficulties included making goals too "abstract," not in the patient's best interests, not mutually agreeable, or beyond the patient's capabilities.

The other two areas of concern in integrating information about the aims of the therapy are qualifications and policies of the therapist (as well as specific procedures and sources of help available other than therapy) and legitimate areas and avenues of protest and dissatisfaction about what is happening in the therapy. Major portions of these areas have to do with the therapist, as distinguished from the therapy as an identifiable, separate process. These we will reserve for our discussions of the therapist as the agent of the therapy.

Assuming the therapy has specifiable aims, which it should have to merit the designation as a psychotherapy, then it is of course the obligation of the therapist to be fully aware of these aims and convey them to the clients. This means a contract between therapist and client which has these aims as essential ingredients. Since contracts are of themselves a major issue, we will explore their details and ramifications in Chapter VI. Here we will simply affirm their implicit and/or explicit existence as part of the process that is to be mentioned in specifying the conditions of therapy.

One possible form of assistance in describing the aims of psychotherapy might appear in the measures of change used in outcome studies. After all, these measures are supposed to be indicators of what is expected (or hoped for) by therapists and clients. But as will be shown, a number of refinements are needed to facilitate this. Waskow (1975) has described the selection of a core battery of tests for outcome measurement. Unfortunately they are not focused on particular dimensions of change, but they do provide measures of a patient's status at the start and completion of therapy from the vantage points of the patient, therapist, a relevant person in the patient's life, and an independent evaluator. The battery is a generalized measure of the alleviation of distress, which suggests the most obvious kind of change, namely "feeling better."

The measures include an indicator of psychiatric status (by an independent clinical judge), patient estimates through a symptom checklist, target complaints, an inventory of psychological disturbances, and some evaluation of treatment effectiveness, such as subjective impressions of the degree of improvement. Therapist measures also included impressions about target complaints, description of goals and the degree to which they were thought to have been met, and a coping-adjustment scale. Then, scales of adjustment and role scales would also be completed by relevant others in relation to the patient.

The core battery is an interesting idea that unfortunately does not supply the practitioner with much specific help in pointing up the particulars of psychotherapeutic change. The battery-makers recognized this, and had a number of recommendations, two of which are pertinent here. They saw a great need for specifying treatment goals for a designated patient, as well as being able to evaluate the extent to which the goals had been achieved. They did not have a method for doing this, but they felt that ideally there should be a way to encompass a variety of possible goals and treatments. As general aims they suggested removal of symptoms, improvement of interpersonal relations, self-acceptance, the development of insight, and congruence between therapist and patient goals for the treatment.

Their suggestions are easy enough to agree with, but the task goes well beyond that. Therapists have to fill in these specifics, arrive at methods, and be quick about it. We are now being asked for clarity and accountability when we have grown accustomed to vagueness and making much (if not most) of the therapeutic progress the responsibility of the patient.

As an article by Parloff (1979) points out, in some ways our troubles are just beginning. He mentions that more and more, society is being asked to pay for psychotherapy. As a result, society has rights and responsibilities to know as much as it can about the therapies. Key questions are: Do they work? and What is involved? We are now expected to answer these questions before we are as prepared to respond as we would like to be.

As far as Parloff can see, at least some of our explanations are encouraging for all concerned. We do know that psychotherapy is better than no psychotherapy, and probably better than nonspecific approaches, although as previously noted, further exploration is needed there. The specifics of therapeutic intervention are far from certain, however; and the ingredients of the "successful" therapist are more in question than we had thought earlier. What it all adds up to is that we are going to have to continue in the face of uncertainties and strong possibilities of change in what we do. Despite that, psychotherapy and psychotherapists are the primary health offerings to ameliorate a host of life's problems, ranging through psychosis, anxieties, depression, drug abuse, and boredom. It must be spelled out as clearly as possible, what the therapy will involve, and what will and will not happen.

Explaining the Aims of Psychotherapy: A Personal View

Now that the needs and possibilities for specifying the aims of the psychotherapies have been described, we will illustrate what we do at the moment. There are many possible variations to this model, but the thrust, the laying out of a plan, is essential.

We are operating from a theoretical base which has technical procedures attached to it. There is a psychoanalytic orientation, meaning that the patient's problems are felt to have developmental roots, and that with an awareness of these origins, and behaviors related to them, insight can be translated into action and change can occur. We believe in the importance of the unconscious, the development of transference, and thus the crucial role of the relationship between the patient and the therapist, and the ultimate possibility of effecting changes in the structure of the personality. The composition and strength of the components of that structure, and their interrelationships, are vital determinants in the applicability of our techniques.

For example, we attempt to appraise the levels of psychosexual and ego development the types and effects of defensive operations, the degree of secondary as compared to primary process thinking, and the patient's style of relating. The more evenly developed, better integrated personality is better suited for the more classical psychoanalytic technique, with its emphasis on making the unconscious conscious, the establishment of a strong transference, analysis, synthesis, and structural alterations. In contrast, the less structured personality requires ego building to ensure the ability to cope with drives and relate to the world. These initial appraisals are tentative, subject to modification. The primary interest is intrapsychic change, but that also means concern with interpersonal relationships and with social and political realities that face the patient.

Considering the frequency of third-party payers, and their requirements to fill out claim forms, we also consider standard diagnostic labels. The criteria of DSM-III soon appear to be realities to be used in the interests of our patients (and our interests as well, considering the desire for payment for services).

Patients have presenting problems of one sort or another, ranging from symptoms to claiming the need for an analysis purely to meet the requirements of a training institute. So, we begin by listening to these, and whatever else the patient has to say at the start of therapy. We explain that a number of sessions will be necessary to form a useful impression of what is bothering them and what might be done about it, with their cooperation. The aim at that point is made explicit in order to form a diagnostic impression (in a broad sense, subject to revision, though a label will be attached if need be), and let treatment follow from there. We receive the patient's consent to do this, after indicating the need to question and to receive as accurate a response as possible. All questions will be explained if the patient does not understand the line of inquiry. After an impression is formed of the client's strengths, limitations, and problems, a tentative description of the cameo of the patient is presented.

For example, we might say to a particular person whose primary presenting complaint is anxious feelings (unexplainable as far as the patient can determine): "I can certainly see that you have been feeling upset, and that these anxious feelings are mysterious and disturbing to you. They seem to affect a number of important areas in your life that we could explore, such as your relationship with your wife and your feelings of personal value. My impression is that the basic source of your anxiety, and some of the difficulties that appear to be related to it, lies in your past, particularly in your relationship with your parents. I believe we can do something about what bothers you, but it will take some time. You will have to help by talking to me as freely as you can, and by trying to discover the connections between your feelings and related events that tie into your anxieties. I will try to help you make those connections and enable you to gain more mastery over your life so that you will not have to feel the way you have described—somewhat 'out of control.' Along the way you may discover some other disturbing feelings, but try to keep in mind that we are in this together to figure out what and who you are, so that ultimately the new knowledge should prove helpful. At times, although your present way of being and feeling is uncomfortable, you may be drawn back to it. This is because often the known problem may seem less threatening than the possibility of the unknown. Tell me if this is happening and I will try to help, since it is important that we keep the process moving. Psychotherapy is going to be work, for both of us, but there can be a joy to it as well. In fact, it presents a number of probabilities, in that it may be exciting, rewarding, frustrating, discouraging, or even ineffectual. But from what I have learned from you so far, I believe we can effect changes that you desire."

As you can well imagine, all this would probably not be said without interruptions by the patient, nor does it have to be said in this fashion. But its purpose—to describe as clearly as possible what is to be attempted—is necessary. Depending on the patient's problems and your theoretical beliefs, certain things would be said, others left out. That is understood, and you may consider this example as one possibility rather than *the* model. Yet, do not let your reservations about this example (or its orientation) block the fact that *your* aims also need to be explained, to yourself and to your patients.

Prospective patients should be encouraged to ask questions about what has been said, or not said, and they do ask. Some examples are given below.

P. "How long is 'some time'?"

T. "Well, I can't be exact because the process has its uncertainties, but it is appropriate to think in terms of years."

P. "Were you indicating that at times I might get to feel worse than I do now?"

T. "Yes, that is certainly possible, but I was also indicating you should finally feel better."

P. "I gather this is a cooperative venture, but what is it that you are going to do?"

T. "Listen a lot, and carefully. Support you when you need it. Tie things together, at times offering explanations. Mainly I am going to help you understand yourself and use that to be a way that works for you, considering all the factors involved in your life."

Other issues need to be explained of course, such as policies regarding the arrangements of the therapy, including fees, vacations, frequency of sessions, and the like. As indicated, all therapists contract in some fashion with the patient; the details of that contracting will be explored in a subsequent chapter.

Regarding cure, the best guarantee possible is a try, since probabilities, not certainties, are issues involved. This point must be clear to both parties. The patient also has the right to question the treatment procedures, and it is important to distinguish resistance from reality in this regard. We stress the mutuality of the enterprise, and try to be alert to where the potential for failure may lie, and subvert it. Of course, such prevention is not always possible, but the aim remains to alleviate suffering and promote intellectual and emotional growth. When such an aim cannot be realized, then this must be faced.

The possibility of misapplication of psychotherapy, which can occur through a variety of sources and can have negative effects, is also explained to the client. But, as will be discussed in the forthcoming chapters on therapists' behaviors, there is considerable possible control over such happenings, and we do our best to prevent negative occurrences. The fact is, risk exists, and patients need to know that (as do therapists, in case they have forgotten). Therapists must be able to deal with the patients' anxiety about these risks, as well as with the risks themselves.

Finally, although trying to effect intrapsychic change, we realize that all human misery is not intrapsychic in origin for the victim. The disease of poverty, for example, results in conditions that may well cause most people to desperately seek some relief, and drugs are one immediate escape. Psychotherapy is not designed to cure such social ills, although it is designed to change people. Thus any patient's reality situation must be considered when the aims are stated, since the efforts are going to take place within an environment that can well be more powerful than any current psychotherapeutic process. In these instances the social and political consciousness of the therapist needs raising, for there may be little psychotherapy can do for these sufferers without societal change (Herron, 1979).

REFERENCES

Bergin, A. E. Some implications of psychotherapy research for therapeutic practice. *Journal of Abnormal Psychology* (1966) **71**:235–246.

Bergin, A. E. The evaluation of therapeutic outcomes. In A. E. Bergin and S. L. Garfield (Eds.), *Handbook of psychotherapy and behavior change: An empirical analysis* (New York: Wiley, 1971).

Bergin, A. E., and Lambert, M. J. The evaluation of therapeutic outcomes. In S. L. Garfield and A. E. Bergin (Eds.), *Handbook of psychotherapy and behavior change: An empirical analysis*. (2nd ed.) (New York: Wiley, 1978).

Bergin, A. E., and Suinn, R. M. Individual psychotherapy and behavior therapy. *Annual Review of Psychology* (1975) **25**:509–556.

Beutler, L. E. Toward specific psychological therapies for specific conditions. *Journal of Consulting and Clinical Psychology* (1979) **47**:882–897.

Bootzin, R. R., and Lick, J. R. Expectancies in therapy research: Interpretive artifact or mediating mechanism. *Journal of Consulting and Clinical Psychology* (1979) **47**:852–855.

Bordin, E. *Research strategies in psychotherapy* (New York: Wiley, 1974).

Cartwright, D. S. Psychotherapeutic processes. *Annual Review of Psychology* (1968) **19**:387–416.

Chessick, R. D. *Why psychotherapists fail* (New York: Science House, 1971).

Corsini, R. (Ed.), *Current psychotherapies* (Itasca, IL.: Peacock, 1976).

DiLoreto, A. O. *Comparative psychotherapy: An experimental analysis* (Chicago: Aldine-Atherton, 1971).

Dittman, A. T. Psychotherapeutic processes. *Annual Review of Psychology* (1966) **17**:51–78.

Eysenck, H. J. The effects of psychotherapy: An evaluation. *Journal of Consulting Psychology* (1952) **16**:319–324.

Eysenck, H. J. The effects of psychotherapy. *International Journal of Psychiatry* (1965) **1**:97–142.

Eysenck, H. J. *The effects of psychotherapy* (New York: International Science Press, 1966).

Frank, J. D. The present status of outcome studies. *Journal of Consulting and Clinical Psychology* (1979) **47**:310–316.

Garfield, S. L. Research on client variables in psychotherapy. In S. L. Garfield and A. E. Bergin (Eds.), *Handbook of psychotherapy and behavior change: An empirical analysis* (2nd ed.) (NewYork: Wiley, 1978).

Gibb, J. R. A research perspective on the laboratory method. In K. D. Benne, L. P. Bradford, J. R. Gibb, and R. O. Lippit (Eds.), *The laboratory method of changing and learning: Theory and application* (Palo Alto, CA.: Science and Behavior Books, 1975).

Gottman, J., and Markman, H. J. Experimental designs in psychotherapy research. In S. L. Garfield and A. E. Bergin (Eds.), *Handbook of psychotherapy and behavior change: An empirical analysis* (2nd ed.) (New York: Wiley, 1978).

Hare-Mustin, R. T., Marecek, J., Kaplan, A. G., and Liss-Levinson, N. Rights of clients, responsibilities of therapists. *American Psychologist* (1979) **34**:3–16.

Herron, W. G. Perspectives on radical therapy. *Psychological Reports* (1979) **44**:925–926.

Hogan, D. B. *The regulation of psychotherapists. A study in the philosophy and practice of professional regulation*, vol. 1 (Cambridge, MA.: Ballinger, 1979).

Karasu, T. B. Toward unification of psychotherapies: A complementary model. *American Journal of Psychotherapy* (1979) **33**:555–563.

Kazdin, A. E. Nonspecific treatment factors in psychotherapy outcome research. *Journal of Consulting and Clinical Psychology* (1979) **47**:846–851.

Kellner, R. The evidence in favor of psychotherapy. *British Journal of Medical Psychology* (1967) **40**:341–358.

Kiesler, D. J. Some myths of psychotherapy research and the search for a paradigm. *Psychological Bulletin* (1966) **65**:110–136.

Kilmann, P. R., and Sotile, W. M. The marathon encounter group: A review of the outcome literature. *Psychological Bulletin* (1976) **83**:827–850.

Lambert, M. J. Spontaneous remission in adult neurotic disorders: A revision and summary. *Psychological Bulletin* (1976) **83**:107–119.

Luborsky, L., Mintz, J., and Cristoph, P. Are psychotherapeutic changes predictable? Comparison of a Chicago Counseling Center Project with a Penn Psychotherapy Project. *Journal of Consulting and Clinical Psychology* (1979) **47**:469–473.

Luborsky, L., Singer, B., and Luborsky, L. Comparative studies of psychotherapies: Is it true that "everyone has won and all must have prizes?" *Archives of General Psychiatry* (1975) **32**:995–1008.

Malan, D. H. The outcome problem in psychotherapy research: A historical review. *Archives of General Psychiatry* (1973) **29**:719–729.

Malan, D. H. *Toward the validation of dynamic psychotherapy: A replication* (New York: Plenum, 1976).

Marecek, J., Kravetz, D., and Finn, S. Comparison of women who enter feminist therapy and women who enter traditional therapy. *Journal of Consulting and Clinical Psychology* (1979) **47**:734–742.

McLean, P. D., and Hakstian, A. R. Clinical depression: Comparative efficacy of outpatient treatments. *Journal of Consulting and Clinical Psychology* (1979) **47**:818–836.

Meehl, P. E. Psychotherapy. *Annual Review of Psychology* (1955) **5**:357–378.

Meltzoff, J., and Konreich, H. *Research in psychotherapy* (New York: Atherton, 1970).

Mintz, J., Luborsky, L., and Cristoph, P. Measuring the outcome of psychotherapy: Findings of the Penn Psychotherapy Project. *Journal of Consulting and Clinical Psychology* (1979) **47**:319–334.

Mitchell, K. M., Bozrath, J. D., and Krauft, C. C. A reappraisal of the therapeutic effectiveness of accurate empathy, nonpossessive warmth, and genuineness. In A. S. Gurman and A. M. Razin (Eds.), *Effective psychotherapy: A handbook of research* (New York: Pergamon, 1977).

Naar, R. What, when, and for what: A suggested multi-modal approach to therapy. *Psychotherapy: Theory, Research and Practice* (1979) **16**:9–17.

Orlinsky, D. E., and Howard, K. I. The relation of process to outcome in psychotherapy. In S. L. Garfield and A. E. Bergin (Eds.), *Handbook of psychotherapy and behavior change: An empirical analysis* (2nd ed.) (New York: Wiley, 1978).

Parloff, M. B. Can psychotherapy research guide the policymaker? A little knowledge may be a dangerous thing. *American Psychologist* (1979) **34**:296–306.

Rachman, S. *The effects of psychotherapy* (New York: Pergamon, 1971).

Rachman, S. The effects of psychological treatment. In H. Eysenck (Ed.), *Handbook of abnormal psychology* (New York: Basic Books, 1973).

Razin, A. A-B variable in psychotherapy: Still promising after 20 years? In A. S. Gurman and A. M. Razin (Eds.), *Therapists handbook for effective psychotherapy* (New York: Pergamon Press, 1977).

Rush, A. J., Beck, A. T., Kovacs, J., and Hallon, S. Comparative efficacy of cognitive therapy and pharmacotherapy in the treatment of depressed outpatients. *Cognitive Therapy and Research* (1977) **1**:17–37.

Sloane, R. B., Staples, F. R., Cristol, A. H., Yorkston, N. J., and Whipple, K. *Short-term analytically oriented psychotherapy vs. behavior therapy* (Cambridge, MA.: Harvard University Press, 1975).

Smith, P. B. Controlled studies of the outcome of sensitivity training. *Psychological Bulletin* (1975) **89**:597–622.

Smith, M. L., and Glass, G. V. Meta-analysis of psychotherapy outcome studies. *American Psychologist* (1977) **32**:752–760.

Strupp, H. H. Psychotherapy research and practice: An overview. In S. L. Garfield and A. E. Bergin (Eds.), *Handbook of psychotherapy and behavior change: An empirical analysis* (2nd ed.) (New York: Wiley, 1978).

Strupp, H. H., and Hadley, S. W. Specific vs. nonspecific factors in psychotherapy: A controlled study of outcome. *Archives of General Psychiatry* (1978) **35**:210–219.

Strupp, H. H., Hadley, S. W., and Gomes-Schwartz, B. *Psychotherapy for better or worse: The problem of negative effects* (New York: Aronson, 1977).

Truax, C. B., and Carhuff, R. R. *Toward effective counseling and psychotherapy: Training and practice* (Chicago: Aldine, 1967).

Voth, H. M., and Orth, M. H. *Psychotherapy and the role of the environment* (New York: Behavioral Press, 1973).

Waskoff, I. E. Selection of a core battery. In I. E. Waskow and M. B. Parloff (Eds.), *Psychotherapy change measures* (Rockville, MD.: National Institutes of Mental Health, 1975).

Wilkins, W. Expectancies in therapy research: Discriminating among heterogeneous nonspecifics. *Journal of Consulting and Clinical Psychology* (1979) **47**:837–845. (a)

Wilkins, W. Heterogeneous referents, indiscriminate language, and complimentary research purposes. *Journal of Consulting and Clinical Psychology* (1979) **47**:856–859. (b)

Wolberg, L. R. *The technique of psychotherapy* (3rd ed.), Parts 1 and 2 (New York: Grune & Stratton, 1977).

Wolman, B. B. (Ed.), *Success and failure in psychoanalysis and psychotherapy* (New York: Macmillan, 1972).

Wray, H. Maryland board says psychotherapy cause for insurance disqualification. *APA Monitor* (1979) **10**: nos. 7 and 8, 1.

III

At Issue: The Behavior of the Therapist

GENERAL CONSIDERATIONS

There is an outstanding, time-worn assumption in the field of psychotherapy about the behavior of the therapist. The assumption is that what the therapist does in the process of therapy is *crucial* to its outcome. This is not overstating the case, regardless of the therapist's reported and/or actual adherence to a variety of theoretical and technical problems. Different schools of therapy may well attempt varying approaches to the therapist variable, but all tend to respect its potential influence, for better or worse. Some schools want to control and minimize the "personal" aspect of the therapist while stressing technical maneuvers, yet even this may be thought of as at least related to a kind of intuitive, subjective knowledge of timed interventions. Other approaches more directly stress the therapist's personality and attitudes as vital ingredients of the therapeutic process. Connected to all the psychotherapeutic possibilities is the strong suggestion that many personal characteristics are the motivators for whatever the therapist chooses to believe in and use as a preferred treatment modality. What these particular personality features are, and how they correlate with particular therapies, is one matter to be subsequently explored.

The assumption by the therapists of a major degree of influence on the therapy is on the one hand a rather grandiose, narcissistic position whose power ingredients probably have quite an appeal to many psychotherapists. And it is a position that has received little challenge, although recently in the research realm the Program Development Model (PDM) has altered a bit of this focus on the power of the therapist. As proponents of the PDM, Gottman and Markman have said: "It ought to be our job as therapy researchers to discover low-cost conditions that produce change, and removing the therapist from the spotlight may facilitate that objective" (1978, p. 35).

Still, there really does not appear to be that much movement toward downplaying the therapist's importance. There may be controversy over whether personal qualities or technical maneuvers are the primary determinants of outcome, but the therapist remains quite visible as the probable major agent of success or failure. So, we have on the other hand, to whatever degree the assumption of therapist power is valid, a potentially frightening situation. For to assume the power often offered by the profession and the consumer alike could mean responsibility and accountability are much more our burdens than the clients' or society's. That kind of power status, considering the state of psychotherapeutic knowledge, can certainly look like a questionable benefit. No wonder we so often opt for psychotherapy as a shared enterprise.

Partial comfort is afforded by this conclusion from the recent review of therapeutic outcomes. "We believe . . . the largest proportion of variation in therapy outcome is accounted for by preexisting client factors" (Bergin and Lambert, 1978, p. 80). Of course, as we knew all along, we are assuredly of significance, but without the proper client attitudes, the results have to be out of our hands. This is too protectionistic a thought, for Bergin and Lambert continue: "Therapist personal factors account for the second largest proportion of change, with technique variables coming in a distant third" (p. 80). We are back on the hook, with an emphasis on personal factors in therapist selection in order to facilitate outcome.

Although the discussion thus far may appear to be aiming at some kind of absolutism, such as ultimate responsibility or constant ambivalence, the actual hope is to gain a realistic perspective on the effects of therapists' behaviors on the process and outcome of the psychotherapies. We want to sharpen the sense of the present and future responsibilities, as well as knowing and acquiring the skills necessary to carry out the work. Considering the broad process of therapy, including its inception, action stages, outcome, and reputation as a helping process, what are the ways in which therapist behavior can have effects?

From the therapist's point of view there is certainly stress on the person designated as the expert to be able to demonstrate some facilitating ability that is reflected in the client's behavior as the therapy progresses. Hopefully the client is going to change, since that is what is supposed to happen in connection with—and to varying degrees caused by—the therapist's efforts. If the client does indeed change, then the therapist will take at least some of the credit. It is more accurate to state that in the main it appears that therapists take credit for *improvement* on the client's part. Therapists are understandably less eager to receive and/or support blame for a client's lack of change, or deterioration. While the patient is blamed for therapeutic failure more often than the therapist (at least by that patient's therapist), nonetheless all therapists must be continually aware of the possibility of their own mistakes. In turn, there is an increasing spotlight on the potentially negative consequences of therapist errors.

Chessick (1971) asserts that the best way to prevent failure in therapy is to improve therapists, as contrasted, for example, with an emphasis on improving theory. Actually, when Chessick talks about "psychotherapists" it appears he is discussing psychiatrists, while giving slight acknowledgment to the rest of the therapist world—a numerical majority. Something similar shows up in his use of the word "psychotherapy," which most of the time he reserves for lengthy, intensive, dynamically-oriented therapy. Again, the reality is that other therapies are more common. So, there is a certain restrictiveness and parochialism about his comments. In particular, the scope of his rather important contentions could benefit from the deletion of such patronizing thinking as displayed in this statement: "I assume that with careful selection, it is not necessary to have an M.D. degree to become a psychotherapist although it is desirable" (p. 40). Nonetheless, he makes it very clear that he believes psychotherapists are not currently being trained in an appropriate manner. He asserts that as a result of such limited training, psychotherapists at times fail their patients. While giving examples of certain therapists in action, mostly he has the courage to openly present his own "failures." These cases are used as illustrations of what can happen. He then has a number of suggestions as to how the negative situation of therapeutic failure can be altered. His solution emphasizes a change in training, and will be discussed in the section on the therapist's training.

Chessick has illustrated, with clinical material, the belief in the concept that the behavior of the therapists is a very important treatment variable. He states: "At present the public is at the mercy of inadequate and untrained psychotherapists who unfortunately do not hesitate at times to tackle very complex problems with harmful (and sometimes lethal) results" (p. 38). He puts the case strongly. Recent comments of other therapists have been in accord with this conceptualization of the strong effect of the therapist on therapeutic process and outcome. For example, the opinions of seventy experts in the psychotherapies were gathered and categorized regarding the possible causes of the negative effects of psychotherapy (Strupp, Hadley, and Gomes-Schwartz, 1977). Most of the factors considered to be associated with negative effects were therapist variables, although the categories were inaccurate and deficient assessment, therapist variables, patient qualities, misapplications and deficiencies of technique, problems with patient-therapist relationship, communication issues, and problems unique to special forms of therapy, as well as miscellaneous problems that may happen in any form of therapy.

By using a number of categories in addition to therapist variables per se, these authors, as did Chessick, recognize the fact that the therapist is hardly the only problem in the doing of psychotherapy. Limited motivation on a patient's part, or patient-induced distortions of communication, are patient variables affecting the therapy. However, scrutiny of all the Strupp et al. categories mainly implicates the therapist. The focus here is on the therapist's behavior, and that includes technical misapplications resulting from combinations of poor training and aversive personality characteristics. Some of the latter, such as narcissism, are discussed in subsequent chapters, while some others, such as the therapist's possible exploitation of clients, will be considered later in this chapter.

From what has been mentioned thus far, it seems clear that a bad therapist is quite a liability. It also seems logical, then, that a good therapist would be an asset, and that all of this does reflect the importance of the therapist's behavior in regard to the process and outcome of psychotherapy. Actually, in the two previous chapters we stressed psychotherapy, rather than the psychotherapist. At this point we will become more specific about therapists' behavior. The emphasis will be mainly on the problems in behavior, for we are saving the last chapter of the book to put forth our version of the good therapist. At the same time, when discussing behavioral difficulties, solutions will be offered, where possible. Naturally these solutions are indicative of effective therapist behavior. So, while consideration of therapists' behavior involves both good and bad, the emphasis for a number of chapters will probably appear to be more on what is done wrong, or is ineffective, and the need to change such behavior.

Earlier, we established a baseline of agreement as to the need to carefully scrutinize therapist variables. Therapists consider themselves important factors in therapy, but in what way are they important? To what degree? These are key questions requiring careful assessment of therapist variables. Research, with the usual reservations, attempts to formulate responses to these questions.

RESEARCH ON THERAPIST BEHAVIOR

As might be expected from previous descriptions of psychotherapy research, studies on the therapist variables share in the problems and limitations. So, before getting to the possibilities and probabilities, we mention the limitations of the current research. Unfortunately, limitations as to conclusions from the research are then present as well. First, the concepts studied are often large-scale, and, in that sense, simplistic. Coupled with a tendency to aim for a few "biggies," such as genuineness, empathy, and warmth, and then hang on to these, the research has lacked sophistication. Relating it to specific goals has been a problem, though there has been some improvement. Generally, it is far too often the case that the therapist variables under scrutiny are mixed in with other therapist characteristics and with a number of unspecified patient variables. Also, the way a therapist uses a professed technique is very frequently left unexplored.

Some specific problems will now be discussed. For example, although the effects of a variable, such as therapist's sex, or the more complex one of sexual orientation, have been depicted as very important influences on the outcome of therapy, there are no studies whose design could be considered appropriate to adequately test this provocative assertion. Then, the level of experience of the therapist, which is an old warhorse in terms of the frequency with which it has been assumed as an explanation of the results of outcome studies, varies from study to study in regard to its explication. And the outcome measures that have been used to support the contention of the value of the experience are so heterogeneous as to make comparisons very difficult.

When mentioning the skills of the therapist, particularly in regard to the Rogerian triad to be discussed later in the chapter, there is a definite connotative confusion. It is often unclear whether the investigator is referring to the attitudes of the therapist which are shown in the treatment setting, or to such fairly discrete entities as traits, techniques, and emotional and linguistic styles.

Finally, the idea of matching the therapist to other variables, such as the treatment method, problem, and particularly the patient, has an appealing logic. In respect to the research evidence for particular patient-therapist combinations, however (for example, what outcome can be predicted on particular demographic matches) little is known.

We have suggested general limitations, and illustrated some specifics, with more to follow. Still, with these reservations in mind, a useful review of research on therapist variables has been compiled by Parloff, Waskow, and Wolfe (1978). They make a general, though overlapping division into therapist variables that are independent of the patient both within and out of the treatment setting, and therapist and patient variables in some combination. Many of the variables have already gained some nearly mythical significance, so it is of great concern to see how they actually fare when under experimental investigation.

The concept of the therapist's behavior having independence from the patient's is an interesting one, for it implies the possibility of "therapist" behavior as distinct from the "personal" behavior of a therapist. The idea is one of a therapist role that is relatively similar across therapists, assuming some identity of therapeutic orientation. Therapist behavior is therefore responsive to the task at hand—the therapy. Of course this is relatively independent, since the therapist is reactive to the patient and the setting, but the therapist characteristics considered in this regard would be relatively constant for all patients, given a particular treatment modality.

THERAPIST PERSONALITY

In the clinical literature a variety of personality characteristics have been suggested, such as objectivity, integrity, humanity, intuitiveness, and perceptiveness. This concept of a constellation of "healing" qualities (and for that matter, the concept of negative qualities as well) has considerable face validity. However, in regard to the "independence" aspect, Parloff et al. state: "We know of no studies concerning the therapist characteristics conducted independent of the patient or class of patients, or independent of the therapist's activities within a treatment setting, which support this conviction" (p. 235).

The probability exists that even within a stipulated treatment modality the patient's behavior results in more therapist behavioral variability than is manifested in a generalized curative therapist personality. At the same time, provided therapist qualities are kept quite general, as psychological health for example, the concept of a therapist type receives some support. There is actually a considerable body of evidence to support the idea that therapists' psychopathology reduces treatment effectiveness, while therapists' mental health increases therapeutic success (Parloff et al., 1978). For example, while Luborsky and Spence (1978) report a paucity of quantitative studies of personal qualities of the psychoanalyst, there is some evidence for "healthier" analysts being of greater help to patients.

Also, psychoanalytic technique has always stressed the issue of countertransference as an interference in the treatment. However, there has been some difficulty in agreeing upon a definition of countertransference for purposes of studying it. The more classical definition is the transference reactions of the analyst for whom a particular patient has come to represent a source of projection for past feelings. This is an unconscious distortion by the therapist, who reacts to the patient in accord with this distortion. A broader definition embraces all personality-type responses of the analyst to the patient. Again, viewing countertransference broadly, or in a narrower sense, there is not much research evidence on it. What exists tends to support the clinical contention of the possible negative effects on treatment of uncontrolled countertransference reactions (Luborsky and Spence, 1978).

The need for consideration of the effect of the patient on the therapist becomes very striking. We have shown in the previous chapter that no particular therapy is successful regardless of the patient and the problem. Sundland (1977) has illustrated the lack of a convincing relationship between therapists' stated theoretical orientation and outcome. Thus, the focus on the therapist contributions tends to be mainly on how the therapist relates to the patient with an agreement on the need to form, in a very broad sense, a positive relationship with the client. The key question is, What are the qualities, behaviors, and so forth that the therapist must display to ensure a therapeutic relationship and therefore effective therapy? There have been a number of attempts to provide definitive answers to this question. Probably the best known, and most frequently investigated, has been the suggestion that client improvement could be brought about if the therapist displayed the attitudes of genuineness, unconditional positive regard, and empathy, and if the patient indeed perceived these attitudes as apparent in the therapy (Rogers, 1957, 1975). Scales were derived to measure these conditions, which were offered as a set of variables to account for all patient change, regardless of variables such as problems treated and techniques employed. So, for example, the analysis of transference would be just one of a number of possible ways to communicate empathy and positive regard. Unfortunately for the causes of specificity and simplicity, the current picture regarding the effect of such interpersonal skills is more complicated than the initial suggestions and research on the Rogerian variables had indicated. The evidence has turned up considerable disagreement about the relationship of these therapist attitudes to the outcome of therapy (Mitchell, Bozarth, and Krauft, 1977).

In addition to contradictory findings in this respect, it also appears that the personality factors do not operate independently of the school of therapy, nor of the level and type of training of the therapist. The absence of high levels of these suggested therapeutic conditions does not automatically mean a negative outcome for the therapy (Parloff et al., 1978).

None of this changes the conception of the general value of a positive relationship between patient and therapist. It does indicate that the ingredients of the relationship are complex, and that variables such as genuineness, empathy, and positive regard are often involved. They are not the whole story, however, nor even as much of it as has been previously thought. What is further suggested is the need to explore the components of this complexity, particularly the therapist's part in the patient-therapist/ problem-treatment method mixture. So, our next step is a look at patient-therapist matching, mainly from the point of view of therapist variables, though now seen more definitely in combination with patient behaviors and characteristics.

MATCHING THERAPIST-PATIENT VARIABLES

Much of the research in this area has concentrated on patient-therapist combinations that would be predictive of outcome. The best known are those involving the A-B scale (Whitehorn and Betz, 1957, 1960). The A therapists are supposedly characterized by personal, active participation and ability to establish a trusting relationship. They work best with schizoid or schizophrenic patients and are distinguished from B therapists on four career scales on the Strong Vocational Interest Blank. The B therapists use interpretation, permissiveness, and an instructional style, working best with neurotics. However, subsequent research has failed to support the differential effectiveness. A refined A-B scale constructed by Stephens, Shaffer, and Zlotowitz in 1975 suggested continued lack of agreement. In a recent review (Razin, 1977) the lack of consistent findings was apparent, and with schizophrenics the A-B dimension was found to lack any significant contribution to effective treatment, whether by drugs, psychotherapy, or the two combined (Tuma, May, Yale, and Forsythe, 1978).

Research using an array of personality instruments, such as the MMPI and the FIRO-B, has been used to explore therapist-patient similarity, dissimilarity, and compatability. These studies abound with methodological problems, and have produced variable and conflicting results. Forming therapist-patient dyads on the basis of similar or compatible personality traits at the moment appears to be more logical than successful. Perhaps therapist-patient similarity and/or compatibility enhances outcome, but there is no consistent body of research that supports the notion.

More obvious than personality variables, though probably intertwined with them, are demographic factors, such as sex, race, and social class. These factors are of particular interest because of prevalent criticism in recent years regarding the possible lack of understanding on the part of the therapist, who was often white and middle class, when dealing with patients who were of a lower socioeconomic level. Also, the fact that the majority of therapists are male and the majority of patients are female is and was another issue. The concern has been that because of their sex, race, and/or class, therapists would have biases, as well as lacking the similar values and experiences of the client. As a result, the mismatch in the therapist-client demographic variables could result in discriminating and ineffective treatment.

Although social class and race are separate variables, they are frequently confounded in both research and practice. For example, blacks make up a substantial amount of the lower class in psychotherapy. So the interaction of the demographic variables really has not been explored. In regard to race, the research has been less than systematic. Evidence has been found to indicate certain benefits in same-race dyads, though evidence has also been discovered that white therapists are of benefit to black patients. The value of same-race pairings in regard to outcome remains unsettled, and the same conclusion appears to be true in terms of socioeconomic matching (Parloff et al., 1978), though as indicated, class and race are frequently mixed so that one variable could be dominant without being apparent. Regardless, there is not at the moment strong evidence of the type of relationship that may exist between these variables and outcome.

There are some hints, however. In the past it has been repeatedly found that lower socioeconomic patients are, in the first place, less likely than middle or upper class patients to be accepted for treatment, and then, less likely to be assigned to intensive psychotherapy if they *have* been accepted for treatment. Finally, they are more prone to terminate therapy before the therapist considers it appropriate than patients from the other classes. These findings suggest therapists are more interested in middle- and upper-class patients. The interest is often justified on the grounds that lower class patients have a higher drop-out rate, and so will not do as well, regardless of the therapist, but for those lower-class patients who stayed in treatment, there is little support for a differential in outcome.

So, while it may well be that therapists who are mainly middle class prefer to deal with patients who share their values, with whom they feel they can communicate better, and whom they construe as better candidates for psychotherapy (particularly of the intensive type), such as approach *cannot* be accepted as the projected functioning behavior of psychotherapists. There is a vast population of lower class patients (or patients who differ from many therapists in other apparentiy significant ways) who need treatment, and there is not a similar pool of therapists to match these patients. In particular, there is a small number of therapists who are interested in dealing with a rather large number of "poor" patients. These interested therapists often have low social class origins, or are paraprofessionals, or are former members of the groups to be treated, as in certain peer-help groups that also have a leader. These therapists are by no means of sufficient number to afford enough treatment opportunities, considering the need, nor is there substantial evidence to support the greater effect of such therapists on outcome, despite the reasonable assumption that shared experiences and knowledge could facilitate a therapeutic relationship. Considering the pool of therapists and potential patients, it seems more prudent to work on the possibility that certain therapists, regardless of class background, might be particularly effective with lower-class patients. Of course we are again looking for a good match, though we are also dealing very much with the issue of therapist motivation. That needs some changing.

While therapists might be a bit addicted to their therapeutic approaches because of faith, a commitment by the therapist to expensive therapy (and most of it is that, regardless of duration and orientation) arises from the desire of the therapist to make money. We consider this an understandable desire. Nonetheless, it has to be made more flexible as part of integrating our functioning as therapists. We are in practice to serve those who need us, not just those who can afford us. Chessick (1971) has pointed out that as far as he can discern, the quality of care in psychiatry (and that could apply to the other psychotherapy disciplines as well) depends upon the patient's socioeconomic status, and such an economic decision violates the human rights of many patients. We can do more for more people by an increased willingness to receive fewer economic rewards. The fat cats need to become leaner.

Assuming this responsibility becomes accepted more readily than has been the case so far, what is it then that we might do to be helpful? First, we have to gain a certain sophistication about this client population, which can be most appropriately designated as the disadvantaged, and which comprises the poor, minorities, and the working class. There is definitely heterogeneity among this large grouping, although in the main they share the problems of not being able to get into psychotherapy with someone appropriate and not being able to stay there a sufficient amount of time to fully utilize what psychotherapy can offer. For therapists to be effective, we must be aware of the particular needs of the minority, low-income levels of society, and our awareness ought to be heightened by the fact that these people have the highest rate of psychopathology in our total population.

Useful in this understanding is a delineation of the prevalent psychological difficulties of different subgroupings of the disadvantaged. For example, the poor, in addition to constant economic crises, are characterized by derogation from within and from others, incompetence, and hopelessness (Gladwin, 1967). In contrast, the working class generally does not face *constant* and severe economic threats, but instead focuses on being independent while getting along in the world—not such a simple task either. While they try to think and operate in pragmatic terms, they have a suspicion of institutions and professionals whom they ultimately may need to call on to serve them. So, although both the poor and the working class can be considered as lacking advantages, their needs and approaches to psychotherapy would be different, and such differentiation appears to apply to minority group members as well. All, however, seem to be less than the favorites of the psychotherapy establishment when it comes to choosing whom to treat.

The point is that psychological problems exist in all segments of society, and if we are to effectively serve the group having the greatest problems, stereotyped notions must be examined and discarded. Instead, the living context of these patients—their situational resources and limitations— must be realistically assessed. Therapists are often uncomfortable with disadvantaged clients because therapists have prejudged them, or the therapists are insistent on treatment procedures that simply do not meet the needs of these clients. The work of Goldstein (1971) strongly indicates that the attitudes of therapists certainly influence the effects of psychotherapy for the disadvantaged.

A number of practical suggestions regarding the effectiveness of psychotherapy have been made by Lorion (1978). Attempts to educate patients by clarifying attitudes and expectations regarding treatment appear to be quite useful. Even more helpful is alerting therapists to their own stereotypes and aiding therapists to perceive disadvantaged clients as having the potential to respond to therapy. While thus far the evidence needs replication, it has also been found that negative therapist attitudes toward the disadvantaged are reversible. It appears that regardless of economic or racial background, therapists can do effective psychotherapy with the disadvantaged (Jacobs, Charles, Jacobs, Weinstein, and Mann, 1972), provided the therapists have their consciousness raised, and are truly interested.

The following therapist characteristics have also been identified as helpful: identifying and dealing actively with issues related to race and class differences between therapists and patients; therapists being task-oriented and flexible; therapists reaching out for their patients and being actively involved with them;

and, a commitment to democratic values (Parloff et al., 1978). Suggestions about psychotherapy with the disadvantaged echo a suggestion about psychotherapy with any patient. It is helpful to have an adequate knowledge of the patient's beliefs, values, and life style. That ought to be obvious, yet the suggestion has not been apparent or eagerly embraced. Instead, there have been negative effects for even the inception of therapy, no less its outcome, if indeed the misunderstood patient is naive enough to persist in the process.

In regard to the actual therapeutic procedures, it seems that with some modification a number of the major psychotherapies can be successful with the disadvantaged. Also, nonprofessionals have been used increasingly in this area. All of these things need to be subject to more systematic study before they can be described as more than promising; however, short-term psychotherapy, behavior therapies, and insight-oriented therapies all seem to have useful possibilities for the disadvantaged (Lorion, 1978).

An example of what can be accomplished is described by Lerner (1972). Over a five-year period, forty-five patients were treated by fifteen therapists using insight-oriented approaches. Of the patients, twenty-three were black and twenty-two were white. Eight of the therapists were highly experienced, while the others had less experience. There were a variety of outcome measures, including a psychometric one. Thirty patients completed treatment prior to the end of the study (with three still involved and twelve dropping out). Of the thirty, significant improvement was shown by twenty-three, with no significant racial differences, nor did same-race or cross-racial matches make a difference in outcome. But the use of nonauthoritarian attitudes by the therapists appeared to be particularly effective.

LEVEL OF EXPERIENCE

One of the variables mentioned by Lerner is therapist level of experience. While not a demographic variable in the sense of race, class, and sex, we want to devote some attention to it at this point because it exists in most other studies, even when not mentioned. That is, in the studies reviewed and cited it is rare that the therapists were equal in experience. But, does this actually affect outcome? Aside from the fact that experience level means different things to different researchers, and that it is confounded with other variables such as the therapist's level of training, there has long been a belief that the more experienced therapist is the better therapist. Two reviews, however, which eliminate studies that were methodologically inadequate, tend to be pessimistic (Auerbach and Johnson, 1977; Parloff et al., 1978). They report there is not sufficient evidence to support the contention that experienced therapists achieve superior results.

SEX OF THE THERAPIST

The therapist's sex is probably the most controversial of the demographic variables. It has been alleged that there is a bias regarding sex, particularly in respect to male therapists treating female patients. The belief is that the therapists are perpetuating sex-role stereotypes and working toward aiding their clients to fit into narrow roles and restrictive situations.

The research on the effects of the sex of the therapist on outcome have been reviewed (Parloff et al., 1978). In five out of seven studies of the relationship between therapist sex—independent of the patients treated—and outcome, no differences were found attributable to the sex of the therapist. The two others did find relationships, but the results are contradictory. Actually the seven studies are not comparable and they have design problems, so the effect of therapist sex on this basis is inconclusive.

Further reviewing of studies on the effects of therapist-patient sex matching on the outcome of therapy continues to indicate contradictory results, though the comparability of the studies is often not a reality. It appears, then, that there is little research evidence to derive any factual conclusions about the effects of same-sex as opposed to opposite-sex pairs on outcome. At the same time it appears sensible that therapists ought to be sensitive to sex-role issues. It is very probable that they could benefit from the acquisition of greater knowledge about the psychology of the opposite sex. This seems to be more frequentiy an issue for males, due to their greater numbers in the profession. However, it works both ways, and extends into other related areas, such as familiarity with homosexual life styles (male and female) for heterosexuals. The probability that therapist attitudes affect the process and outcome of therapy still seems quite feasible, but the manner of this effect is not yet explainable, other than by possibilities.

In this connection, Whitley (1979) has reviewed current research on the effects of sex-role stereotypes on mental health judgments. In 1970 (Broverman, Broverman, Clarkson, Rosenkrantz, and Vogel), evidence was reported that psychotherapists shared society's sex-role stereotypes as part of their definition of mental health. The implication was of a bias by the therapist that would automatically result in discriminating activity in therapy. Thus, the first issue is the existence of evidence for different mental health standards for men and women which would be based on sex stereotypes. Twelve studies have tested such a hypothesis, and found support for it, but Whitley considers their methodological flaws a definite limit on their validity. If, however, this hypothesis is accepted, then there is the possibility that cross-sex-role behavior would be judged as pathological. Twenty-four studies explored this issue, and the hypothesis was generally supported for nonprofessionals, but not for mental health professionals. Then, five studies explored the possibility that treatment goals tend to be related to sex roles, but this was not generally supported. However, some specific goals were sex typed.

Whitley concludes that while mental health professionals may share the sex-role stereotypes of the society, these stereotypes have little effect on their judgment regarding psychopathology and goals for treatment. Of course this is no guarantee as to what happens in the process of psychotherapy, or what the outcome will be, but it could be a hopeful sign. What may be happening is that therapists' attitudes are becoming more flexible than they had appeared. It may be that sex-role congruence in the stereotyped sense no longer is as strongly associated with mental health, and that the emphasis in therapy is moving more toward the client's personal aims as to how sex roles will be enacted. At the same time, paraprofessionals, who often have a great deal of contact with people suffering from considerable psychopathology, appeared quite locked into stereotypic roles as standards of mental health. *Furthermore, this appeared to be the case for all mental health workers when it came to judgments and therapeutic goals for children.* The problem, then, is certainly existing rather than in definitive resolution.

OTHER MATCHING VARIABLES

A number of other patient-therapist characteristics have been considered in regard to their congruence. One of these is expectations, with the assumption being that if patient and therapist expect the same thing from the therapy, it is more likely to be a successful venture than if their expectations are markedly divergent. One group of studies set up congruent and incongruent therapeutic dyads before the start of therapy and then compared the number of patients in each type of dyad who derived some benefit. Another group of studies assessed expectations at the outset and then examined their relations to outcome. Neither of these groups of studies found a relationship between congruence of expectations and patient improvement, though congruence does appear to limit the dropout rate (Parloff et al., 1978). However, a third group of studies concentrated on preparation of the patient for therapy in an attempt to induce congruence. These showed a stronger effect of congruence on both maintaining the patient in therapy and on improvement. These findings have led to an attempt to increase congruence by preparation, particularly for the disadvantaged because of their previously reported tendency to terminate therapy quickly. Such procedures appear to have value (Heitler, 1976), especially if therapists are prepared for possible difficulties in therapy (Jacobs et al., 1972).

A promising area of research appears to be cognitive matching. Carr (1970) found that therapist-patient compatibility on conceptual differentiation enhanced outcome, and a similar finding was reported for conceptual levels by McLachlan (1972, 1974). However, studies on cognitive congruence and personal constructs suggested a value in dissimilarity (Parloff et al., 1978). The value of the cognitive variable is definitely supported, but it seems to be a multifaceted operation. The studies under consideration used different tests, samples, and cognitive variables, so they are difficult to compare. But, conceptual differentiation and levels appear to emphasize the complexity of cognitive structures. Similarity here could enhance communication, while dissimilarity may block and reduce treatment effectiveness (Posthuma and Carr, 1975).

The cognitive dissimilarity appears useful in regard to cognitive perception, such as the perspective of the therapist which provides an evaluative basis for the patient's possible need to change. An ultimate convergence in constructs appears related to positive outcome, although that may be a function of adopting values approved of by the mental health community. A similar finding appears regarding convergence of values, where patient and therapist values differ at the start of therapy, but as therapy progresses the patient moves toward the therapist's values (to whatever degree they are apparent). Thus, improvement is construed as convergence with the therapist's view of mental health, and as illustrated in reference to the disadvantaged and to the adoption of sex roles, this is far from infallible. So, it appears that the existence of values as an integral part of therapy is known, but their manner of impact on outcome is not, at the moment.

Before leaving the promising but less than definitive area of therapist-patient matching, the work of Berzins (1977) is useful as an indicator of the probable utility of the matching, or prescriptive concept. In this four-year study there were measures of avoidance of others, turning against the self, depending on others, and turning toward others and the self as four interpersonal roles typically used by patients. Eight patient-predictor scores were derived in reference to these four roles, with pretherapy assessment of 751 patients. Predictor scores for ten therapists (six males and four females) were derived from the Personality Research Form, which covers characteristics such as impulse expression, caution, and acceptance, among others. Patients were randomly assigned to therapists and after the last therapy session, both patients and therapists completed therapy rating scales. The psychotherapy can be characterized as short-term crisis intervention with college students. Generally the best outcome was with pairs having need complementarity, particularly submissive patients and dominant therapists, as well as the reverse pairing. But, there was a sex difference. Considering the role pattern of turning toward the self and others, complementarity existed for male patients, while female patients with male therapists favored need similarity. Thus, some possibilities for matching are suggested and this approach may yet become a practical reality.

IMPLICATIONS FROM RESEARCH

One of the most prominent conclusions from research on therapist variables is that the mental health of the psychotherapist affects the progress and outcome of the therapy. Of course, this is and has been an accepted clinical assumption, often voiced by supervisors and therapists alike, so the research evidence largely confirms it. It is also quite general and points primarily to the probability of emotional difficulties on the part of the therapist interfering with the therapy. Specifics are not so available, nor is it clear what is the best solution to this problem. However, this conclusion is a lot more convincing as an affecting variable than others that have been suggested, such as therapist's sex, level of experience, and in-treatment styles. The tendency has been to study therapist variables in relative isolation from one another, which many times leads to inconclusive findings. The therapeutic relationship viewed from the therapist's behavior appears more complex than it has often been thought. Many of the variables suggested as important, as therapists' attitudes and values, are not negated by the research literature. It is just that they are not given that much support, either. In our efforts to understand therapist behavior in the therapy, and so make it more effective, we are left struggling with questions and complex interactions of therapist and patient behaviors. Of course we need to attempt more and better research into these issues, but in the meantime, the practice of our craft goes on. Considering that fact we will take the hints we have that seem supported by clinical experience and/or research, and do with them what we can.

First we will explore how therapists are trained. Since there are numerous schools and techniques of psychotherapy, and therapists to match all this diversity, there are numerous types of training. What is of interest is a training requirement of some specificity which could be evaluated by its effect on the psychotherapy. Psychoanalysis has that, with its insistence that the psychotherapist have a "personal analysis." The value of this is questioned by Parloff et al. (1978) because of meager and contradictory research evidence. The study by Garfield and Bergin in 1971 is an example of the type of research that has been done on this issue. The therapists were eighteen graduate students, four with no personal therapy, seven with from 80 to 175 hours of therapy, and the other seven had from 200 to 450 therapy hours. The therapists were divided into three groups on this basis. Client change measures were the depression (D) and K scales of the MMPI, and a five-point scale of disturbance, rated at the beginning and end of therapy by both client and therapist.

The sample is obviously small and the data descriptive. But, the clients of those therapists who had no therapy demonstrated the greatest change, while the clients of the therapists who had the most therapy tended to show the least change. The authors asserted these results suggest personal therapy for the therapist is negatively related to outcome for the patient. Yet it also suggested that these results were more a function of the therapists' preoccupations at the moment, and that personal therapy does ultimately pay off in greater ability. Considering the methodological limitations of the study, the conclusion would have to be: no substantial proof for any of the assertions. The patients are treated as equivalent except for differences in their therapists, who are also treated the same way except for differences in the amount of their personal therapy. These equivalencies are unjustified and the study is indicative of its imperfections.

Garfield and Kurtz, writing in 1976, are more tentative about this earlier study, now considering the findings as requiring cautious interpretation, and wanting further data. These authors reported in their 1976 study that the majority (but not a large majority) of psychotherapists have undergone psychotherapy themselves. Furthermore, those who have had it value their personal therapy as a training experience more than those who have not had the experience. Theoretical orientation also enters in, with the psychoanalytically oriented therapists seeing personal therapy most positively, followed by the humanists, and the behaviorists giving it the lowest marks.

While the persistence of the idea that personal psychotherapy is valuable for the potential psychotherapist is at the moment based mainly on personal conviction, there has been no adequate research confronting this issue. More vital is the issue behind it, which is supported by clinical and research evidence. That is, what is to be done about the problems of therapists which interfere with the implementation of therapy?

Lest one still doubt that in treating their patients, therapists have problems that are particularly related to the therapists themselves, consider these opinions:

Therapists often cling to their professional orientation, structuring patient behavior so that it is open to only one interpretation. Therapists dare not be imaginative in technique, for the advantages of dependency and kinship in professional adherence are too great. All this, and more, are the allegations of Gottsegen and Gottsegen (1979) in their appeal for risk taking and experiencing by the therapist. Whatever the proposal, the message is similar. Therapists can and do mess up the therapy, and this situation needs to be changed.

Chessick (1971) suggests a model curriculum for training psychotherapists. It is actually designed for psychiatrists, but the expansion of coverage of material is applicable to all disciplines. Over a four-year period he suggests personal psychotherapy, individual supervision of patients being seen by the trainee, and clinical seminars. The practical work seems scarcely debatable, though some may argue about its duration, longer or shorter being possible suggestions. As for theoretical study, he advocates practical sciences, humanities, language and abstract studies, logic, game theory, and philosophy. All this is in addition to readings in psychiatry and psychotherapy. It is an arduous proposal whose value is supported mainly by Chessick's personal testimony, and the need for something other than what has been done in the past.

The most complete look at the teaching of therapeutic skills is provided by Matarazzo (1978). Again, the problems in studying this area are enormous, beginning with attempting to agree on what are "therapeutic skills." Thus, the variables that may be considered, while fairly numerous, are customarily hard to define and difficult to measure. The therapy situation is a shifting one that restricts replication, and samples tend to be small. In addition, most of the research has been with therapists in training, rather than with more experienced therapists. The latter are unfortunately less available and less cooperative, which in turn limits our data base for studying more complex therapeutic skills. As we have discovered from some of our own research attempts with therapists already in practice for some time, they seem more private about what they do than most of their patients.

Various explanations are offered for the therapists' disinterest or unwillingness to be involved in another person's research efforts, the most common being criticism of the proposed research. We cannot call it unequivocally a fear of scrutiny, but it certainly is a reluctance. It is an understatement to say that it would be helpful if psychotherapists aided the field by allowing more of a look at what they do. As we have indicated, the "accountability people" are just around the corner, and research data would be very useful in dealing with those kind of issues. Finally, we are not going to be at all sure of the value of our training programs unless we can select therapist behaviors that receive systematic validation from working, experienced therapists. We will illustrate this concern further when we discuss the therapist's choice of a theoretical orientation.

Although psychoanalytic schools of therapy tend to be the most precise and insistent about their training requirements, they have done next to nothing to validate their training models. Instead, research on training is clustered in three areas, the first two of which are rather closely related. The three are the client-centered, didactic-experiential program, the microcounseling program, and behavior modification training. The first uses graded procedures to teach trainees defined characteristics and behaviors that the proponents of this program consider effective in bringing about positive client changes. These characteristics are empathy, warmth, respect, genuineness, confrontation, self-disclosure, immediacy of the relationship, and concreteness of expression. Basically the program involves very specific didactic training in these therapeutic conditions, supervision with the supervisors themselves demonstrating these attitudes toward the supervisees, and a group experience designed to relieve the anxiety of the trainees (Carkhuff, 1972; Truax and Carkhuff, 1967).

The microcounseling technique, developed by Ivey (1971), uses a similar approach of teaching specific skills, but these skills are somewhat different from those taught in the client-centered program. The microcounseling techniques are also more rapidly taught and have more obvious behavioral referents. The actual skills are attending, verbal following, minimal activity, open inquiry, and reflection of feeling.

Finally, there are programs for teaching behavior modification methods, with previously demonstrated effectiveness, to various environmental agents (such as parents) in order to enable them to bring about behavioral change in others (such as children). In these, the professional therapist usually has the role of trainer rather than change agent. There is a specification of observable behaviors, reinforcing environmental stimuli, and what behaviors should be effective in changing the reinforcement pattern. These three programs are similar in their teaching methods. They use didactic work first, then modeling, role playing, observed practice with immediate feedback, and audiovisual recording involving replay and feedback.

The advantages of the didactic-experiential method lie in its definition and measurement of some important therapist variables, the stimulation of considerable research, and the value of the relatively precise teaching method. The value of the actual therapist characteristics taught is much more questionable. The same may be said for microcounseling, though the characteristics taught are even easier to measure because they are well-defined behaviors. Both approaches have really focused on teaching interviewing skills to beginning therapists. As indicated, how and what more advanced therapists learn is much less well known. Finally, the behavioral approach also seems to be a useful teaching method, though the conception is a fairly narrow one and would appear dependent on the quality of the relationship between trainees and trainers. More attention to that issue would be helpful in evaluating the behavioral programs.

In summarizing the training research, Matarazzo has several conclusions. One is that effective teaching of psychotherapeutic skills requires objectives that are clearly stated, with progressive learning steps, measurement of achievement, and feedback to the trainee. The importance of good supervision as part of effective training also seems clear. While varying somewhat with the skills being taught, it is vital that the supervisor be able to attend to the person being supervised, and that the supervisor be able to display the therapeutic skills supposedly being taught through the supervisory process.

Of course, we are still left with the tentative nature of our knowledge about effective therapist behaviors. In turn, that limitation makes it hard to select therapists on the basis of specific characteristics. As trainers and therapists we nonetheless have the definite impression that personality characteristics of the therapist are important ingredients in successful therapy. But what personal qualities?

Matarazzo's opinion is that the skills of facilitating communication and relating are indeed important, stating that, "psychological good health, flexibility, open-mindedness, positive attitudes toward people, and interpersonal skills are associated with success as a psychotherapist" (1978, p. 960). Added to this would be possessing certain kinds of knowledge and being able to impart it to the patient, as well as being able to confront and to reassure patients. Matarazzo goes on to state: "The therapist should be warm and reinforcing, attentive and understanding, should encourage the client to do most of the talking, should demonstrate good listening ability, and should be genuine, emphasize the client's assets, and encourage discussion of the specific. . . . " (p. 962). All of this distills to the need for the therapist to be able to relate to the client in such a way that they can work together toward an agreed-upon goal, defined as explicitly as possible. The patient has to perceive the therapist as someone who is competent enough to aid the patient. While the skills summarized by Matarazzo can be used as general guidelines, and efforts must be made to translate them into behavioral terms, there is still going to be an idiosyncratic mix for each patient-therapist dyad (or group, which is even more complex). This is a problem that has been barely touched by the psychotherapy research field, and clinical lore is at the moment our greatest guide. Much of that embraces some kind of theory, an issue that is now open for some consideration, since most therapists do have a professional theoretical orientation, even if they insist it is "eclectic," and regardless of how they actually practice.

THERAPISTS' THEORIES OF PSYCHOTHERAPY

The therapist's theory, such as psychoanalytic or behavioral, is a frame of reference for understanding behavior. As we have indicated, it does not seem to have much differential significance when it comes to outcome. Yet therapists continue to have these philosophical orientations and utilize techniques supposedly espoused by the theories.

Why do they choose particular theories? The most "above it all" answer appears in this statement by Lazarus. "I have chosen my treatment approach, not for its intrinsic fascination, but because these methods are effective, and I have data to substantiate their effectiveness" (1978, p. 360). And don't we all, for we do what we do because we believe it works, and think we have evidence to support our belief. But, as we have shown, there is considerable parity among psychotherapies. Thus, it is apparent that many other reasons enter into the choice of a theory, and they can be loosely organized under personality factors. They actually include opportunity, interest, the influences of one's therapist(s) and/or supervisors, degree of satisfaction derived, and comfort with the philosophy and techniques espoused by the theory (Cummings, 1978; Herron, 1978; Steiner, 1978; Strupp, 1978). Despite considerable opinion, as usual not much data exists on the subject. Walton (1978) did find significant personality differences between rational-emotive and psychodynamic therapists. The latter viewed themselves as more serious and complex Coan (1979) found behavior therapists distinct from analytic and experiential therapists on a therapy orientation survey. The behaviorists tended toward objectivism, such as a factual and quantitative orientation, while the other two groups were more subjective. This means those two groups favored human distinctiveness and a qualitative orientation. The terminology of the distinctions is the researchers' and does not imply universal meaning. Also, the distinctions mentioned are not complete descriptions of the discovered differences, but they do show probable personality preferences for particular theoretical orientations. This is scarcely the answer, however, as Strupp points out, when it comes to how people practice psychotherapy. "It is now abundantly clear that no two therapists, even if their training has been in the same 'school,' practice in the same way. Instead,. ..the process and outcome of a given patient-therapist relationship is determined to a far greater extent by factors other than the therapist's theoretical orientation" (p. 314).

The practice is one complex of factors, and the theory another, although they are related. A recent issue of *Psychotherapy: Theory, Research and Practice,* edited by Barron (1978), was devoted to "The Theory and Personality of the Therapist." This issue makes it clear that quite a number of factors contribute to the therapist's choice of a theoretical orientation. In essence, the therapists who wrote in that journal believed in the value of a theoretical orientation based on their personal experience. The value of personal psychotherapy was reaffirmed a few times as well, but as previously pointed out, there is little research support for their faith, or ours. Also, therapists generally agreed that many therapists often say one thing and do another. We are a vulnerable crew in many of these areas, and simply have to begin systematic scrutiny of issues such as the value of theoretical orientations and the congruence between them, training in them, and actual practice.

Of course we do therapy our particular way because, primarily, we believe in it. But, as illustrated, other beliefs are both possible and plausible. Nevertheless, they do not *feel* as good, right now anyway, and so we are skeptical of their truth. Still, many may have to change their minds, and their feelings. After all, it is our responsibility to try to become aware of the "best truth," which may indeed be out there, beyond the current truth. If and when that occurs, and it is certainly our continuing duty to seek out the best for clients, then we will have to use it or become something other than psychotherapists. Barron (1978) has suggested that a philosophy and value system are the basis for every theoretical orientation. This foundation is intertwined with the social, historical and cultural aspects of the therapist. The result of this interaction is a chosen theoretical orientation, the practice of which is variable within certain limits and also influenced by a variety of factors. For many the value issue is fairly subtle, particularly in a rather customary school of therapy, such as psychodynamic or behavioral, or if we maintain we are eclectic, just in case we want to justify a certain conception or procedure that does not fit too well into the more discrete molds. For some therapists there are no pretensions to even relative freedom from a definitive philosophy of living which they want their clients to espouse. Following are two illustrations of this type of therapist's theory, that is, feminist therapy and radical therapy. Both have been stimulated by reactions to various areas of neglect apparent in the more traditional therapies.

Feminist therapy stresses an awareness of both individual and social contexts. Thus, symptoms are considered as part of the situations in which they arise. The authenticity of the suffering is recognized and the therapeutic goal is the changing of roles or expectations. In fact, certain symptoms may often be a part of the steps necessary for a woman to define a freely chosen life style. Self-esteem tends to involve redefinition of the ideal and the source. Thus the self-image of a woman is conceptualized in terms of autonomy, realistic appraisal of potentials, flexibility, and freedom from stereotypes, rather than adjustment to a role predetermined by society. Whatever the woman's role, emphasis is placed upon her choice, and the fulfillment of competence and recognition needs.

In the interpersonal area, concern is given to relating to both sexes, to the use of assertiveness, and to the sharing of experiences. Other important issues are the woman's use of skills in making decisions and solving problems, as well as developing her ability to enjoy her sexual and sensual being. The essential task of feminist therapy is to deal with issues for women which appear to have been neglected previously, and to provide women with nonbiased, effective psychotherapy (Johnson, 1976; Kaschak, 1976; Klein, 1976; Kravetz, 1976; Waskow, 1976).

As indicated, there is not a body of research evidence to strongly support a sex bias in treatment, and little research evidence for any relationship between sex of the therapist and outcome of the therapy. Most of the evidence has appeared in the reports of patients who feel they have been subjected to sexist therapy and the reported sexist attitudes of therapists, most of whom have been men. Our impressions are that sexism in therapy and therapists does exist, but that it is decreasing through an awareness of its potentially harmful effects. We do not believe that the therapist and the patient need to be of the same sex to ensure effective therapy. But therapists need to understand the psychology of each sex, and the psychology of women has been neglected in the education of most therapists. Women have often been oppressed without much choice, and sex-stereotyping in therapy can certainly foster such restriction. While it is not "therapy" to insist that the client be indoctrinated into an exclusive value system, it is the therapist's obligation to make the patient aware of alternative values. Thus, in working with women it is essential that the therapist provide exposure to feminist values.

In practice, what does this mean, at least for the therapist? If a woman is in an unproductive or dangerous marital situation she should consider all options, and then choose the one she feels would work the best for her. We would neither insist she get out of the marriage, nor would we demand she stay in it, but would encourange her to look at all the alternatives available to her. Stereotyping is bad therapy and should be avoided, for many of our clients have already been the victims of social straitjackets. Illustrations of this problem, along with some suggested remedies, are certainly available, as for example, Guidelines for Therapy with Women provided by the Task Force on Sex Bias and Sex Role Stereotyping (1978).

Furthermore, we believe this issue goes beyond doing therapy with women, though they have been both perceptive and assertive enough to highlight it. Men who dislike their stereotyped roles face a similar problem. The advocates of various nonstandard sexual behaviors have been subject to negative psychological labels for many years, although homosexuals have begun to make psychotherapists rethink this issue. The theories and practices are too often reflective of a narrow scope of understanding. We recommend to all psychotherapists our version of a checklist of therapeutic goals developed by Klein (1976). She calls it: *"Things every therapist should ask about female patients* (and every researcher should consider as well)." We consider it applicable to all clients.

1. What is the relationship between the patient's reported problems, intrapsychic factors, and the actual life situation?
2. Are some of the symptoms, such as anxiety, reflective of attempts to make useful changes in life styles?
3. How internally generated are the patient's estimates of self-esteem?
4. How stereotyped, sexist and otherwise, are the patient's values?
5. Does the client's interpersonal behavior allow for a full range of behavioral styles?
6. Can the patient relate to both sexes as people?
7. Is the patient's life reflective of important personal needs integrated with freely chosen alternatives?
8. To what degree is the client open to personal skills for problem solving?
9. Has the client come to terms with gender-role and sex-role identities?
10. Is the client truly aware of all the options in life?

The goals of feminist therapy are compatible with the goals of therapy as we practice it, although the methods of implementation will undoubtedly vary across therapists. It is also obvious why many female therapists, who themselves may have been objects of sexist discrimination, would struggle to implement these goals for their clients. However, it also seems that with a change in the way therapists, regardless of their sex, approach their clients, the major aim of feminist therapy, namely a nondiscriminatory approach, should be incorporated into any reputable psychotherapy. These procedures should be both psychodynamic and nonsexist, which is both possible and necessary. The issues of personal values, therapeutic practices, and theoretical orientations, do not have to be in conflict in this area. For example, psychoanalysis is a living body of theory and practice designed to change with the acquisition of knowledge. Based on the growing information about the psychology of women there are continuing reformulations in the psychodynamics of female clients, as there are for other groups that have in the past been imperfectly understood. That process can continue, and in fact, must continue for therapy to really be of value. However, for us, integrating radical therapy is more of a problem, as the word "radical" may suggest. The position taken by radical therapy is that the structure of a capitalistic society causes interpersonal problems. Thus, society must be changed to bring about emotional health, and the therapist has a definite view about this which is transmitted to the client.

For example, Hurvitz states: "Radical therapy means that the therapist introduces a particular world view—one that encourages the client to recognize the role of the social structure in causing his problems, and supports his efforts to change the social conditions which affect him—right into the therapy experience" (1977, p. 72). Capitalism is seen as the culprit, and socialism as the savior. The therapist is pictured as a very active agent of social change, and intrapsychic factors are largely ignored. In a recent article Hurvitz (1979) has made it clear that his social and political philosophy necessitate his embracing and practicing radical therapy. He works with the disadvantaged, mainly black people, and he feels that he is successful. His commitment is impressive, and through the medium of private practice, he does what he believes in. His position is clear, and his therapy value-laden—a necessary therapeutic condition for radical therapists (Agel, 1971; Clark and Jaffe, 1973).

We do not see the work of psychotherapy as strongly espousing one sociopolitical view over another. In fact, we do not believe there is sufficient knowledge of how social systems affect personalities to support the kinds of interventions proposed by radical therapists. We can even question whether radical therapy can be considered "psychotherapy" considering the definitions for psychotherapy that are customarily given and have been cited in this book. However, none of these objections eliminate a very basic issue highlighted by radical therapy. A radical therapist, such as Hurvitz, is trying to aid the disadvantaged directly through what he considers to be psychotherapy, and he is doing this although he is white and not disadvantaged. His motivation is a value orientation, and he attempts to solve a very real problem, to which, as we indicated earlier, we all must attend. His willingness to work with the disadvantaged and his particular interest in their problems are certainly behaviors that need to be woven into the mainstream of psychotherapeutic practices.

Our approach is to keep in mind the necessity of broadening our conceptions beyond the interpersonal and intrapsychic. We also consider the social and physical situations of the person with a problem. People can change society, and we are encouraging of their efforts to constructively alter their lives through many avenues. As stated in regard to feminist therapy, the need is apparent for a change in the perspectives of many of us. For some, perhaps quite a large number, change may indeed seem "radical."

Discussing theoretical orientations and the therapist's choice of a stated theoretical approach has led us into two therapies that have arisen in response to apparent exploitation of particular groups of patients. It seems appropriate to close out this chapter on the behavior of the therapist with this issue of exploitation, especially the form of it which has tended to garner the most public notice. That issue is sexual relations between the therapist and the patient.

SEXPLOITATION

The rules are clear. The American Psychiatric Association, the American Psychological Association, and the Association for Sex Educators, Counselors and Therapists, have specified that it is unethical to engage in sexual intimacies with clients. Also, such behavior has constituted malpractice. As of 1978 there had been about 100 suits brought for negligent treatment, about ten of which were for sexual involvement (Hogan, 1979). While certainly not a large number, these suits have drawn a great amount of negative publicity and further adverse reaction to our profession.

Actually, considering the less than wonderful image that the psychotherapy profession has many times had, it is somewhat surprising that therapists are not consistently beset by malpractice suits. Therapists are not, and while the suits are increasing, Hogan states, "no reported decisions exist in which a psychotherapist has been successfully sued for negligence in what was said to a client during the therapeutic process. As long as therapists restrict their practice to talk, interpretation, and advice, they will remain nearly immune from suit, no matter how poor their advice, how damaging their comments, or how incorrect their interpretations" (1979, p. 27).

Hogan's review of malpractice suits, with his conclusion as to the past and present relative immunity, is scarcely a reason to stop scrutinizing. Confusion may be an individual's ally in being able to avoid a malpractice suit or judgment, but there is a constant obligation to validate allegedly therapeutic behavior. The profession is beginning to be more reactive, especially in regard to the issue of sexual intimacies between therapists and patients. This reaction appears to have been set off particularly by the *Roy v. Hartogs* case (in 1976) in which the therapist was convicted of malpractice for prescribing sexual intercourse with the therapist as the patient's treatment.

Sexual intimacy had been suggested as a treatment technique in certain cases by McCartney in 1966, and subsequentiy a few therapists, such as Shepard (1971), have been depicted as not really against it. But these public examples are quite isolated, as was the knowledge that such behavior did occur in the context of therapy. The first person to bring this up appears to have been Dahlberg (1971), who described nine cases of male therapists having sexual relations with female patients. The men tended to be middle-aged, suffering from depression, and having strong needs for proof of their sexual adequacy. Robertiello (1975) reported seeing, over a year's time, a number of patients who described having had sexual involvements with their previous therapists. These therapists tended to keep these patients in therapy while their sexual encounters were taking place, but insisted the patients keep quiet about the sexual interactions. While the patients certainly appear to have been exploited, they did not display hostility toward the therapists who had done this. By the time they were seen by Robertiello, the main characteristic of the patients was a very uncertain self-concept marked by strong uncertainty regarding their own judgment. Their therapists were well-credentialed, well-known, and generally enjoyed good reputations. Yet for certain needs of their own the therapists took advantage of their patients in a very sociopathic manner, which was in turn disadvantageous to the patients.

Robertiello mentions another group of patients who reported sexual contact with their therapists, but the therapists reacted with guilt, which certainly seems more appropriate. These therapists showed concern for their patients and tried to make up for what had happened. Treatment was terminated and referral made to another therapist. Of course treatment was disrupted, but the therapists were less exploitative and there was less harm to the patients' self-concepts.

In addition to this anecdotal material provided by Dahlberg and Robertiello, Hare-Mustin had previously examined the ethical considerations involved for therapists attempting to use sexual contact as a psychotherapeutic technique. She stated: "I think we must conclude from a review of principles relating to competency, community standards and the client relationship that genital contact with patients is ethically unacceptable" (1974, p. 310).

Taylor and Wagner (1976) reported surveying every instance of therapist-patient contact that they were able to find in the literature, and they discovered thirty-four cases. They attempted from the descriptions available to rate the outcomes of such relationships. Mixed effects occurred in 32 percent of the cases, with negative results in 47 percent, and positive outcomes reported for 21 percent of the situations. While the finding of positive outcomes is a bit startling, the authors suggest that the outcome of a relationship depends on the resemblance of fantasy to fact, and whether the people involved have similar expectations, and that this could extend to all relationships, including psychotherapy. However, they point out that despite the fact that not all sexual relationships between a therapist and a patient have negative results, it is high-risk behavior and the complexities approach the insurmountable. As such it is to be avoided, but if it does occur, then that therapeutic relationship is to be terminated with referral to another therapist, and with the understanding that the patient has the freedom to discuss what happened. Many times, however, while therapy with that therapist may be terminated, the patient has an investment in keeping this material secret, particularly if it was a disappointing experience. So, the attempted remedy may not occur, which further suggests the value of not attempting a sexual relationship as part of a psychotherapeutic one.

Butler and Zelene (1977) were able to develop a volunteer sample of twenty therapists (psychiatrists and psychologists), two of whom were women, who admitted to sexual intimacies with their patients. Structured interviews with these therapists indicated they had a very high need for affection and love, as well as currently unsatisfied personal sexual and/or love relationships. It appears that the therapists derived their gratifications from their patients because the therapists were feeling vulnerable and needy. Despite some rationalizations, the therapists did not really see their behavior as therapeutic for the patients, but less than half the therapists terminated the therapy. Referrals were not made as they should have been, nor did the majority of therapists seek help about the problem from professional colleagues. Almost all of the therapists did feel guilt and conflict, yet many continued their behavior with successive patients.

Some positive effects were reported, namely sharing a relationship that was complex, but in the main the effects were considered negative. These included the unequal nature of the relationship, a great amount of conflict experienced by both therapists and clients, and after the relationship ended, strong feelings of anger and hurt on the patient's part.

A larger survey dealing with the broader area of physical contact produced responses from 703 people. Of these, 347 were male and 310 were female, while 9 did not indicate their sex. About half indicated that nonerotic contact, such as hugging, kissing, or affectionate touching, could be beneficial to both male and female patients. Male therapists were more prone than female therapists to see it as beneficial, but as having the possibility of being misunderstood by the patient. As might be expected from their customary therapy techniques, the majority of psychodynamic therapists believed such behavior might be misunderstood, while the majority of humanistic therapists thought it would rarely, if ever, be misunderstood. Humanists were also the group that engaged in this behavior the most often. Overall, 27 percent of the sample at least occasionally engaged in what they considered nonerotic touching with their clients (Holroyd and Brodsky, 1977).

In contrast, only 4 percent of the respondents thought that erotic contact might benefit patients, and that dropped to 2 percent for the treatment of same-sex patients. The possible benefits proposed were the alleviation of a specific sexual problem, or the promotion of some type of personality growth, such as enhancing the patient's self-concept. In actual practice, nineteen male and two female therapists had intercourse with their patients in the course of treatment. The results are similar, for male psychologists, to those found by Kardener, Fuller, and Mensh (1973, 1976) in their survey of male physicians.

Thus it appears that there is a small group of therapists who believe in the value of erotic therapist-patient contacts, and a smaller group who have such contacts. Those who do are predominantly male, have intercourse with female patients, and tend to repeat their behavior. We do not know the true frequency of such behavior, but surveys probably underestimate its occurrence. Butler and Zelen (1977) suggest that one out of every five therapists engages in erotic behavior with patients, but that strikes us as an overestimate. The opinions of the vast majority of therapists who have offered comments is that erotic contact between therapist and patient is not therapeutic and therefore should not occur.

Despite some evidence that the outcome at times may be positive, the actual behavior is designed to fill the *therapist's* needs. At times it may also fill complementary patient needs and produce something positive, but that is a result of the characteristics of the match, which in these cases is not planned, and so the positive outcome is not a function of therapeutic skill. Rather, it is that once in a while a dyad gets "lucky" in this regard, but most of the time, that is not what occurs. Instead, the "therapy" as such has ended, which is the most appropriate course. The therapist has an obligation regarding the patient's further therapy, which now will have to be with some other therapist; the therapist also has an obligation to himself (since it is usually a male) to attempt to solve his problem. Not only is the behavior of the therapist likely to be negative for the patient, but also such behavior is certainly not in the therapist's best interests. As the profession has become more aware of this form of potentially self-destructive exploitation of patients, it seems appropriate to do more than announce its unsavory and unethical aspects. While therapist-patient sex certainly points up the power of the therapist to exploit, it also illustrates the vulnerability of the therapist to his or her unresolved needs. We have to recognize our vulnerabilities, and as a profession find ways of managing them which does not run the risk of damaging patients or destroying therapists. Marmor (1972) has illustrated the necessity for the recognition of the therapist's needs that foster physical closeness with patients. If psychotherapy is defined as we have been defining it throughout this book, then satisfying the therapist's sexual needs is not psychotherapy for the patient. Thus, simple as it may sound, the solution is for therapists to focus on the task at hand, which is not exploiting the patient, but doing effective psychotherapy.

Therapists obviously do not find that so simple to carry out, however. In the next chapter we will deal with the vicissitudes in the life of the therapist, the temptations, struggles, and problems that are relatively singular to the profession of practicing psychotherapists. We will explore a number of important areas, such as the connections between practicing psychotherapy and the therapist's other relationships, and consider how they affect us and what we can and should do about such effects.

FINAL COMMENTS

First, the behavior of the therapist is considered by both therapists and patients as a very important influence on the process and outcome of the psychotherapy. To be accurate about the influence, however, it is necessary to see therapist behavior as interactive—*as part* of the total process of the therapy rather than conceiving of the therapist as *the* therapy. In one sense this means there is no such entity as the "therapeutic personality"; at the same time, however, there are therapist behaviors, which, taken in combination with other variables, do significantly influence the therapy. These behaviors are of major interest. We have already developed many clinical impressions, but they need validation, and we look to research to provide better answers.

Because of the numerous limitations in the studies of therapist variables, help has been limited. The available research has indicated that the power of certain variables to affect outcome is either less than we thought (or hoped), or has not really been appropriately tested. For example, on a gross level there is support for the idea that the therapist's emotional wellbeing influences the therapy, for better or worse. There is little support for the superiority of any major theoretical orientation, but there is agreement as to the value of all therapists establishing a positive therapeutic relationship with clients.

While the display of therapist behavior is related to factors such as theoretical orientation, degree of adherence to prescribed technical procedures, and patient perceptions and responsiveness to the therapist, we can make some generalizations about therapist behaviors that will tend most often to increase or decrease chances of a successful outcome. On the negative side, personality characteristics that exploit the patient while catering to the needs of the therapist, such as excessive hostility, seductiveness, and avoidance of self-scrutiny, are prominent, along with technical errors, such as the failure to be explicit about goals, rigidity, and communication problems. The remedies available at the moment focus on the need for better selection and training, and various forms of self- and peer-examination, such as personal therapy and supervision. The remedies apparently do not work as well as one would like, nor are there guaranteed preventive measures.

A major reason for these limitations is lack of validation for the positive therapist behaviors. Nonetheless, high probability can be given to the combining of therapist behaviors that include the elimination of stereotyping, adequate knowledge of the client's needs and life situation, genuine interest in the patients being treated, and facilitative personality characteristics, such as clarity, warmth, concern, and a sense of appropriate responsibility. Finding the workable therapist-client match still seems to be a very good idea, but it has not been made clear what the ingredients must be, other than indicating the complexity and variability of the possible dyads and their relation to the outcome of the psychotherapy.

Faced with uncertainty and the pressure to do a good job, therapists obviously have to use some pattern. We believe in establishing a therapeutic relationship that has as its ingredients that it is warm, empathetic, and has a "fit" for us and for the client. There must be an appropriate exposition of procedures, including discussion of the goals, possibilities, and probabilities of any particular therapy situation to be considered or attempted. A theoretical orientation is needed, as well as techniques connected to it, but there must be flexible application of both theory and techniques. Personal therapy, supervision, peer discussion, and patient feedback are valuable aids to understanding our role. Formal continuing education has also proved useful.

REFERENCES

Agel, J. (Ed.). *The radical therapist* (New York: Ballantine, 1971).

Barron, J. A prolegomenon to the personality of the psychotherapist: Choices and changes. *Psychotherapy: Theory, Research and Practice* (1978) **15**:309–313.

Bergin, A. E., and Lambert, M. J. The evaluation of therapeutic outcome. In S. L. Garfield and A. E. Bergin (Eds.), *Handbook of psychotherapy and behavior change: An empirical analysis*, 2nd ed. (New York: Wiley, 1978).

Berzins, J. I. Therapist-patient matching. In A. S. Gurman and A. M. Razin (Eds.), *Effective psychotherapy: A handbook of research* (New York: Pergamon Press, 1977).

Broverman, I. K., Broverman, D. M., Clarkson, F. E., Rosenkrantz, P. S., and Vogel, S. R. Sex-role stereotypes and clinical judgments of mental health. *Journal of Consulting and Clinical Psychology* (1970) **34**:1–7. Butier, S., and Zelen, S. L. Sexual intimacies between therapists and patients. *Psychotherapy: Theory, Research and Practice* (1977) **14**:139–145.

Carkhuff, R. R. *The art of helping* (Amherst, MA: Human Resource Development Press, 1972).

Carr, J. E. Differentiation similarity of patient and therapist and the outcome of psychotherapy. *Journal of Abnormal Psychology* (1970) **76**:361–369.

Chessick, R. D. *Why psychotherapists fail* (New York: Science House, 1971).

Clark, T., and Jaffe, D. *Toward a radical therapy* (New York: Gordon & Breach, 1973).

Coan, R. W. *Psychologists. Personal and theoretical pathways* (New York: Irvington Publishers, 1979).

Cummings, N. A. Adoption of a psychological orientation: The role of the inadvertent. *Psychotherapy: Theory, Research and Practice* (1978) **15**:323–328.

Dahlberg, C. Sexual contact between patient and therapist. *Contemporary Psychoanalysis* (1970) **6**:107–124.

Garfield, S. L., and Bergin, A. E. Personal therapy, outcome, and some therapist variables. *Psychotherapy: Theory, Research and Practice* (1971) **8:**251–253.

Garfield, S. L., and Kurtz, R. Personal therapy for the psychotherapist: Some findings and issues. *Psychotherapy: Theory, Research and Practice* (1976) **13:**188–192.

Gladwin, T. *Poverty U.S.A.* (Boston: Little, Brown, 1967).

Goldstein, A. P. *Psychotherapeutic attraction* (New York: Pergamon, 1971).

Gottman, J., and Markman, H. J. Experimental designs in psychotherapy research. In S. L. Garfield and A. E. Bergin (Eds.), *Handbook of psychotherapy and behavior change: An empirical analysis*, 2nd ed. (New York: Wiley, 1978).

Gottsegen, G. B., and Gottsegen, M. G. Countertransference—The professional identity defense. *Psychotherapy: Theory, Research and Practice* (1979) **16:**57–60.

Hare-Mustin, R. T. Ethical considerations in the use of sexual contact in psychotherapy. *Psychotherapy: Theory, Research and Practice* (1974) **11:**308–310.

Heitler, J. B. Preparatory techniques in initiating expressive psychotherapy with lower-class, unsophisticated patients. *Psychological Bulletin* (1976) **83:**339–352.

Herron, W. G. The therapist's choice of a theory of personality. *Psychotherapy: Theory, Research and Practice* (1978) **15:**396–401.

Hogan, D. *The regulation of psychotherapists. Vol. III. A review of malpractice suits in the United States* (Cambridge, MA: Ballinger, 1979).

Holroyd, J. C., and Brodsky, A. M. Psychologists' attitudes and practices regarding erotic and nonerotic physical contact with patients. *American Psychologist* (1977) **32:**843–849.

Hurvitz, N. The status and tasks of radical therapy. *Psychotherapy: Theory, Research and Practice* (1977) **14:**65–73.

Hurvitz, N. The radical psychotherapist and the American dream. *Voices* (1979) **14:**66–76.

Ivey, A. E. *Microcounseling: innovations in interviewing training* (Springfield, IL: Charies C Thomas, 1971).

Johnson, M. An approach to feminist therapy. *Psychotherapy: Theory, Research and Practice* (1976) **13:**72–76.

Jacobs, D., Charles, E., Jacobs, T., Weinstein, H., and Manu, D. Preparation for treatment of the disadvantaged patient. Effects on disposition and outcome. *American Journal of Orthopsychiatry* (1972) **42:**666–674.

Kardener, S., Fuller, M., and Mensh, I. A survey of physicians' attitudes and practices regarding erotic and non-erotic contact with patients. *American Journal of Psychiatry* (1973) **130:** 1077–1081.

Kardener, S., Fuller, M., and Mensh, I. Characteristics of "erotic" practitioners. *American Journal of Psychiatry* (1976) **133:**1324–1325.

Kaschack, E. Sociotherapy: An ecological model for therapy with women. *Psychotherapy: Theory, Research and Practice* (1976) **13:**61–63.

Klein, M. H. Feminist concepts of therapy outcome. *Psychotherapy: Theory, Research and Practice* (1976) **13:**89–95.

Kravetz, D. Consciousness-raising groups and group psychotherapy: Alternative mental health resources for women. *Psychotherapy: Theory, Research and Practice* (1976) **13:**66–71.

Lazarus, A. Style not systems. *Psychotherapy: Theory, Research and Practice* (1978) **15:** 359–361.

Lerner, B. *Therapy in the ghetto* (Baltimore: Johns Hopkins University Press, 1972).

Lorion, R. P. Research on psychotherapy and behavior change with the disadvantaged. In S. L. Garfield and A. E. Bergin (Eds.), *Handbook of psychotherapy and behavior change: An empirical analysis*, 2nd ed. (New York: Wiley, 1978).

Luborsky, L., and Spence, D. P. Quantitative research on psychoanalytic therapy. In S. L. Garfield and A. E. Bergin (Eds.), *Handbook of psychotherapy and behavior change: An empirical analysis*, 2nd ed. (New York: Wiley, 1978).

McCartney, J. I. Overt transference. *Journal of Sex Research* (1966) **2**:227–237.

McLachlan, J. C. Benefit from group therapy as a function of patient-therapist match on conceptual level. *Psychotherapy: Theory, Research and Practice* (1972) **9**:317–323.

McLachlan, J. C. Therapy strategies, personality orientation and recovery from alcoholism. *Canadian Psychiatric Association Journal* (1974) **19**:25–30.

Marmor, J. Sexual acting out in psychotherapy. *The American Journal of Psychoanalysis* (1972) **22**:3–8.

Matarazzo, R. G. Research on the teaching and learning of psychotherapeutic skills. In S. L. Garfield and A. E. Bergin (Eds.), *Handbook of psychotherapy and behavior change: An empirical analysis*, 2nd ed. (New York: Wiley, 1978).

Parloff, M. B., Waskow, I. E., and Wolfe, B. E. Research on therapist variables in relation to process and outcome. In S. L. Garfield and A. E. Bergin (Eds.), *Handbook of psychotherapy and behavior change: An empirical analysis*, 2nd ed. (New York: Wiley, 1978).

Posthuma, A. B., and Carr, J. E. Differentiation matching in psychotherapy. *Canadian Psychological Review* (1975) **16**:35–43.

Razin, A. M. The A-B variable: Still promising after twenty years? In A. S. Gurman and A. M. Razin (Eds.), *Effective psychotherapy: A handbook of research* (New York: Pergamon Press, 1977).

Robertiello, R. C. Iatrogenic psychiatric illness. *Journal of Contemporary Psychotherapy* (1975) **7**:3–8.

Rogers, C. R. Empathic: An appreciated way of being. *Counseling Psychologist* (1975) **5**:2–10.

Rogers, C. R. The necessary and sufficient conditions of therapeutic personality change. *Journal of Consulting Psychology* (1957) **21**:95–103.

Shepard, M. *The love treatment: Sexual intimacy between patients and therapists* (New York: Wyden, 1971).

Steiner, G. L. A survey to identify factors in therapists' selection of a therapeutic orientation. *Psychotherapy: Theory, Research and Practice* (1978) **15**:359–361.

Stephens, J. H., Shaffer, J. W., and Zlotowitz, H. I. An optimum A-B Scale of psychotherapist effectiveness. *Journal of nervous and Mental Disease* (1975) **160**:267–281.

Strupp, H. The therapist's theoretical orientation: An overrated variable. *Psychotherapy: Theory, Research and Practice* (1978) **15**:314–317.

Strupp, H., Hadley, S. W., and Gomes-Schwartz, B. *Psychotherapy for better or worse. The problem of negative effects* (New York: Aronson, 1977).

Sundland, D. M. Theoretical orientations of psychotherapists. In A. S. Gurman and A. M. Razin (Eds.), *Effective psychotherapy: A handbook of research* (New York: Pergamon Press, 1977)

Task Force on Sex Bias and Sex Role Stereotyping in Psychotherapeutic Practice. Guidelines for therapy with women. *American Psychologist* (1978) **33**:1122–1123.

Taylor, B. J., and Wagner, N. N. Sex between therapists and clients: A review and analysis. *Professional Psychology* (1976) **7**:593–601.

Truax C. B., and Carkhuff, R. R. *Toward effective counseling and psychotherapy: Training and practice* (Chicago: Aldine, 1967).

Tuma, A. H., May, P. R., Yale, C., and Forsythe, A. B. Therapist characteristics and the outcome of treatment in schizophrenics. *Archives of General Psychiatry* (1978) **35**: 81–85.

Walton, D. E. An exploratory study: Personality factors and theoretical orientation of therapists. *Psychotherapy: Theory, Research and Practice* (1978) **15**:371–374.

Waskow, I. E. Summary of discussion following workshop. *Psychotherapy: Theory, Research and Practice* (1976) **13**:96–98.

Whitehorn, J. C., and Betz, B. J. A study of psychotherapeutic relationships between physicians and schizophrenic patients when insulin is combined with psychotherapy and when psychotherapy is used alone. *American Journal of Psychiatry* (1957) **113**: 901–910.

Whitehorn, J. C., and Betz, B. J. Further studies of the doctor as a crucial variable in the outcome of treatment with schizophrenic patients. *American Journal of Psychiatry* (1960) **117**:215–223.

Whitley, B. E., Jr. Sex roles and psychotherapy: A current appraisal. *Psychological Bulletin* (1979) **86**:1309–1321.

IV

At Issue: Occupational Hazards

UNAPPRECIATED BURDENS

In this chapter we discuss the fact that the therapist's behavior is reactive to the process of psychotherapy. We have already discussed how the therapy is reactive to the therapist. In so doing we suggested that the therapy can also put the therapist at risk. Thus, behavior in and outside the therapy may be a function of doing therapy, of being a therapist. Some of these behaviors can be major problems for the therapist, and these difficulties are considered.

These problems have been given limited attention in the literature about psychotherapy. They are accepted as probabilities, but their impact on the therapist has been given little notice. They are too often dismissed as far less serious issues than they really are, and when included, are melded into a focus on how the therapy is being affected. The usual conception is that the therapist is to "work out" personal problems so that they do not negatively affect the therapy.

As illustrated previously, patients are exploited by therapists who apparently have not sufficiently solved their own problems. In fact, all therapists bring more or less imperfect selves to the practice of their therapies. The therapy situation itself provides endless opportunities for these personality factors to be played upon and exhibited. Some therapists take the opportunity to gratify their needs in ways that are detrimental to the process, with one striking example, sexual exploitation, described in the preceding chapter.

Most often, the therapy situation is a stimulus for feelings and actions not consciously intended to be harmful to the client, though they may be. Primarily, they are struggles for the therapist, in which the burden is on the therapist, and damage first accrues to the therapist. Ultimately the *damaged* therapist may well become the *damaging* therapist, doing ineffective or harmful therapy. But the initial trouble is the therapist's, and our concern in this chapter is preventing that, with the belief that such prevention will benefit the therapeutic enterprise.

By not paying sufficient attention to rather obvious potential problems, such as the ways the therapeutic situation may contribute to most therapists having feelings of boredom, fatigue, anxiety, or anger, a powerful potential source of negative therapeutic effects is certainly ignored. Generally, therapists are simply told to learn *not* to be inappropriate. The probability that the therapeutic situation is creating repeated opportunities for less than therapeutic feelings and actions on the therapist's part, is really glossed over. Furthermore, what happens to the therapist in the therapy may be carried out of there by the therapist and into personal life in a deleterious fashion, only to finally return to the therapy and limit its outcome.

The therapy situation is considered something that the therapist has to manage, and in a major sense this is certainly true. But the ingredients of the therapy situation, or beyond that, of an entire therapy practice, are not completely handled by the usual procedures of getting the therapist well-equipped and putting her or him into action. None of us, whatever measures we use or have used, are that well-equipped. We all run into trouble, such as feeling tired, bored, anxious, angry, distracted, impulsive, neglected, unrewarded, and a number of other feelings that are both personally unpleasant and have the potential for interfering with the doing of psychotherapy. At times therapists act on these feelings inappropriately. It is insufficient assistance to the psychotherapist to assign these feelings and actions a label, such as countertransference, and apply only the customary remedies of more personal therapy and supervision. We believe the therapy itself is liable to cause problems to any and all therapists. We must recognize these problems and make them far more visible than has been done in the past. And we must seek remedies for these which involve restructuring modes of therapeutic practice or personal lives, or both. The feelings tnat occur in the therapist, and are suppressed or repressed in the interests of the therapy, may well create havoc in the therapist's life outside therapy. Such situations are not conducive to the mental health of the therapist and, as we have seen, pose a threat to the welfare of patients. We believe the awareness of the impact on the therapist of doing therapy can lead to ways to lessen the negative possibilities. For example, the most helpful way to do therapy is not to accept the fact that you are always tired in the afternoon while seeing patients. It is much better to find ways not to be tired, even if that means not seeing patients at that time, or eliminating something pleasurable, such as a luncheon martini, which you discover makes you tired at the time you are seeing patients.

This, and other difficulties, will be explored, but first we want to look at what the therapist brings to the therapy, some of which in turn can be viewed as vulnerabilities. We will assume the equipment is as good as our training facilities can produce, which still means limitations. Even if the therapists are as good as we know how to make them at the moment, they will feel stress from the very process of being psychotherapists. The questions are: How will they inevitably be subject to stress? and How can we minimize the stress effects?

Therapist Characteristics

The most extensive survey of psychotherapists has been reported by Henry (1977; Henry, Sims, and Spray, 1971, i973). This survey covered over 4,000 therapists from psychiatry, psychoanalysis, psychology, and social work. They were an urban population, with primarily a psychodynamic orientation. The majority were Jewish and had been exposed to at least one set of cultural influences besides those of the United States. In general, the sample had a high socioeconomic status, upward social mobility, and a liberal political stance. Their degree of emotional instability was no greater than the general college-educated population.

Personal motivations for becoming psychotherapists included the desire to help people, need for affiliation with others, desire to understand people and society, the gaining of an identity, and an interest in self-examination. The latter was affirmed by 74 percent of the group having undergone personal therapy.

The idea that psychotherapists engaged in therapy because they had particular problems themselves, such as a need to compensate for previous lacks in their own lives, was not supported. Henry states that their investigation concluded in a view of psychotherapists as, "a reasonably balanced group of educated persons with a positive sense of their own competence and identity" (1977, p. 56).

The findings of Henry and his co-workers are supported by an earlier work on 148 psychiatrists and 35 analysts (Rogow, 1970). Some contrasts are found in a survey of clinical psychologists by Garfield and Kurtz (1974). In particular, the predominant psychodynamic orientation was replaced by avowed eclecticism. Also, Kepecs and Greenly (1975) found urban-nonurban differences among psychiatrists. Only 16 percent of the nonurban sample were Jewish, and there was less personal analysis and political liberalism than in the urban sample.

Thus, there is not a great amount of data to go on. The Henry data are really limited to urban therapists with a predominantiy psychodynamic orientation. However, within this context some interesting conclusions are reported (Henry, Sims, and Spray, 1973).

1. For these therapists their relations with spouses and their children seemed less exciting and less emotionally charged than their relationships with patients.
2. The relationships with patients were asymmetrical, meaning there was intimacy without the therapist having the risk of revealing personal feelings to the patient.
3. Relationships with the therapist's family focused on intellectual pursuits and recreational activities rather than shared emotional expression.
4. Therapists tended to select patients based on the patients' compatability to the therapists' perspective of life, which generally meant the patients were capable of insight, had good verbal ability, a psychological approach, and a certain communality of feeling states. The outward signs of probably fitting together well were a high educational level and similar religiocultural backgrounds.

5. These therapists were generally uninterested in professional societies and the routine activities of home and community. They were not very interested in, or adept at, ordinary socialization. Instead, they were primarily intrigued with their work with their patients and were most comfortable in the psychotherapeutic relationship.
6. Some distinctions appeared between therapists who were in private practice, who were in the majority, and therapists working in institutions. The latter tended to feel less responsibility for, and involvement with, their patients.

In essence, then, the therapists in the Henry sample were committed to a psychodynamic approach, were very invested in their patients, and evolved this interest through the medium of psychotherapy. At the same time, they appeared afraid of close emotional relations outside the therapy, which may have been taking most, if not all, of what they had to give. So, it would appear that they were "better" interpersonally as therapists than when they were being husbands, wives, mothers, fathers, or socializing persons. It is impossible to tell whether the therapeutic process causes this, or whether the outside relating process causes the therapist to want to "escape" into the therapy because it is seen as a less risky outlet for emotional investment.

What does seem apparent is that these therapists felt and behaved differently in doing therapy than in other interpersonal situations. Of course the generalizability of such a conclusion is quite limited. As indicated, these were urban therapists with a predominant psychodynamic orientation. Nonurban psychotherapists tend to have different backgrounds. Also, subsequent to this survey there have been more serious attempts to recruit people from disadvantaged groups into the psychotherapeutic profession, though they undoubtedly remain a minority. While statistical information is not available to support this, the probability is that the majority of psychotherapists are still middle class and Jewish in origin, but that other backgrounds are achieving larger representation.

Also, Sundland (1977) has illustrated that by this time the surveys of therapists' professed theoretical orientation show a majority of therapists choosing an eclectic approach. Thus, psychodynamic, and any of the other "school labels," represent a minority of therapists who actually respond to surveys. But Sundland indicates a response bias in terms of the various professions, with psychologists, pastoral counselors, and social workers responding more frequently than psychiatrists and psychoanalysts. Since the responses tend to come from between only 30–50 percent of those asked, it may even be that eclectics are not the majority of psychotherapists but are merely more cooperative in responding to surveys.

In essence we are left with some scattered samples of evidence about psychotherapists' personalities. There is some support for the concept of a relationship between certain personality variables and different theoretical orientations, but the evidence is too limited to depict even a relatively comprehensive picture. The research data available do not provide sufficient information to describe definite personality structures that could form the stage for the process of psychotherapy. Demographic data are more available, but how that affects therapists' personality traits is really not known. Nor are the effects of training procedures at all established.

For example, Gurman and Razin state: ". . . we see evidence of the dearth of empirical attention that has been paid to the personal therapy of professional psychotherapists . . . perhaps someone will be courageous enough to dispassionately examine some of the many important issues involved in therapists' own personal therapy" (1977, p. 219).

The question of whether therapists bring particular personal needs into the doing of psychotherapy that would make them more reactive and vulnerable to the situation is not at the moment open to a clear answer. Henry (1977) has indicated no particular support for this idea, but Burton (1972) suggests it, though for a sample of only twelve, and Wheelis (1956) believed that psychoanalysts had a particularly strong desire for self-mastery along with needs for intimacy. That is an impression, and there appear to be no studies of the actual effect of the therapy on the therapist, particularly in reference to behavior outside therapy. Studies on the therapist and the process and outcome of therapy merely give the inference to support the impression that therapy does affect the therapist, as well as the patient. We will now explore specific effects that we have observed.

FATIGUE

Is is very true that doing psychotherapy can be zestful, fascinating, and packed with jumbo shrimp for the spirit. When it is that way, it is a pleasure and a facile activity for the psychotherapist. But it can also be very tiring, and when that occurs the therapy suffers because the therapist is struggling with something in addition to, or instead of, the patient's problems. The therapist is desperately trying to stay awake. At the very least this means looking alert, not yawning, and managing intelligible responses when they are called for. Many patients who lie on the couch and cannot see their therapist may have the idea that sleep may have overtaken their customarily avid listener. These patients are not always wrong. In addition, there are partial "turnoffs" by the therapist's receptors because in some fashion the therapist is tired and cannot tune in as completely as the treatment requires.

The fact of therapist fatigue needs to be considered for probable causes and remedies, since the patient is entitled to an awake therapist, and since we have established that the therapist's aware presence is a very vital factor in the probable outcome of any of the psychotherapies. Each therapist will have to gauge his or her own fatigue quotients, and get familiar with the influence of time on their degree of usefulness. It is obvious that, other than within broad limits, the use of time by therapists varies widely in all of its dimensions. Thus, there is no universal "best time" for practice, but their are individual ones.

The situation of the therapy is a determiner of when time will be spent with patients and when it will not. So, if you are a therapist in an institution your working hours may well be set by the institution. If you are in private practice and are in the process of developing a hoped-for number of patients, you may find it necessary to be most available when the possible patients are most willing to come. This is often early in the morning, in the evening, and on weekends. These can also be times when you are more likely to be less awake, particularly if you are working elsewhere during the inbetween hours, and that work is supposed to be your "full time" job, with the private practice of psychotherapy as an "extra," even though ultimately you would want the practice to be primary. Therapist fatigue comes from three main sources. The first of these is a major characteristic of psychotherapies, namely that the patients are suffering. They come to therapy because they are in some kind of pain, and they suffer while they are in therapy, and when the suffering is relatively minimal, they leave therapy. So, although all of the therapy does not involve hearing about problems, grief, distress, and the like, most of it involves just that. Such content can and does wear at the therapist. The money received and the excitement and pleasure involved in aiding another person and sharing their intimate struggles and victories are certainly sources of satisfaction. But these, and whatever else that is positively derived from the therapy relationship by the therapist, do not eliminate the possibility that the content may make you weary. How much of this you can handle is an individual matter, but for each therapist there is a tolerance range. Moving beyond that puts you in psychic jeopardy.

It is not so easy to notice either what is happening to you, or to believe in the possible negative consequences once you become aware that you are feeling tired. English (1979) has suggested a number of reasons why therapists "find" themselves with an overload of clients. These include pride in your ability to handle many patient hours, a feeling that you need the money, a sense of importance that does not seem to be available from other sources, and an inability to turn people away if they seek help from you. Also, once you have developed a large practice you may become very habituated, even though you are also becoming very fatigued. You stay in the routine and lack conviction about the value of more time for other pursuits, such as recreation or meaningful relations with people outside those you see in therapy.

The possibility, if not probability, of taking on too much therapy time, is there for all of us who are serious about doing psychotherapy, and indeed like what we do. In the beginning there is the challenge of establishing yourself in the variety of ways offered by the practice of therapy, such as building a successful practice and reputation, or being the best therapist in a clinic by, among other things, seeing the most patients. However, the profession is much too demanding to just keep charging on without reflection. Thus, in respect to overload, while the specifics are indeed a matter of individual differences, it is crucial for the therapist to have a schedule that is not grueling and does not make the therapist tired on a regular basis. There are occasional exceptions, because therapy with even only one patient may present unexpected time demands. In general, however, therapists have considerable control over the time to be devoted to seeing patients. This power must be exercised to maximize the therapists' effectiveness, and the prerequisite is that the therapists arrange their lives so they are rarely, if ever, tired when seeing patients. Therapists obviously have trouble doing this, due to the pull of interest, dedication, status, power, money, and whatever else.

A second source of fatigue is those particular patients who make the therapist feel tired. Different types of people do this to different therapists, but most therapists have had clients who were boring or irritating in a demanding way, or who are so needful and disturbed that our energy is at some point overused. A certain amount of this behavior is expected and tolerable, but too much is exactly that. In the personal, narrow sense, these people make many other people tired as well, thus provoking a universal response. Yet, with their current therapist they are doing something which may well defeat the therapy. There appear to be a number of ways to avoid getting tired this way. For example, Cleaves (1979) has suggested that sometimes it is a matter of poor client selection on the part of the therapist. He states: "For me, boredom and that burnt-out feeling result from being with someone with whom I cannot make contact, the patient from whom I get no nourishment. . . . I now understand that attention to my needs, both in patient selection and within the therapeutic hour, is important for my survival as a therapist" (p. 90).

The second possibility is that this dimension of the patient's character be confronted by the therapist. Some of the therapy will then focus on attempting to aid the patient to see how the behavior appears to others, and how others will respond to it. This can be seen as an early attempt to foster increased cause-effect perception of situations where the patient has problems in living. English (1979) pointed out that over the many years of his practice he has attempted to emphasize the idea with his patients that their lives could be more enjoyable and that they indeed could be different. Of course the type of patient we are describing is very exacting and resistive to changing their style, so the therapist has to be open to the possibility that one's best efforts are futile. In essence, if the boring patient fails to turn into an interesting person, then there is no value in the therapist wearying herself or himself into oblivion, for after a while there would seem to be a vested interest. Perhaps Ellis (1979), who has a work schedule that makes us tired when we envision it, has the right idea when he talks of ways to fend off fatigue derived from dealing with disturbing clients. These include accepting frustration as part of the reality of psychotherapy, and accepting challenges, but not berating himself if his efforts do not bring about change every time or in everybody. And to this we add the therapist's acceptance of boredom as part of certain patient-therapist experiences, although we might like it otherwise.

Doing psychotherapy is an activity with a proclivity to consume the therapist, even when the client is pleasant and cooperative. We have also become quite aware that some form of resistance to change is a repeating behavior for all patients, but that is really not what makes us tired. Instead, patients who frequently give us very little by way of something to work with, and who often turn our efforts aside, do wear us out. Ideally we would choose the appropriate moments and use the appropriate phrases, and all would be well, meaning that the therapy situation would be workable rather than fatiguing. Instead we sometimes miss out, sometimes hesitate and work tired, and sometimes have to terminate the situation as unworkable. Why don't we do better than that? Well, we certainly try, but some patients just have a way of slowing therapists and keeping them in a weary place. As Cleaves notes: "It will always be difficult for me to tell someone I don't choose to work with him or her, and anxiety producing to confront someone during the therapy hour with my negative feelings" (1979, p. 90).

The third source of therapist fatigue is more encompassing. It is a feeling of being tired of doing whatever psychotherapy one is doing, a desire to get away from it and either do something else as an occupation, or do psychotherapy, but with different people in a different place and in a different way. It is a constant fatigue, a depression and a resentment connected to doing what was once very appealing.

The probability with this kind of fatigue is that it signals powerful unresolved emotional problems on the part of the therapist. Misperceptions of patients and their problems will seem to be occurring with painful repetitiveness, and there will be a growing, unpleasant sense of the therapist's inability to be involved in any therapeutic endeavor resembling success. Nothing seems to work out for anybody, particularly the therapist. By this point the signals are very strong that tiredness is covering over something that is very disturbing to the therapist. While busy at being therapists we have neglected ourselves to the point of needing to rebel against it all. Bar-Levav points out: "When we, therapists, tire excessively it may well be not from too much work, but because we work in a way which yields too little for our unconscious needs, whose very existence we may deny" (1979, p. 56).

The first step is the recognition by the therapist of probable emotional difficulties that are being triggered by the process of doing psychotherapy. The struggle with these difficulties makes a person tired, and in this case the person is the therapist. The meaning of this generalized fatigue, apparently connected to the doing of psychotherapy, has to be discovered. This can be done by whatever form of self-examination the therapist chooses. (For example, we discovered that when we were having conflicted personal relationships with others outside therapy, it was harder for us to do therapy. We did it, but it was rarely effortless in its feeling tone for us. Yet when our interpersonal lives were more fulfilling, the same time spent in therapy, often with the same patients who previously seemed to be fatiguing us, was much easier and had a comfortable flow to it.)

Szckely (1979) suggested that the therapist's tiredness will occur more often when the ego has to work with particular integrative tasks. Some of these she cites are significant changes in relationships, or in roles, or in the environment, or in one's body image. She offers a number of possible remedies, as a supportive relationship, a challenging task, or a religious experience, all of which aim for the expansion of the boundaries of the ego. Criswell (1979) suggests a range of possible solutions, from paying attention to simple needs by relaxing, playing, exercising, and completing unfinished business, to a large-scale revision in our style of living if fatigue has become too pervasive.

Fatigue is a problem we all share and need to combat. There are a number of somewhat imperfect ways to do this (we do not know of any perfect ways); the emphasis above has been on paying sufficient attention to yourself—the therapist—so that you do not have to get tired very often. The solutions are there, but the beginning has to be recognition.

There are two inventories that have been proposed as ways to estimate your fatigue status as a therapist. One is by Tirnauer and Cheek (1979), the other by Bach (1979). Such conceptions seem useful to us, so we have borrowed from these two and suggest the following ten as our own "tired signs." If you recognize these, you are in trouble, or soon will be.

GROSS SIGNS OF A TIRED PSYCHOTHERAPIST

1. All clients seem annoying, more or less.
2. When the therapy day begins, you wish it had ended.
3. You doubt any of your patients will change significantly, and you doubt you know what change is, anyway.
4. You sense interventions you could make, but they do not seem worth the effort.
5. You do not discuss your feelings with colleagues, but in fact use up energy disguising what you really feel about your clients.
6. You schedule every hour you can, charge whatever comes into mind, and toy with the idea that psychotherapy is certainly a ripoff of lots of people.
7. You do not take days off. When you are sick you always work.
8. You feel needed by everybody to the point of oppression, yet you wonder why people came to you in the first place, and particularly, why they keep coming.
9. Your fantasy is to earn as good a living, or better, some other way.
10. During each therapy session you watch the clock more than anything or anybody else in the room.

If you experience all ten of these, the syndrome is clear, and the problem is acute. The other two measures we mentioned are a bit more elaborate and "softer," giving you some ground to ponder. All of us are nonetheless attempting to face the same issue. It is more of a fact than most therapists have been willing to acknowledge that psychotherapy is seductive in draining your energy. Rather insidiously you can find yourself too tired too often. The demands of practicing psychotherapy can be inherently fatiguing, by content, by clients, and by the process stirring up unresolved emotional problems of the therapist. Greater attention has to be paid to the therapist's vulnerability to factors such as fatigue. No one knows, for example, the degree to which the tired state of the therapist has been an influential variable in therapeutic outcome. What we do know is that all therapists get tired, that it is a disease of the occupation, that it bodes ill for all concerned, and that the therapists have to do more about it than hide the fatigue from the patients. As O'Connell has said: "You can't do this work safely and well, unless you realize what you are getting into . . . we need to face straight out that the profession of psychotherapy is demanding, time consuming, and that it can be a risky way to be, eventually, sometimes" (1979, p. 37, 40). Fatigue is inherent in the risk. The dangers of this "taken for granted" problem have been underestimated. Fatigue can decimate therapists and therapies. When it can be avoided, and it often can, then we have to stop working when we are fatigued.

PERSONAL RELATIONSHIPS

While we are not sure of the numerous factors that appear to motivate people to become psychotherapists, we are sure they want something out of it in addition to, or other than, monetary rewards. As indicated in the previous section on fatigue, there are personal needs of any therapist, and the therapy process itself is related to their gratification, or lack of it. The report by Henry (1977) contains the suggestion that therapists are at their best, interpersonally, when they are doing therapy. Therapists' intimate relationships outside therapy, such as marriage, appear not to be as successful. We are not suggesting that therapists are less adept at these social, interpersonal relationships than the rest of the world, but being a therapist can, and often does, pose problems for personal relationships outside therapy. For example, the Snyders (Snyder and Snyder, 1971–72) describe the two sides of their marital relationship. She comments: "Not only could I now consult with an authority on the problems of adjustment to marriage but in the future I also had a handy problem-solver. . . . It was ideal. It wasn't ideal. Oh, he was an ace at solving problems but unfortunately they always belonged to other people" (pp. 23–24). Her husband, who is the therapist (problem-solver), stated: "Initially, I assumed that a wife would not require me to 'therapize.' I was wrong" (p. 25).

Fox (1971–72) has also articulated the problems faced by spouses of therapists. They complain that their therapist-partners are not willing to be as patient, compassionate, and understanding with them as they are with their clients. They also complain that therapists, when involved in solving problems between themselves and their partners, have a rather restrictive methodology. They believe only in talking it out together, and resent any insistence on other behaviors, such as privacy and silence, that their partners may consider to be solutions.

Kornrich has some very open and pertinent comments about himself and his relationships. He states: "I became interested in psychology because of my parents marital discord. I am about as distant with my wife and three sons as I felt in my family of origin. I am against marriage and children. I am for noncontractual, open and free relationships. I resist being typecast in the role of husband, father, etc., and have my behavior predictably flow from the expectations these roles elicit from others. Must my needs, in order to be labeled mature, husbandly, fatherly, and loving, be subordinated to family needs? Man is absolutely not monogomous. Love does not endure. Often, even mutual affection, admiration and respect die. Intensity . . . in relating and sex wane rapidly for most people. I love my parents. I love my sons. I'd even like to love and live the idea of a family. You'd never guess, would you?" (pp. 73–76).

Auster comments: "I think Allen Wheelis's speculation in *The Quest for Identity* that people in our profession have substantial difficulty with intimacy except in clearly structured situations is relevant here" (1971–72, p. 77).

Robertiello feels that a primary motivation for most therapists entering the field is trying to find a way to deal with their own problems. On the one hand, personal knowledge of emotional problems can help their understanding of patients and increase their empathic abilities. But "since it was often their personal insecurities and faltering self-image that led them to become therapists in the first place, many or even most of them retain these insecurities about themselves as people (1978, p. 124).

We have cited these examples to illustrate the fact that therapists, and people close to them, have reported the existence of personal struggles for therapists. Therapists do bizarre things, and behave in unusual ways, such as marrying their former patients. They behave very much like the rest of humankind, and there really are no special gods to protect them from their own humanness. Perls, Rado, Moreno, and Freud all make Robertiello's list of insecure people, without his contending they were or are poor therapists. It seems that therapists' psychotherapeutic behavior can be isolated from personal behavior, which may be ineffective. The potential separation of the behaviors is not, however, guaranteed. If personal difficulties are serious and frequent, then the probability increases of negative reverberations into the doing of therapy.

The therapy situation itself can frequently make it hard for therapists to have enjoyable and successful personal relationships outside the therapy. Robertiello illustrates this in respect to therapists relating to their partners in intimate relationships. He believes psychotherapists are drawn to problem people, insecure and immature when compared to the therapists. The therapists tend to be supportive, while their partners tend to be dependent, or at least that is how it seems to work in the beginning. Therapists get narcissistic gratification from the admiration and the superiority of control, but it is too one-sided and eventually can self-destruct because the therapists also want to have fulfillment of dependency needs. Being supportive all the time leaves no room for this. After a series of days of primarily attending to the needs of others, who actually tend to have a very positive image of the therapist in numerous instances, it is difficult and often unappealing to pay attention to the needs of still another person. By not being supportive, the seeds of disillusionment are planted. The partners did not expect, and do not like, demands from their therapist-mates. Frequently they cannot, or will not, meet these demands when the therapists want to take rather than give.

Another pattern relating to mates and families is really not to relate, to distance and busy oneself in other activities, such as becoming a famous person through the professional societies, or writing books that attract attention and positive regard, or in general dashing about and becoming well known. The therapist's self-image is enhanced without the enhancers getting particularly close to the therapist. Of course we do not mean that everybody who does these activities has such motivations, but it is one way to increase self-esteem that certain "famous" psychotherapists probably use at the expense of their personal, potentially intimate relationships.

Some therapists go into the therapy situation in a highly needful state and derive gratifications from doing therapy which they are unable to obtain elsewhere. At the same time, the gratifications of therapy are limited by the type of relationship endemic to the psychotherapies. It is true that the boundaries of the psychotherapeutic relationship can be both stretched and contracted, and often are, usually in the name of therapeutic necessity. Yet it is quite possible that the delineation of the therapeutic situation may also be designed to meet certain needs of the therapist. The use of time is an example of this. One could certainly ask why the 50–minute hour has become 45 minutes for so many therapists? It could probably be argued that the time spent with a particular patient ought to be variable from session to session, depending on patient needs at the time. But that approach would neglect therapists' needs, for such variations could wreak havoc for many a therapist's schedule. So, a regular time is stipulated and expected. It is believed that such regularity has more benefits for the patient than varying the time, but the schedule is not maintained by therapists solely for the posited value for the patients. The regularity, and the time per session, are variables that at the moment therapists find conducive to their work needs, and that has a tendency to reduce continued scrutiny of whether or not the current procedures are the "best" for the therapy.

However, most of the variations in psychotherapies and psychotherapists are rather limited if therapists wanted to construe therapy as a gratification source for their basic needs. Sexual satisfaction of any major sort is out of the question, despite some therapists foolishly attempting it. Warmth and praise are available, but tempered over the course of the therapy by anger and criticism of the therapist. Patients who spend any length of time in therapy exhibit a range of emotional reactions to the therapist which are by no means synchronized to how the therapist is feeling at particular times. In many psychotherapies the technique requires the therapist to be relatively ambiguous in order to serve as an object of the patient's projections. While it is true that such procedures alleviate the risk of revelation by the therapist, they also mean the therapist is frequently misunderstood in regard to what the therapist really thinks and feels about the patient. Unreal negative attitudes and attributes are assigned to the therapist by the patient as part of the therapeutic process.

When a patient is being difficult with the therapist on the basis of distorted perceptions of the therapist's feelings, the therapist may wish to be disclosing with the hope of stopping the patient's anger and restoring the therapist's well being. There are, of course, other instances in which the therapist may consider possible self-disclosure. Actually, there is a considerable difference of opinion about the amount and type of self-disclosure that can and should be made by therapists to patients, with humanistic orientations being the most open and encouraging of this practice, and psychodynamic the least. However, all approaches debate its appropriateness as a therapeutic tool in terms of its effectiveness for the patient, but do not encourage it if it is primarily something therapists have a need to do for themselves.

Thus, if therapists want to be self-disclosing, they have to find a "therapeutic" justification. Some is provided in a general way by the research indicating that mild to moderate degrees of disclosure are positively related to better mental health (Jourard, 1964). Weiner (1969, 1972) believes in the value of some self-exposure by the therapist, but requires developing a rationale that will serve the needs of the therapy. He feels that therapy with adolescent and borderline personalities calls for giving information that establishes the therapist as more of a real person than a transference figure. He is against a great deal of self-exposure under any circumstances, however, and feels that such exposure without an adequate therapeutic alliance or during negative transference would be a mistake.

It seems that considerable anonymity is the most accepted "rule," though actual practice may not adhere to this as rigidly as most therapists would profess. In addition, there are events that occur, such as marriage, divorce, death, pregnancy, and childbirth, which patients can and usually do discover whether or not the therapist tells them directiy. Pregnancy is one of the most obvious, yet a review of the literature by Lax (1969) found a minimal amount of material on the subject. What there was then, as well as subsequent exploration, makes it clear that the pregnancy of the therapist, and similar events, do have an impact on patients and certainly merit discussion, yet do not have to serve as contrary factors in patients' therapy.

Flaherty (1979) discusses the possible motivations and effects of the disclosure of his marriage upon different patients whom he was seeing at that time. In a number of instances he informed his patients (whom he was seeing in a hospital outpatient setting) because he believed they would probably hear about it anyway and therefore it would be better for their therapy if he told them. In two cases where he did not tell patients, they did discover he was now married. In all cases the patients were reactive to the information, and their reactions appeared to be related to the state of the therapeutic process. But it did not seem that the revelation by the therapist was a necessary procedure to ensure the effectiveness of the therapy. Flaherty suggests that borderline and schizophrenic patients have more of a need to see the "real person" of the therapist, and self-disclosure is more useful with these types of patients than with others. It also appears that the difference between the practice of self-disclosure and the frequent "official policy" of anonymity may make many therapists uncomfortable about their self-disclosures, when they do occur.

It is clear that we are offering a service to clients where the purpose is to help them. If self-disclosure by the therapist is useful for the clients, then we ought to do it. The problem is, we really do not know how helpful, nonhelpful, or possibly even trivial, it indeed is. What we do suspect, however, is that most therapists have a need to do some of it, to share, to equalize the relationship, to make the patients more comfortable, to relieve themselves in some fashion, and other possible reasons for telling something about themselves. In order to meet this need, the therapists then find "therapeutic" reasons to reveal themselves. In contrast, we also believe there are therapists who are interested in being secretive and mysterious for reasons of their own, and they use the "therapy" to avoid disclosure.

As a guiding rule, we return to the belief that therapy is conducted to help the patient, and therefore self-revelations should only be a part of that schema. Thus, at times we have shared our personal experiences with patients. This was deliberate, with the idea of achieving a therapeutic purpose, such as the relief of debilitating anxiety, extreme grief, or overwhelming guilt as the patients felt too alone and separated in their feelings and behavior.

Obviously an exact line cannot be drawn in regard to specific material. What appears comfortable and appropriate for some therapists and their clients may be either too constricting or open for others, but the focus has to be on what is good for the therapy, and self-disclosure ought not to be treated lightly as a whim of the therapist's mood. Of course endowing personal statements by the therapist with so much importance may cause therapists to think that the same disclosures, made outside therapy, are of similar high value to the nonpatient world. They are not, but in making the transition therapists may still feel uncomfortable about possible reactions to their self-disclosures. There is some basis for this discomfort. We have already indicated certain of the unmet expectations that are held by people married to and living with therapists. Other people in the "outside" world also have expectations, and therapists can grow wary. There may be feelings on the therapists' part of needing to maintain an image of superior mental health (or at least normality) with many people who are relatively unsophisticated about the humanity of therapists. With colleagues there is the possibility of competition, and so again, there can be the need to appear a certain calm, unruffled way. The not infrequent stereotype of psychotherapy as quackery and psychotherapists as the quacks increases reticence in social relations. Thus, it is not so surprising that many of us may be particularly careful about where and with whom we share our personal feelings. In truth, of course, we are reactive beings, as illustrated by the story of the fictional psychotherapist, Saul Bergman. In active practice, Bergman, on the day following his sixty-fifth birthday, is told by his son that he is leaving his wife. Bergman is devastated, and shows it.

Ansell (1979), telling the story, had previously described Bergman this way. "He had been listening to voices over a score of years and he had in time learned to settle into a clinical view, in which he conjured mental maps that permitted him to trace the flow of passions backward and forward, from an imbedded anxiety to the revealed symptom, from a welter of painful thoughts to bland defense. He had been in a cool preoccupation with examining what he heard under a variety of lenses . . . the behavior of humans, thought and deed, was a tangle of knotted fibers which he was charged to loosen and free" (p. 266).

But, to his son he replies: "You have absolutely no consideration for anyone but your own damned self . . . !"

And his son retorts: "You're giving me your hurt as if that's got to control my life . . ."

His son later goes on: "I thought maybe you'd understand. I don't know, but I thought that you would understand . . ."

"What was I to understand?"

"That things like this happen. They happen all the time . . ."

"I know things like this happen, but not in my generation. In your generation. Not mine" (pp. 267–268).

That Bergman could not pull it out at that moment, for himself or for his son, is an example reinforcing our impression that therapy indeed takes its toll of therapists. Of course many people would have reacted as Bergman did, but the point is, he was a psychotherapist, and there is the implication that because of this, he was supposed to, above all, understand. Instead, he felt his own pain and revealed it, making it obvious that we can be sensitized in our personal lives and have none of the magic that those who would be intimate with us may expect. We are in an exacting position in our profession and we are often in need of refreshment. Some of it does come in the joyous parts and times of the job, but we look outside the job for other very significant parts. And sometimes we are very needy.

As we listen to patients we recognize our own vulnerability to behaviors that are disturbing them, such as separation, loneliness, divorce, abortion, guilt, sexual inadequacy, depression, anxiety, and an unfolding list of other problems. Some of these difficulties have been ours directly, and others have fortunately passed us by. But we know better than to be complacent about any of it. What happens to them can happen to us. The fact that we function well as therapists is no guarantee that the rest of our lives will be a source of satisfaction for us.

Most, if not all, psychotherapists have major interpersonal struggles, and therapy can stimulate personal problems, as well as having a healing function for the therapist who must "plunge" into work. Although you are a practicing therapist you will have to contend with relationships with your parents, your spouse, your children, your friends, some strangers, and some enemies, in ways that can expose your vulnerability, involve high risk, and may mean great pain. You have to solve the same or similar problems for yourself that your patients have to solve for themselves, and with more or less the same equipment, namely your own hard work. Always keep in mind that being a therapist carries the potential for causing problems in your personal life. No one has any perfected remedies for this, but awareness of your needs can help a lot, and so can the right people, if you make sure you find them.

There is personal therapy designed to help you function as a total person, not just as a therapist. And there is the time to translate what you have learned in therapy into your living process. As a therapist you will be subject to anxiety, anger, depression, boredom, and frustration (as well as, and hopefully in the main, a host of positive feelings and behaviors). You will require an antidote in your personal life to the negatives of the therapy experience. That is the special burden of psychotherapists. It is generally inescapable, but also, generally open to solution. The ways are diverse, and have to be searched out, with trial and error, and then individualized. The only real folly is believing that being a therapist is making you the least bit invincible, or that it ever will. Vulnerability and the need for further self-expression and for great love are the most likely personal consequences, along with the possibility of a great amount of personal satisfaction, joy, and excitement in being alive.

THE ROOT OF ALL EVIL

Money is the customary payment for services. However, for therapists this has traditionally been a problem, and it still continues to be. There are a number of reasons for this, the most obvious being the possible appearance of hypocrisy in the therapist's image. The therapist is the helper, the giver, the devoted person who truly cares about the patient. This clashes with the image of the taker, especially when the taking is quite overt and concrete. Asking, in fact *insisting*, on getting paid is blatant taking.

Rewards that look more subtle, and sublimated—joy in seeing patients improve their lives, stimulation of intimate participation in others' life struggles, learning about diverse worlds, the happiness and excitement of sharing and being seen as knowledgeable and helpful—all are generally considered compensation for being a psychotherapist. That is, these rewards fit the "good parent" image of the psychotherapist, and that is a very popular one among patients and therapists. Although it is clear in most definitions of psychotherapy that there is a *process* involved which includes technical skills and theoretical applications by therapists, the focus is so often and so much on the therapist-client relationship that too many therapists think of themselves as the therapy. Our review of the literature on the process and outcome of therapy cited in previous chapters makes the complexity of the process very definite. There are many skills involved, with the use of the therapist's person certainly being one of them. But, being a "good" person does not a therapist make. There is more to doing therapy than being warm and caring, or confronting and elucidating, or whatever flashes of personality therapists do demonstrate. We do not want to downgrade therapist qualities, but it appears that when it comes to getting paid for having carried out the skills of therapy, therapists often feel guilty. They act as if they are getting paid for merely being themselves, particularly if their self-image is one of a caring person, which it generally seems to be. When it is not, then they are really getting paid for not being themselves, and they might keep that in mind. Again, there is much to be said for authenticity, but more to be said for behaving as a therapist and thereby doing psychotherapy. Also, it seems that therapists are frequently made aware that the structure of society may have contributed to the client's difficulties, and there they are, taking in the money, conceivably perpetuating the capitalist ethic and a few possible social evils as well. Radical therapy has already pushed up the guilt quotient in that area. And then, therapists can actually be viewed as benefiting from the suffering and misery of others—the essence of anti-altruism. No wonder many psychotherapists only decide to take the money and not feel good about it.

For example, Arbuckle states: "I like to be paid money for my services as a therapist. . . . And yet, somehow, there is a feeling of crassness in being paid money for offering one's fellow person the milk of human kindness. . . . Somehow I feel that what I offer is not a 'service,' and that I don't really 'provide' anything but me" (1979, p. 21).

Feeling guilty about getting paid for doing therapy can foster a variety of approaches that have as their aim the exclusion of money from the process of therapy, at least as far as the therapist is concerned. One way is to stay out of private practice, thereby working for agencies who pay the therapist a salary, and it is the agency that has to deal with collecting fees from the patients. Another possibility is to use a sliding scale, and keep the top of it low, so that no one is likely to register a complaint that your fees are too high, and thereby avoid any implication of greed on your part. Various middlemen, and middlewomen, can be utilized, as the postal service, receptionists, secretaries, and collection agencies. Barter systems can be employed, with clients returning something of value (other than money) for the "whatever" they got from the therapist. Still another possibility is "soaking the rich" while seeing the poor for little or nothing. Actually, this last approach has some limitations because so many of us work with the middle class.

What all of this indicates is that receiving money for psychotherapy is an enormous problem for many therapists. They have quite a need to justify getting paid, particularly if the payment is directly from the client to the therapist, and if the payment is relatively substantial. The most prominent justification of the past has been that the fee was an essential motivator for the patient. The belief was that without the fee, or if the fee was too low, therapy would be ineffective.

However, Mintz (1971) raises some questions about this premise. He indicates that a relationship between patient sacrifice as supposedly indexed by the fee and therapeutic effectiveness has not been demonstrated. The fee is undoubtedly part of the patient's efforts, but certainly not all of the story as regards motivation. The possibility exists that in some instances the existing fee structure is a problem for the patient's therapy, although the therapist would like to keep the fee arrangement as it is. For example, considering the fee as a potential force against the resistance of missed appointments, and using it this way, does not deter some patients from repeatedly missing appointments anyway. In fact, it provides the material for an additional type of resistance because these patients pay for the missed appointments and declare they have thereby discharged their responsibility to the therapeutic process. Whatever reason they have stated as to why they missed, they then consider this the end of any discussion regarding not being at a session, and they use the payment as a way to avoid seeing their major responsibility of appearing at the sessions in order to participate fully in the therapy. In these cases the fee does not work as a motivator for the therapy, but instead is turned into a way of resisting the possibilities of the therapy.

Mintz concludes that therapists have continual problems in their financial transactions with their patients for historical, cultural, and personal reasons. Historically, the psychotherapy of today had its origins in private practice, and that direct-fee-for-service model remains prevalent. There is a considerable amount of socialized mental health care, but it is directed primarily at the disadvantaged and the most flagrantly ill clients. The quality of it is both questioned and questionable, with consumers and providers alike elevating the value of "private" therapy. For example, Herron (1976) found that psychologists who were training to be psychotherapists and were at that same time mainly working in institutions, had a negative response to therapists who worked in institutions, while they perceived private practitioners as the most competent psychotherapists. It appears that most therapists see private practice as better than practicing in an institution, even when the therapists are the same.

Furthermore, psychotherapy has originated and developed mainly in societies stressing the economy of the marketplace. Thus, in these societies the making of money is expected, yet financial matters are also treated rather privately. It is not "good form" to talk about one's personal financial situation, which appears to lead to less than open discussions with patients regarding their attitudes about payment to the therapist. Then, on a personal level, therapists want certain things, ranging from economic sustenance through possessions to various degrees of financial security. The ability to satisfy these wants is vested in money. The reality of the value of money also merges with its symbolism for sexual and power drives. Having a lot of money does fit the fantasy of many therapists, but, as indicated, there is considerable guilt about this, even as a fantasy. The dissonance felt by therapists in giving and getting has kept money a relatively taboo topic, and led to strange and awkward interactions with patients around financial matters.

Schofield (1971) supports Mintz in the observance of the frequency of relative secrecy by psychotherapists in regard to fees. He feels that some of this may be due to the fact that a lot of psychotherapy is indeed commercialized friendship. If this is indeed the situation and is so recognized by the therapist, then it is quite possible that the therapists will feel ashamed about being paid.

We have indicated how the relationship factor of the treatment fosters an atmosphere of concern about why we are getting paid. The result of this concern appears to have been avoidance or justification on therapeutic grounds. Schofield disputes the justification of the fee being essential for the therapy to work, stating: "I have been unable to observe any systematic difference in my approach, in how hard I work, or how responsive my clients are as a function of whether they are receiving 'free' or expensive therapy" (p. 10).

Kornrich has said: "I was brought up on the notion that there must be a charge, even 50 cents, for the patient to value treatment. I believe I have read one study not supporting this. Nor do I feel that I give inferior therapy when I see a patient for no fee" (1979, pp. 34–35).

Finally, Cutter states: "I do not believe, and, in fact view as unfounded, the theory that the 'fee for service' is the incentive to 'work in treatment' and that, without it, clients make little progress and/or coast along in a dependent manner somehow 'taking for granted' the help provided" (1979, p. 63). So, if the justification for having a fee does not directly lie in the effect the payment has on the patient, then it is fairly obvious that the fee is for the benefit of the therapist. Of course, by making the therapist happy the probability of the therapist working better is increased, but the idea that therapists are in it for the money to any significant degree is repellent to many therapists themselves. They want to feel that the money is incidental, though they still want to get it. Thus, other justifications appear on the scene. We have mentioned a number of nonmonetary ones, and there are undoubtedly others where the therapist can stress their primacy, and play down the money. Still, there is the fact that these "other" rewards will not do by themselves, because, as we have noted, therapists want the money as well. What seems to be happening is that, guilty and uncomfortable, a large number of therapists worry the issue around until they have a "good enough" reason to feel justification for their fees.

In most instances the reasoning involves therapists taking stock of their efforts and deciding that they are indeed "worth it," though just what "it" is going to be remains hazy and open to negotiation. Apparently quite a bit of the negotiation is with the self rather than with patients, though some of that goes on as well. Therapists seem to agree that they need income to be able to live, and somewhat reluctantly agree that doing therapy is the "job" which will provide their income. But, how much income, and who is to pay what?

DiBella and Seitel (1979) have discussed the problem of money issues for psychotherapists. Their experience has been that therapists feel anxiety over dealing with money in an open manner. Criticism by patients of proposed fees is often discomforting, and their proposed remedy is a fee policy that has taken into account your impression of the value of your time, the market price, the amount of money you feel you need, and a host of particulars, such as the use of a sliding scale and charges for cancellations. They advocate candid discussion of fees with clients, and the awareness that you indeed are in business and therefore are interested in money. In fact, money is an issue arousing considerable feeling in all patients, probably throughout the course of the therapy, and ought to be discussed as openly as any of the other issues involved in patients' therapies. Often it is not so discussed, nor was it considered in any detail in the training of the therapist.

In two current texts on psychotherapy the money issue is kept brief, so that the importance of the issue is still downplayed. Wolberg (1977) has roughly a page on arranging fees. He advocates open discussion of fees, the use of a sliding scale, and the understanding of the therapist's feelings, but he does not go into detail about these feelings. Indicating that moral and ethical values are involved in the fee situation, he leaves their resolution to the individual therapist. Fees get another page later in the book. Considering this is a 1343–page, two-volume set, money does not seem to get its due.

Kramer (1978) gives fees about two pages, while furnishings get four, so the trend continues. His idea is that he charges for his time, rather than his services, which he attempts to keep constant. Thus, he makes a similar attempt with his fee. Kramer states: "The size of my fee is determined by the particular local, social standards for psychotherapy fees and by my particular evaluation of myself and my experience" (p. 28).

While we can certainly agree that it is a neglected issue in training, and that therapists are not as prone to be as open about money as some other emotional issues, we have often talked about money to each other, and to other therapists. Thus, for us at least, money is not an untouchable topic, though we certainly understand the emotional loading attached to it. Our approach is to attempt to have a standard fee, which has been rising with inflation. We attempt to charge that fee to each new patient, and we try not to raise it for as long a time as is possible. However, since we prefer to do long-term therapy, and since we only want to work a certain number of hours, we do find at intervals that we have no room for new clients, who, due to the rise in our standard starting fee, would be higher paying patients. When that occurs to a significant degree, we will raise fees, keeping our income proportionate to our needs at the time. The reality of the economic scene is that these needs have never decreased.

Our fee policies are flexible. While our standard fee is not based on our estimate of the prospective client's reported income (which, from our years of previous service in clinics, we have learned is very difficult to accurately determine, anyway), but rather on what we want to get paid, we are aware that the patient has to be able to pay us. If the patient is not, yet we believe there is more reason for one of us to see this person as opposed to any other available source, we will do it for a lower fee. The reason could be their need or ours, as, for example, if one of us had a particular interest in the patient, or even if we simply needed the money that would be paid. Fortunately, we practice in an area where people expect and generally can afford to pay the fees we ask as our standard. Also, in recent years we have been as busy as we desired, so the issue of being paid a fee lower than we really wanted hasn't happened very often. As far as we can determine, the infrequency of this for us has eliminated the possible resentment that could be felt if it seemed to us we had "too many" low-paying clients. What that number would be is obviously a subjective phenomenon. Even in regard to raising fees, we currently have a sufficient range in our income that we can afford to keep working comfortably with some patients who may not be able to afford a raise when we want it. That number is small and so not a significant stimulus for negative feelings on our part.

The parent discipline of the psychotherapist results in differential self-valuing based on probable consumer values in the marketplace. So, psychiatrists are valued more than psychologists, who in turn are valued more than social workers, who are more valued than psychiatric nurses, and on through the heirarchy of mental health practitioners. We disagree with the idea that this should be the case, but we recognize it, and have to deal with the fact that it is. Uniform training standards could eliminate the distortions arising from the fact that not all psychotherapists are "doctors," or that all "doctors" are not perceived as equal. It would also establish minimum levels of competence that are not presently assured the consumer, yet ought to be.

We are not free from anxiety about money, but most of the fears about what we should and/or would charge, and the concerns about how prospective clients would react to our fees, were active when we had fewer patients than we wanted. People seeking us out and working with us for long periods of time through difficult phases of their lives made us feel more worthwhile than the fees we received. What the money does for us is to enable us to live our lives as we want, which mandates sufficient time for ourselves. So, it is life styles that really set our fees.

There are some pertinent questions that most therapists have struggled with and, sooner or later, answered somehow.

1. *Do you feel anxious about discussing money with clients?*

Yes, but not most of the time. We feel anxious when we suspect the patient will be resistant to whatever it is about money that we want. A case in point at the moment is raising fees. One of us recently had some need for more money, but did not want to take on additional patients. So, the alternative was to raise fees of existing patients. The clients selected were those in once-a-week therapy who had not had any raise in their fees within the past two years. As once-a-week patients they were paying less than people coming more often who would have a heavier weekly burden if their fees were raised. The therapist felt a raise was necessary and that the procedure was fair, yet was anxious about telling the patients. With each patient involved the entire rationale was explained, starting with the therapist's need for the additional money. Anxiety was highest in regard to one patient who worked as a therapist in an institution and had always had definite negative feelings about what therapists charged in private practice. While she did complain, a number of very useful sessions then followed dealing with her feelings about money and her own value system. She also accepted the raise in her fee.

2. *Would you have chosen psychotherapy as an occupation if it was low paying?*

Certainly. We got into it out of interest, and at first it was low paying. But, our lives changed, and we wanted more, and living has become more expensive, and so money is now a bigger part of our motivation. If fees were cut in half tomorrow, we would stay with doing psychotherapy. We like it. We would adjust our life styles.

3. *Do you feel uncomfortable or guilty about being in the private practice of psychotherapy?*

Yes, though not most of the time. Some of our discomfort is about the insecurity of a practice, such as the possible instability of referral sources, the unpaid vacations and sick days, and the sporadic timing of actual payments. The insecurity results in our attempting to reduce such anxiety by instituting procedures that could make us feel more secure. An example of one of these is charging by the month for group therapy, rather than a per session, weekly fee. Over our years of doing groups we have found that people not infrequently act out their anger in group therapy by leaving or threatening to leave the group. If this occurs now, we only have to deal with it once a month and it is usually the last session of the month, that being the most economically sensible one for the client to choose. Also, it seems that group members beginning will more readily stay at least through the month, since they are paying for it anyway, and so time is gained to possibly work out difficulties. Furthermore, it appears that absenteeism is less in four week months than five, since the charge is the same, regardless of whether there are four or five group sessions in a given month. Such behaviors do give the impression that the motivational aspects of the fee are still something to consider. Such a procedure has made us more secure about the continued existence of our groups. We suspect that is the main reason for our use of such a structure. In addition, it does appear to facilitate the group's cohesiveness, and we do believe that if it was harmful to the group we would not risk their therapy for our comfort.

As far as guilt goes, we dislike the system that prevents many people from getting the best possible therapy. The disadvantaged do not come to us in our practices because, we suspect, they already know what we are looking for in terms of payment. The clients that we already have, and those who are likely prospects for the future, can afford our fees. It is the clients we don't have who could use our services who provoke guilt, because we are not approached by them for economic reasons. Their appraisal may well be correct.

However, we do not feel guilty about getting paid well for doing psychotherapy. We see how it is quite possible to conceptualize incongruities between "giving" therapy and "taking" money, but we do not conceptualize getting paid for rendering psychotherapeutic services as incongruous. If you are having trouble receiving money for what you do, then take a new look at what you do. If it indeed is psychotherapy then you deserve to get paid for it.

CONCLUDING COMMENTS

We could have added to the previous paragraph that a prime reason for getting paid is that the doing of psychotherapy is hard work. Of course, pay is not always proportionate to the effort involved, but there is a logic to such a relationship. In fact, what this chapter has aimed at is the revelation of major occupational hazards. The occupation is psychotherapy, and the problems scrutinized were fatigue, effects on the therapist's interpersonal relations, and the role of money in the therapist's life.

These problems accentuate the work aspect of psychotherapy as well as its demanding essence. They also reflect upon the image of the psychotherapist, who has some affinity for being seen as filled with the joy of living, basking in the glow of warm, intimate relationships, and deriving ultimate satisfaction from the therapeutic relationship, enabling someone else to become more of a person. The therapist wants to be seen as a "together person," but that will scarcely happen by denial of the fact that one can get tired, angry, depressed, and anxious about money, all from doing therapy. We all share these problems, or the potential for them, and we need to be aware of that, as well as doing something about them. We have made some suggestions, always starting with an emphasis on understanding what is going on with you, the therapist. These are not the only possible occupational disorders. Other issues are explored in the next chapter.

REFERENCES

Ansell, C. Counter-transference. A story. *Psychotherapy: Theory, Research and Practice* (1979) **16:**261–268.

Arbuckle, D. S. Ethics, money, and therapy. *Voices* (1979) **14:**21–23.

Auster, S. L. A letter to the editor and Mrs. Anonymous. *Voices* (1971–72) **7:**77.

Bach, G. The George Bach self recognition inventory for burned-out therapists. *Voices* (1979) **15:**73–76.

Bar-Levav, R. Invigorating the tired therapist. *Voices* (1979) **15:**54–57.

Burton, A. *Twelve therapists* (San Francisco: Jossey-Bass, 1972).

Cleaves, C. M. Intervision: Response to the problem. *Voices* (1979) **15:**90.

Criswell, G. E. Dead tired and bone weary. *Voices* (1979) **15:**49–53.

Cutter, C. G. Fee for service and other problems. *Voices* (1979) **14:**62–65.

DiBella, G. A., and Seitel, K. Anxiety of therapists over openly dealing with money issues in the psychotherapy relationship. *Voices* (1979) **14:**16–20.

Ellis, A. The untired rational-emotive therapist. *Voices* (1979) **15:**34–35.

English, O. S. I do not consider myself to be a tired therapist. *Voices* (1979) **15:**20–25.

Flaherty, J. A. Self disclosure in therapy: Marriage of the therapist. *American Journal of Psychotherapy* (1979) **33:**442–452.

Fox, R. Lessons from a therapist's wife. *Voices* (1971–72) **7:**36–37.

Garfield, S. L., and Kurtz, R. A survey of clinical psychologists: Characteristics, activities, and orientations. *The Clinical Psychologist* (1974) **28:**7–10.

Gurman, A. S., and Razin, A. M. (Eds.), *Effective psychotherapy: A handbook of research* (New York: Pergamon, 1977).

Henry, W. E. Personal and social identities of psychotherapists. In A. S. Gurman and A. M. Razin (Eds.), *Effective psychotherapy: A handbook of research* (New York: Pergamon, 1977).

Henry, W. E., Sims, J. H., and Spray, S. L. *Public and private lives of psychotherapists* (San Francisco: Jossey-Bass, 1973).

Henry, W. E., Sims, J. H., and Spray, S. L. *The fifth profession: Becoming a psychotherapist* (San Francisco: Jossey-Bass, 1971).

Herron, W. G. Trainees' impressions of psychotherapy and psychotherapists. *Psychological Reports* (1976) **39:**491–498.

Jourard, S. M. *The transparent self* (Princeton: Van Nostrand, 1964).

Kepecs, J. G., and Greenley, J. R. *The Wisconsin study of mental health careers* (University of Wisconsin Medical School, 1975).

Kornrich, M. A family therapist—Ha! *Voices* (1971–72) **7:**73–76.

Kornrich, M. Twelve monetary moments. *Voices* (1979) **14:**34–35.

Kramer, E. *A beginning manual for psychotherapists*, 2nd ed. (New York: Grune & Stratton, 1978).

Lax, R. F. Some considerations about transference and counter-transference manifestations evoked by the analyst's pregnancy. *International Journal of Psychoanalysis* (1969) **50:**363–367.

Mintz, N. L. Patient fees and psychotherapeutic transactions. *Journal of Consulting and Clinical Psychology* (1971) **36:**1–8.

O'Connell, V. The taste of the strawberry. *Voices* (1979) **15:**70–72.

Rogow, A. A. *The psychiatrists* (New York: Putnam's Sons, 1970).

Robertiello, R. C. The occupational disease of psychotherapists. *Journal of Contemporary Psychothempy* (1978) **9:**123–129.

Schofield, W. Psychotherapy: The unknown versus the untold. *Journal of Consulting and Clinical Psychology* (1971) **36:**9–11.

Snyder, S., and Snyder, C. R. The therapist at home: Her side and his. *Voices* (1971–72) **7:**23–25.

Sundland, D. M. Theoretical orientations of psychotherapists. In A. S. Gurman and A. M. Razin (Eds.), *Effective psychotherapy: A handbook of research* (New York: Pergamon, 1977).

Szekely, H. Comment. *Voices* (1979) **15:**68–69.

Tirnauer, L., and Cheek, A. The Tirnauer-Cheek checklist on how to keep fatigued. *Voices* (1979) **15:**70–72.

Weiner, M. F. In defense of the therapist. *Psychosomatics* (1969) **10:**156–159.

Weiner, M. W. Self-exposure by the therapist as a therapeutic technique. *American Journal of Psychotherapy* (1972) **26:**42–46.

Wheelis, A. The vocational hazards of psychoanalysts. *International Journal of Psychoanalysis* (1956) **37:**171–184.

Wolberg, L. *The technique of psychotherapy*, 3rd ed., Parts 1 and 2 (New York: Grune & Stratton, 1978).

V

At Issue: The Therapist's Narcissism and Its Consequences

INTRODUCTION

In 1974 Bellak, in writing about the life of a psychotherapist, said: "It is as close a vantage point on the human condition as there is. As you listen to a life history and to the symptomatology, you have a ringside seat all day, every day, to the human drama" (p. 7). He writes, too, of the feeling of competence to intervene, of doing something worthwhile, of intellectual pleasure and "the emotional experience of a sense of a Greek drama unfolding in its inevitability before you" (p. 7). These observations are familiar, yet, while they certainly seem an accurate account of what a therapist experiences, the description feels strangely incomplete. Perhaps it is because it is nearly impossible to succinctiy describe such an experience. After all, it is in the process of therapy that there is an intense, often disturbing mixture of therapists' emotional and interpersonal responses to their patients. When these responses are described, the confusion of health and pathology is definitely possible. Words are beggars at describing the mix, but words are what we have to offer here.

It is true indeed that the therapist is an observer, albeit a participant observer. It is true, too, that after the novice's initial grandiosity and subsequent feelings of powerlessness, over time, a therapist does feel an ability to help and make some sort of human contribution. And it is true that there is, over the long haul, a kind of drama unfolding. On the other hand, the rational observations and sentiments expressed by Bellak (1974) unwittingly point up some of the problems that therapists bring to their work: the "need" to help, the conflict about closeness and intimacy, the intellectual operations as a defense against emotional response, all of which fall under the umbrella concept of the therapist's narcissism, the self-involved use of self with patients—the defensive use of self. In describing such behavior we use mainly psychoanalytic terminology, since the problem, when addressed, has customarily been couched in these terms. But the problem is by no means restricted to the psychoanalytically oriented. The terms and concepts bear translation to all approaches to the psychotherapies.

Sometimes in the privacy of the therapist's solitude, often in the inner sanctum of the therapist's unconscious, yet rarely in the light of consciousness or in print (Greben, 1975; Lipp, 1978) the therapist asks, "What's in it for me, this business of doing psychotherapy?" Although the question is seldom raised or addressed, its essence repeatedly manifests itself in the therapeutic relationship. The question in fact reflects the importance of understanding the therapist's narcissistic needs—needs that perhaps have drawn him or her to the field, but needs that can work against the best interests of the patients treated and, ultimately, against the therapist. In exploring the therapist's narcissism our aim is not to indict the therapist. Rather, it is to clarify the dynamics of the narcissism and suggest how the dynamics, in repeating themselves through relationships with patients, impede the relationship through inhibiting the full development of the patient and the therapist.

That the therapist's narcissistic needs arise during the process of therapy is not surprising, for they are always present in one degree or another, even in seasoned therapists. To paraphrase Sullivan, therapists are, after all, like everybody, more human than otherwise. It is not uncommon, however, to hear it intimated that therapists have more than their share of narcissism. While to our knowledge therapist narcissism has not been measured on a scale, it has been observed repeatedly, and is seen by some theorists such as Mehlman (1974) and Sharaf and Levinson (1964) as an inevitable dimension of the therapy situation, especially for the novice therapist, relatively helpless, relatively unknowledgeable about him or herself, patients, and a treatment process, where, unlike most, doing less is doing more. Certain theorists (Ford, 1963; Jones, 1951; Lewin, 1958; Marmor, 1953; Miller, 1979; Sharaf and Levinson, 1964) in one way or another think that the therapist's narcissism is a problem to be reckoned with if indeed the therapy that is engaged in is to prove a therapeutic experience for the patient. Still others, (Miller, 1979; Searles, 1976/1979), through a variety of formulations equivalent to the concept of narcissism hold that the therapist's choice of profession is itself intimately bound up with his or her narcissism.

The point is that in the therapeutic relationship, as in any relationship, the quality and creativity of the relationship is dependent on the ability of the persons to participate through an unencumbered use of self. By that we mean there is sufficient self-object differentiation and confirmation so the relationship can indeed be a relationship, not a quasi two-person experience, whereby one person is an extension of the other or in the emotional service of the other. At the same time, with the security and self-esteem that comes with confirmation and differentiation there arises the ability for nondefensive or healthy fusion by way of empathy—the automatic, if momentary, experiencing of the other. Obviously, when a patient comes into treatment, he or she is not in a position for such a relationship. The therapist has a responsibility to become aware of how his or her narcissistic stance in the relationship helps determine the course and outcome of the therapeutic process. To this end, we will discuss narcissism as a personality feature in general and of therapists in particular, the obsessional brand of narcissism so prevalent among therapists, and the therapist's need to be a therapist. In the process, through discussion of developmental narcissism and what went wrong, and presentation of ways in which the therapist's narcissism manifests itself during treatment, we hope we will bring some clarity to the issue of the therapist's narcissism.

NARCISSISM IN PERSONALITY

Narcissism can be seen as pathology and as an essential part of development. Often a concept difficult to grasp, it has nonetheless captured the imagination and intelligence of major theorists such as Freud (1914/1957), Kernberg (1975), and Mahler (1968), to mention a few. As Blanck and Blanck (1979) imply, the study of pathology will yield greater knowledge of developmental narcissism and vice versa. Normative narcissism and its sometimes pathological vicissitudes after all are considered dimensions of the organizing process in personality development.

That narcissism as a feature of personality is of more than one type or level has been postulated by Blanck and Blanck (1979). They theorize five levels of pathological narcissistic formation in a developmental framework (apparently Mahler's, 1968) ranging from the symbiotic phase, through the differentiation, practicing, and rapprochement subphases, to object constancy. While such a continuum could be useful, at this point the Blancks have not developed the levels sufficiently to make clinical application an easy matter. The idea, however, has a good deal of merit and recalls work done by Bursten (1973, 1977). In his 1973 paper he postulated there were four types of narcissism on a continuum ranging from a more primitive end of personality organization to a more advanced end. Further, though he classified each type (craving, paranoid, manipulative, and phallic) as narcissistic personality, it is not until the second paper on the subject in 1977 that he modified his view so that what he seems to be hinting at, but stops short of saying, is that narcissism is an integral part of various levels of personality organization.

From our work with patients and clinical supervision of therapists it seems clear that narcissism is part of various personality constellations, some more primitive in their organization than others. In other words, though perhaps there is a theoretically pure "narcissistic personality" there is a developmental, dynamic core of narcissism in all personalities, some more primitively expressed than others, depending at which end of the continuum the personality would be organized and classified.

Although Bursten (1977) implies the obsessional character has less narcissistic need than other character types, such has not been our observation over the years in our supervisory and treatment work with therapists. First, although we have no hard data on which personality type goes into the therapy field, our observation and that of many colleagues is that the field attracts obsessionals far more than other personality types. This is neither good nor bad; it just seems to be that way. There are a number of possible reasons: what would appear to be thinking operations taking precedence over feelings, the intrigue with figuring things out, the relative structure of the therapist-patient relationship and the need for closeness in small doses, are several that come to mind. Although we do intend later in the chapter to discuss certain dynamics in the parent-child relationship existing during developmental narcissism (which we believe result in a person inclined in a therapist direction), now our point is only that the obsessional personality type seems most prevalent in the field.

In this regard, one of the most striking observations is that the particular brand of narcissism the obsessional has, and the facility in using it, gets the therapist into trouble with patients. Since these obsessional dimensions of a therapist's character do cause a good deal of trouble, severely limiting relatedness with patients, it is useful to present the dynamics of the narcissism in the obsessional defense. In so doing, we will point out where in the course of developmental narcissism things go wrong and stay that way despite what would appear to be a level of sophistication implying development without such strong narcissistic residual.

Instead of presenting all views, we have tried to use those references which seem to bear relation to certain features of our formulations. In addition, we feel compelled to mention that we are amazed at the obtuse ways theorists have explained various theories of narcissism. Faced with such "autistic" presentation, we cannot guarantee that our formulations have not been said before in any way. Further, the writings can certainly make one wonder about therapists (including us) who choose to write about narcissism. All we can say is we will try to be clear without being simplistic and complex without being convoluted, and to the degree we accomplish that task we will consider that our interminable analyses have paid off.

NARCISSISM IN THE OBSESSIONAL DEFENSE

A patient, who is also a therapist, reported the following during a session when she had been describing how she finally noticed a gulf between her and her patients: "As a child I remember feeling perplexed when I heard my uncle say that what he loved best was to have his family all around him. The words seemed inconsistent with his behavior; although he was pleased when he saw us he never seemed quite 'with' us, never quite in touch. The distance between him and us seemed greater than the miles separating his city from ours. I sensed, I guess, that something was missing in the relationship and in him, despite all the words spoken and experiences exchanged when we were together. Actually, he didn't know us very well, nor we him for that matter. The image I consistently had when he'd say all that was, 'him' in the center of a circle of 'us,' his family. I pictured him turning round and round looking at us 'out there' surrounding him, there, as distant objects of his pleasure." Narcissism neatly depicted is our impression.

This therapist had always considered herself quite different from her uncle, until, as a young adult in her first session as a patient in a psychotherapy group, she had an illuminating experience. There she sat, aware of feeling detached, having a fantasy: she was in the center of the circle, turning round and round in her prettiest cool blue lingerie for the group "out there" surrounding, distant objects of her pleasure and she, elusive object of the group's curiosity and pleasure. Narcissism returning in case the patient did not see it in herself.

Although narcissism is at the central core of the obsessional defense, it is well disguised. It is only on deeper acquaintance with the obsessional character structure that it becomes possible to identify the narcissism and understand how it operates for and against the person in human relationships, for and against the therapist in relationships with patients. Contrary to the popular notion of narcissism as a focus purely on oneself, and narcissism in some schools of thought as the opposite pole of object relatedness (Freud, 1914/1957), narcissism is not a "one person" phenomenon. As the saying goes, there is no sound to one hand clapping. Narcissism does not in fact occur in a vacuum (Klein, 1952) in its developmental or extended state, although at first glance, it would appear to be a solitary experience. We agree with Kemberg (1975) when he concludes that "one cannot analyze narcissism as if it were a drive independent of internalized object relations" (p. 338). Therefore, narcissism manifests itself through one's interpersonal relationships, or, to quote Kemberg (1975), "Normal and pathological narcissism always involves the relationship of the self to object representations and external objects" (p. 341). Developmentally, narcissism arises as the natural tendency of the human infant to fuse, then blend with the mother in such a way that assures getting enough of what is needed to eventually separate from this emotional storehouse. Two sub-phases of the early narcissistic state are postulated. In the first, called normal autism by Mahler (1968), there is perceptual fusion of the infant with the mother. In other words, there is no distinction between self and object; there exists instead what has been termed a self-object; in the infant's world the self and object are one. As the infant matures to the sub-phase of symbiosis, he/she recognizes a separateness between the mother and the now developing "self." However, the object mother is now considered separate from but existing to serve the self. Thus, the self is still conceived of in relation to another, the self is still a self-object in a sense, a rather powerful one in fact.

In working with obsessional patients, and with obsessional therapists as patients and as supervisees, we have come to think that, developmentally, it is in the phase of symbiosis where their troubles begin. Their difficulties in living, which are considerable, stem from an extraordinary desire to establish relationships where the other person is there in the service of the self. For whatever maternal reasons, during normal symbiosis, the obsessional does not seem to have been in the position of having the object in his or her service. Often, indeed, the positions are reversed, which probably heralds the beginning of what will later be the therapist's "life of service." Although this reversal does not interfere with the development of a self it noticably influences the quality of the self that develops. As Balint (1968) might say, the "basic fault" has been lack of fit in the mother-child unit. The mother, unyielding in her emotional position, is unable to bend with the rhythm and child. Furthermore, the dynamics at work turn the child into a mother, a role reluctantly accepted, and though well carried out, a role unconsciously resented.

In fact, at some level the person who becomes obsessional is forever locked into the struggle to make the mother serve the self. In a sense, life is spent trying to wrench from others what during development was not forthcoming from the mother. Not item for item so much as the state of receiving; the obsessional feels the other should fit into his or her system. Such an attitude is not only determined by the desire to get in fact what was needed early in life, but by a "right" which is now felt due. A sense of righteous indignation develops that regulates self-esteem (Lax, 1975). "Outbursts of righteous indignation enable the child-adult self of these patients to merge again and again with the idealized 'righteous one' (parent), to whose grandeur they had submitted and whose grandeur they still want to attain" (p. 288).

The obsessional has identified with the mother in whose service he or she was as an infant. Consequently, the person is in the difficult position of having identified with the mother without getting from her what was needed, having had only a hint of what it is like to get what one wants. Often this results in a kind of compliant state, in the development of what has been termed by Winnicott (1960) a "false self." With self-feeling not validated, self-esteem remains vulnerable. Aggression becomes directed at the search for and acquisition of the object rather than a tool aiding in separation, individuation, or the development of the self on its own. In other words, the aim of the aggression is to maintain a symbiotic bond by identifying with the mother, whereas, ordinarily, the identification facilitates separation.

Through identifying with the mother the person tries to right the situation—to right the wrong done, the injustice perpetrated. In the mind's eye the situation will be redressed by trying to be better to others than his or her mother was to oneself, a motivation not unfamiliar in the life of a therapist. However, the focus is still on the self—still in effect to prove a point to the mother.

By all this, you might conclude that the person does not feel whole, that a self-object is needed to feel a sense of psychic integrity. In fact, that is not entirely the situation. The object has been internalized, therefore there is a sense of object constancy, making it possible largely to function separately from the mother (unlike the schizophrenic personality who cannot function with object loss). The problem is that emotional separation is incomplete because the obsessional lives with the nearly pathologic hope that the mother will come through, as seen in relationships with others. Virtually all behavior central to the obsessional way of life bears this out, although (in true obsessional complexity) the meaning and source of the behavior is far from clear. The quest for perfection is directly related to the obsessional's narcissism for it is not actually for "self" satisfaction that perfection is sought. In the obsessional mind and heart the hope never quite dies that if one is perfect, *then* the parents will show their devotion and give their approval. The corollary is that early in life the obsessional has the idea that the reason for maternal (and later, paternal) deficiencies lie in himself or herself, not in the parent. To recognize that the mother would not or could not allow the infant's needs to intrude on her own, that is, on her system, would fill the child with rage and anxiety beyond the then current developmental capacity. (This is useful to remember in treatment and supervision, to respect that the obsessional truly feels he or she will surely fall apart in experiencing anger, rage, or anxiety—so much so, that secondary anxiety can occur as soon as the feelings break through.)

What is sought as a child and later as an adult is recognition that indeed he or she is a person with a need to be taken seriously, a need for respect of and tolerance for feelings not necessarily shared by the parents. Because there has been little recognition or validation of this "separate-self" concept, what start out as human needs become repressed, then to be distorted through detachment, isolation of affect, and a list of rights due which underlies the defensive quest for perfection.

The obsessional's narcissism affects psychic and interpersonal function and makes therapy a lengthy and difficult process. For the obsessional therapist, treating patients creates a situation where there looms constant threat to his or her narcissism. For example, to acknowledge that there exists an emotional tie, even an emotional reaction to one's patient, may be nearly impossible. Not that it does not occur, but to acknowledge it would be admitting that a person has somehow been admitted to the inner sanctum of the therapist's emotional life, that the barrier has been permeated.

Not only have we heard our patients talk about their therapists in the most rational and intellectual terms even after years of contact, but all too often we hear therapists talk about their patients as if someone else were seeing them. We're reminded of such a therapist, who, when referring to the therapist he'd seen for many years, made it clear that the therapist was "bright, perceptive, perhaps not always accurate, but on balance, doing his job well." Clearly, this sounds like a defense against an emotional bond, as though the bond were not growing anyhow, testimony to Kernberg's (1975) point that attachments were originally pure affect cathexes, we think now being defended against because of the nature of the original affect.

Contrary to what one might expect, that the defense prevents the development of an emotional bond, the intellectual defense allows for the "secret" development of the emotional connection. It acts in the same way as a screen-memory, that is, the intellect shields its accompanying or allied feeling just as one memory may shield an allied, emotionally laden memory. In operation, this means that even the therapist with strong obsessional defenses develops an emotional bond with the patient, sometimes quite a surprise to the therapist. It has been noticeable to us that once such a therapist has "discovered" an emotional bond, he or she becomes angry. Thus, often the first noticeable and acknowledged genuine countertransference reaction that comes to the therapist's attention is a negative one. But why the defense against the emotional involvement in the first place, and why the anger? We think the defense serves several purposes. It protects the therapist from another taking over, robbing him or her of any autonomy, not respecting his or her existence. That anger is perhaps the first acknowledged countertransferential response is not surprising either, for it is a response to having somehow been caught, if only by oneself, at having dropped one's vigilance and allowing another's entry. In addition, the anger being released is an expression of the rage at having had one's "self-feeling" unconfirmed and self development thwarted. Further, perhaps it replicates, now in a way distorted by rage, a major dimension of the original emotional attachment, the original narcissistic state, that is, aggression which shouts, "Look, I exist, damn it; respect that, recognize that."

Relating on an intellectual level helps protect the feelings of the obsessional, for it does not allow the other access to his or her heart. Further, it does not allow the therapist access to feelings and emotional perceptions which may frighten or threaten, perceptions which for security's sake are not to be noticed. Thus, in a way, the intellectual defense protects, defends, and perpetuates the original parental bond, the original narcissistic state of relations. All this is at great emotional and interpersonal expense personally, and great empathic expense professionally. Perception of the therapist's feelings and affectual dimension of cognitive experience are constricted, as is perception of similar patient experience. Such perception would threaten the viability of the intellectual defense as a means of isolating the affectual portion—pleasure or pain—of an experience. Thus, it can be concluded that something is present on one level and missing on another in the therapist-patient relationship. This makes for complicated distortions by both patient and therapist.

MANIFESTATION OF THE THERAPIST'S NARCISSISM

Major features of the therapist's obsessional defense as it arises through the therapist-patient relationship, have, at their base, narcissistic dynamics. One central feature is control. In order to feel in control, the obsessional, by necessity, must control the world around him or her (Freud, 1909/1957; Salzman, 1968). For the therapist with a largely obsessional character structure, this task can reach mammoth proportions, for there are thousands upon thousands of perceptions, thoughts, feelings, and actions of patients to keep in check lest they touch off the therapist's unwanted perceptions, thoughts, feelings, and actions. In other words, because the therapist is not free to experience certain aspects of living, he or she unwittingly imposes a similar restriction upon the patient, thereby assuring that the patient will not surpass, threaten, or psychologically leave being in the therapist's "service."

Actually, this is the kind of unconscious control that happens in subtle ways and, in part, accounts for the many reported incidents of how patient and therapist, each in their own therapy, simultaneously deal with the same issues. As the therapist is more free to experience dimensions of self without feeling threatened "permission" is unwittingly granted to the patient. While the parallel experience is not happenstance, it is not simply brought about by therapist control. The paradox is that it also occurs because of therapist readiness to lessen control. As Searles (1966/1979) says, "One does not become free from feelings in the course of maturation or in the course of becoming well during psychoanalysis; one becomes, instead, increasingly free to experience feeling of all sorts" (p. 35).

The demands therapists place on patients have both rational and irrational components. For example, the patient is "supposed" to use the therapist as an emotional supplier. That makes sense: after all, the patient needs help and is coming for it. On the other hand, the therapist in therapeutic zeal may impose his or her dedication on the patient (Searles, 1967/1979). An inordinate need to help and the guilt, anger, and anxiety at being rejected by patients who, at certain times, cannot accept help obscures the therapist's ambivalence and self-interest in treating patients in the first place. Further, the need to help distracts the therapists from the mixed mission of contacting yet keeping at a safe distance the projected dimensions of his or her self. Often the therapist foists upon the patient the role of his or her own marred parent, who, through the therapist's ministrations will be made whole, or at least well enough to provide the goods needed.

This parent image, flawed though it is, has enormous power. A supervisee told of how anxious he was for months during a period when a patient he was treating would not let him help. Not only did the patient start out with reasons for rejecting the assistance, but in addition, he had sensed the therapist's need of him. This was the need to be needy so the therapist could identify with him and be taken care of on his terms, something the therapist's mother had been unable to do for him. On another level, it became clear that what the patient sensed was the therapist's narcissistic need to show him up—to be a better mother than he, the patient, was, which of course meant the therapist would be a better mother than his own.

The patient, through letting the therapist help, could at once show the therapist's mother "how to do it right," prove to the therapist's mother that by comparison she was no good at her job, and to boot, get whatever goods were available by being the good, therapeutic child (a theme to be developed in a later section of this chapter). All this power was to be had simply by being the patient to be helped! Little wonder the patient reeled under such a burden of contradictory expectations and little wonder too that the therapist felt so anxious and feared punishment out of proportion to what the patient was handing out, though admittedly, the patient found expert ways to strangle the therapist with his own needs. It was only when the therapist could extricate himself from the demand he unconsciously made, and could allow himself to feel the anger and disappointment with his own mother that he could perceive the patient as just a patient. Far from a disparaging attitude, this perception, in effect, meant the patient was a regular, life-sized person on whom the therapist did not have to lean, one who did not have the giant-sized proportions of a powerful parent in the eyes of a helpless child.

So, then, it is conceivable that the therapist may genuinely want to help, while on another level the desire to help is based on self-interest resulting in the therapist's so-called dedication reaching controlling proportions.

Such dedication was obvious in this example. A therapist was a few minutes late for her supervision appointment. When she arrived she said she had been exhausted lately and seemed inordinately upset about the latest snow. She then reported she was upset, too, and worried about making what seemed to her to be too many interpretations and premature interpretations with her patients. (She had good reason to be upset, according to her supervisor!) She had noticed the problem previously, but that day it seemed worse and in her mind, related to her getting to work late the day before. "I felt as if I should have gotten there on time; the snow storm shouldn't have mattered. I figure if I had left three hours early instead of two I'd have made it on time. I felt so surprised and angry that the snow interfered. It was after that when I noticed how much I was interpreting, as if to make up for lost time."

Actually, the problem went beyond the lost time. It was interesting that it did not occur to her that no matter what time she left she might not have made it. The idea that nothing is predictable, that external events sometimes interfere with reaching a goal, that something could come between goal set and goal achieved was alien to her, though unconsciously she proved to know it only too well. How dare snow, a patient's unconscious, or a mother's unyielding behavior impede simple, human desires such as getting to work, helping a patient become aware, and seeking emotional goods needed for growth. So she, like her mother before her, was trying to force the world to fit into her system, to feel in control by controlling the world around her, and in so doing recapturing the narcissistic experience of childhood in all its intensity. No wonder she was exhausted.

At some point it is necessary for a therapist to recognize the need to control, reaching the point in personal therapy where the need is seen as a defense and reaction-formation against being out of control as well as a need based on a desire for self-confirmation and esteem. One such therapist comes to mind. No sooner had she begun to realize she feared losing control of herself and others than it became clear why she had been so anxious of late with a particular patient. It seems that the patient had recently "turned" on her. In retrospect, she now understood what was meant in supervision when she had been advised that to be so nice to this particular hard-nosed, contemptuous patient seemed condescending, maybe even hostile, a subject often addressed by Searles (1975/1979) in his writings and in his supervisory demonstrations. Furthermore, she was advised that if she were as ingratiating as she sounded, she would eventually pay for the attitude and its inherent controlling quality.

The therapist came to realize that the value of her controlling behavior was to prevent her from putting herself at the mercy of the patient. Just as the development of self-esteem rests on how the mother responds and reacts to the growing child, the therapist's self-esteem seemed to rise and fall on the patient's reaction to her. Just as the child in effect is at the mercy of the parent, the therapist felt at the mercy of the patient's view of her. She was neither nice to the patient because she liked or valued him, nor was she nice for his benefit at all. Her behavior was self-serving. In the weeks that followed, it became clear that when the patient was accepting of her she felt great about herself, whereas when he rejected her, she would have thoughts of how ugly she was. She would think twice about whether or not she should say something he might not like. Although she fretted that his rejection was because of what she had or hadn't done, she later realized her distress was about the rejection because of what she was or wasn't. She admitted in fact that the main reason she wanted supervision was so she could become perfect, for then she would win the patient over.

Her reaction to the patient appears to be a reflection of the problems in developmental narcissism where the child keeps trying to have an impact on the impenetrable, unyielding mother, who gives what and when she wants. A mother in this god-like position is capable of yielding sufficient power to create or destroy a person; and from a developmental standpoint, this is very pertinent.

Little wonder the therapist experienced the patient's rejection as an invalidation of her very being.

Closely akin to the need to control is *power-stuggling*, which, unfortunately, is a frequent component of therapy. The struggle seems to come out of nowhere, escalating quickly. The issue is of little import for it can literally be anything ranging from what one might consider benign, such as where the person(s) will sit (or lie—good for prolonged struggling) to a difference of opinion over an interpretation. The struggles occur most with patients who also have the tendency, though a "skillful" therapist can bring the inclination out in almost anyone. In a capsule, what occurs is that each person is trying to place the other in each other's orbits. Obviously, the therapist, with a background of this kind of narcissistic oppression is not going to like once again being on the receiving end, and in any event, tends to be compelled to start or enter a struggle because of the very history he or she abhors. The "other" gives the "self" life, as in the original symbiotic bond. The aggression then, is directed at sustaining the struggle (the bond, the life) rather than stopping. If the struggle stopped, the business at hand could proceed and the aggression could be used productively for the therapist's development, for the development of the relationship, indeed, to do therapy, or whatever. Obviously, however, to stop implies giving in, losing control, as well as the bottom line—emotional separation. And for the person locked into the struggle to bring the other around, to have the other acknowledge one's very being, to stop struggling is a narcissistic impossibility.

Although many power struggles are easy to identify, others are difficult because they are covert and linked to negativistic stances. Take the following instance: A therapist had been distracted for some time with a problem supposedly unrelated to overt power struggles she had been having with her patients. The situation was this: At a university where she taught she had applied for a sabbatical, and despite the fact that the department chairman was dragging his heels, it looked like she was going to get it. She was pleased, though not without anxiety. Then, suddenly, her department chairman died, after which she felt incredibly guilty about leaving and could not stop thinking that if he were alive she'd not feel so guilty about taking the sabbatical. Although the guilt had no rational basis and could be interpreted on a number of levels, the essence seemed to be that if the chairman were alive and she left on sabbatical she would carry the struggle—thus him—with her through this ostensibly autonomous move. It became clear that taking the step because she wanted to and not in opposition to him implied separation about which she felt guilt and anxiety. Just as the opposition or negativism bind the child to the parent, so the guilt and preoccupation bound this therapist to her chairman.

She was also having trouble with patients, struggling with several, one of whom was a rather smoothly controlling 8–year-old child. One day, they decided to take pictures with two cameras she kept in the office. The child proceeded to take some pictures and then said such things as, "Oh look, that's the kind of thing you like; why don't you take that picture?" The therapist found herself thinking she wouldn't take any pictures he told her to take, then progressed to thinking she wouldn't take any pictures altogether because he wanted her to, and finally she found herself not knowing what she found interesting to photograph. Her rage obliterated the child's presence as she gazed through him.

To this therapist, a suggestion was a command, and while the child probably was issuing a directive, albeit one consonant with the therapist's taste, it was well aimed—namely, at a person who would dig her heels in and become entangled with him in an unending narcissistic struggle for power. Were she to, as she said, "knuckle under" and do what he wanted, even if it were what she wanted, she could not help feeling in his service—an intolerable, yet emotionally familiar position against which she had been well defended most of her life. Consciously, it did not occur to her that to assume a negativistic stance would still put her in his service, though in the guise of standing up for herself. Her unconscious knew better.

Interestingly, it did not occur to her she could do what she wanted even if he did happen to get satisfaction from it. Conversely, at least some of the time it would seem she could do what she wanted (even if it was not what he wanted, and though he might not like it), and so long as she did not make a project of it or do it for hostile reasons, such a show of her "autonomy" would not be such a bad experience for the child. Again, the therapist was locked into a narcissistic system reminiscent of the unyielding parent; in the therapy she felt herself at once her mother, at once her defenseless self, and saw too, both those dimensions in the child she was treating. Her major aim had been to be confirmed, now entreating this child-mother, "Look mother, acknowledge me, consider that I am a person, at least person enough to know what I want to photograph!"

Discussion of power struggling and negativism leads naturally to another problem area for the therapist, what we consider the *fear of being influenced* but it heads there by way of *fear of compliance*, which is the other side of the coin of negativism. While negativism would appear not to bind child to parent, compliance leaves no doubt and is, therefore, willfully defended against. A therapist we know, while bright and scholarly, always resisted trying any new techniques. In a session describing why he was reluctant he said, "I feel like I need to try something new, but if I try the technique and it doesn't work out immediately I'll feel ridiculous, so I'd rather not try. In fact, it's worse than that, I can't bring myself to try." Obviously negativistic on its face, the declaration indicates the therapist cannot try something new even if he wants to. He is fighting even his own desire; he is still reacting against complying with his internalized mother who is "pushing him around" so to speak, and against separating from her to do what he alone might want and rationally knows is best. Thus the negativism, in one operation, continues the symbiotic bond, allowing the flavor of autonomy while militating against compliance. Furthermore, when what one independently wants coincides with what the parent would have wanted there is a dilemma, for the person is surely in a double bind. If he or she does what the parent wants, he or she can't win; if he or she does what he or she wants, there's no winning either. The way out of course is to be able to do what one wants for oneself, neither for nor against the parent, which, however, implies a degree of separation to be aimed for but one not easily attained. With this therapist, there was also an identification with his mother's fear of risk. Therefore, his problem was compounded to the point that indeed if he but tried new techniques it implied leaving mother.

By this time, it is surely obvious that while fear of influence can permeate a therapist's narcissistic position, it is fueled in operation by interpersonal patterns not immediately associated with such a fear, viz., power-struggling and fear of compliance. The fear of influence impedes the therapist's ability to let the patient take the lead in setting the pace and determining the direction and flow of the therapy. The therapist, like the mother during developmental narcissism, cannot allow the influence of the child. On the other hand, identifying with the patient's effort and narcissistic need to have a mother there in his or her service gives the therapist an idea once again of the frustration of having no influence. The therapist is now both that child who craves the mother and ideally, the desired mother in the child's (patient's) emotional service. It is little wonder that therapists flee from the emotional paradoxes so reminiscent of their childhood positions, that they seek to influence in concrete ways through advice-giving, through overinterpretation, through rigid behavior modification techniques, through prescribing medication, through defensive detachment, through eight-session cures, through having all the answers or none of the answers.

Having all the answers or none of the answers are, as defenses, another pair of features within the obsessional, narcissistic defense. Actually, they are attitudes reflecting the problem of *certainty versus indecision and doubt*. The certainty is a defense against indecision and doubt and accompanying feelings of powerlessness. Said another way, the sense of certainty is built on a weak base of self-esteem. Yet the indecision is a defense against having identified with the certainty of the unyielding parent. On a dynamic level, this two-sided coin is a replication of the position of the child during narcissistic development: For it is as if "someone"—a parent—will come along and make the "right" decision, have the "right" answer. The child, however, unsatisfied in his attempt to influence the parent and angry at imposition of answers, cannot, will not, be sure the answer or decision is right. On the other hand, with such an all-knowing, all-powerful parent, how can the child, short on self-value, be sure his or her own answer or decision is "right." In short, either way, there exists the feeling of fighting the "other," fighting to be recognized and respected, plus the idea that somehow the answer or decision at any minute may be made or snatched away without one's ken or control.

When therapists start their careers some may have a grandiose sense of what they know and how they can effect a cure. With adequate supervision and therapy this attitude dies, often to be replaced by the feeling that they know nothing and can have no effect on patients. A replication of the original narcissistic position in reverse, this helpless, ignorant phase is acutely uncomfortable. We have heard therapists describe what hot shots they were (or so they thought) when they started out, yet years later, with their grandiosity shattered, they felt they knew nothing and could have no effect on patients.

One therapist felt utterly helpless and ignorant when faced with her first outpatient group, despite years of in-patient group experience and several publications. That she could recognize the group as more ostensibly like her than were the psychotic patients she had been treating was probably the trigger for the discomfort. She became silent in early sessions, shrinking in fear, identifying with the disturbed children these formidable mothers were describing. Although her silence and feelings of stupidity activated how indeed she felt with her mother who was supposed to take care of her, yet could not yield her needs to her child's needs, the therapist's immobility was also a defense against her rage—her desire to force the mothers to be influenced, to value her presence, her brilliance, her.

The grandiosity then, is a defense against the helplessness and lack of adequate self-confirmation and self-feeling, but the helplessness and lack of adequate self-feeling is itself then used as a defense against forcing another to be influenced. This means it is conceivable a therapist starts a career with compensatory grandiosity and feels devalued and impotent when faced with patients beyond his or her capacity to deal with. At this level, the helplessness is a rationalized defense—a good one because indeed it reflects the valid feeling of impotence which is a few layers down. This intermediate level helplessness is used as a defense against the anger and defensive aggression that the grandiosity also served to hide. Once the desire to vent the rage at and "run over," influence, "the mothers" becomes clear, the deepest level of the impotence is felt. It is only then, when the therapist is in touch with his or her own helplessness against parental forces that it becomes possible to entertain the notion that maybe psychotherapeutic work, at its best, is not so gratifying as one might have wished.

A word about the therapist's *anger* seems in order. Though it is not our intention to elaborate on the varied dimensions and defenses against anger, it does seem pertinent to our theme to mention that the therapist is often afraid to experience anger, which instead is rationalized by saying it would not be useful for the patient. The merits or demerits of such revelation aside, it would seem that the main issue is that the therapist is afraid of losing control because the patients may return the anger, thus stirring up the therapist's residual rage. We wonder though, if the problem does not go beyond the activation of rage, which in itself may have been an unacceptable affect. The more intense problem appears to be that the patient has penetrated, not only stirring up anger, but stirring up the memory of a mother-child bond characterized by the mother's emotional intrusiveness, controlling or forcing the child into her orbit. With such memory would come the recollection of an impenetrable mother, a characteristic therapists do not want to notice in their parents, their patients, and certainly not in themselves.

That a therapist's *detachment* can be defensive is best supported by a vignette from the therapist of the group mentioned earlier in the chapter. "When I felt part of what was going on in the group, the interaction, I couldn't seem to figure out what was happening in the group. But when I could figure it out I felt—and was—so removed that when I pointed anything out or made an 'appropriate comment' nobody seemed to hear me. I was like two separate people, two aspects of myself I couldn't put together. They all knew it too; in fact when I finally asked them what it would take for them to listen to me they told me all right. The 'spokesman' as I call her, said I seemed to be playing a role, as if from a book, so why should they listen to me when I was obviously an amateur or a dilettante. She couldn't have said it better and I got so anxious at her 'knowledge' of me I thought, 'Why in hell am I in this work? If all this anxiety is what being a therapist is all about, who needs it?' "

Heretofore, this therapist had rarely felt discomfort with patients, for her detachment provided emotional distance sufficient to ward off feeling intruded on. The earlier detachment had prevented her from feeling involved while being involved; or to put it another way, it allowed her to be involved without knowing or feeling the experience. The progress, yet problem, now that she had had several years of therapy and supervision, meant that she began to take notice when she was involved. She would become anxious at the recognition only to retreat to a broader, "better" detachment. Since it became clear it was at those times she made her interpretations or interventions, it was unconsciously obvious to the group she was not "with" them. Her clinical comments, accurate as they might be, served her own detachment needs rather than the needs of the patients. Ostensibly, she aimed to be helpful to the patients, but her fear of being overwhelmed by them compelled her to fend them off. In essence, the comments this therapist offered were recognized as emotionally fraudulent and the intent perceived as only helpful to herself. Thus, the whole narcissistic problem was relived in the therapist's eyes: the powerful, unyielding mother (group) to whom the child (therapist) responded with fear and frustration, from which the child (therapist) imperfectly escaped through detachment, surely itself an unyielding state.

Though obviously detachment does occur it does not work as well as a therapist who needs it may realize. While it may protect the therapist from uncomfortable self-other perceptions the result provides only partial protection, that is, it does not necessarily interfere with patients' perception of the therapist, only the therapist's recognition of the process.

We assume at some level the therapist is "known" to the patient, at least along certain dimensions. Though the therapist may indeed be pathologically detached or may appear "natural," it is a fallacy that the therapist is a blank screen (Goz, 1975). Clinicians such as Searles (1965/1979), in working with schizophrenic patients, have repeatedly noted ways in which the patient's behavior and content often reflect the therapist's unconscious. Not that the patient (or the therapist for that matter) is necessarily aware of the perception or knows what to do with it. But to disclaim that patients and therapist are actually working "unconscious to unconscious," to borrow a Winnicott (1965) phrase, is to disavow a level of relatedness to which it would seem patients, through the therapeutic process, would aspire. Such denial would indicate the kind of rigidity of roles that is antithetical to emotional mutuality and, in a sense, the complexity of human response and communication. In short, just as it is neither possible nor useful for a therapist to be "uninvolved" with a patient, except at the expense of a detached state of relating (Dorpat, 1977), the patient does perceive more than either therapist or patient may realize. The therapist is revealed to the patient whether or not either chooses to consciously acknowledge it or use the knowledge constructively.

Speaking of perception leads us now to a brief discussion of how the therapist's narcissism accounts for problems in *empathy deficit*. Although recent reports

(Gomes-Schwartz, 1978) indicate that the function of the therapist's empathic ability as a predictor of therapy outcome has been over-rated, it seems to us that empathy is a major component in human interaction (Charny, 1966). As such, it is a vehicle through which one feels understood by another. Empathy, therefore, can be seen as a process and mode of communication, albeit an unconscious one. It is here you will note that we diverge from a major research definition of empathy (Carkhuff, 1969; Rogers, 1961; Rogers and Truax, 1967) although it is clear there is no universal operational definition of the concept. (In fact, the construct validity of a major scale, Carkhuffs Empathic Understanding Scale, has been seriously questioned [Avery et al., 1976], to add a measurement problem to the conceptual confusion.)

The most frequently used research definition assumes that empathy relates to the therapist's sensitivity to the patient's internal state and not necessarily to the internal state of the therapist. Lewis (1977) amends this concept of "cognitive empathy," to state that what is involved is the therapist's ability for accurate perception of the patient's manifest feelings. Psychoanalytic writers, such as Sullivan (1939/1953) and Greenson (1960) maintain that empathy relates to the ability to experience the other, the capacity for affective arousal—"affective empathy" (Paul, 1967–68).

While it is possible for the therapist to intellectually appreciate the patient's manifest feelings and even the patient's internal state without necessarily resonating with the patient, we think it is probably the resonance which is perceived by the patient as most meaningful. Consequently, we see empathy as a combination of cognitive and affective empathy. In other words, empathy is that state which occurs in one person and is "caught" and felt by another as his or her own during any given moment of interaction. Such an experience, then, is automatic, unconscious, and cannot be taught, which is in contrast to cognitive empathy where techniques for its development are taught (Lewis, 1977). In our definition of empathy, the objective of the therapist would be at some point to recognize the state as emanating from the patient, and to utilize the empathy—this unconscious emotional communion or bond, as it were—both by simply allowing its occurrence as an end in itself (Havens, 1974) and by recognizing the experience as a subjective clue to objective understanding and analysis of the patient.

Langs (1976) has described projective and introjective identification, in empathy, referring to the empathic process in both patient and therapist. Our focus of concern is more with an apparent empathy deficit in the therapist. Given a developmental background where, for survival, one has had to be inordinately tuned in to parental emotional states, one would think that such persons who become therapists, would have keen, active, empathic ability. In operation, the reverse seems to be the case, for finely honed obsessional features militate against such skill (Lewis, 1977). Rather, intellectual defenses become the barrier against affectual experience. The empathic experience would be seen as equivalent to being taken over by the mother's needs, in effect to be negated, not confirmed, rendered impotent; to once again be in the mother's emotional service.

The therapist fears losing the control inherent in an empathic process (Katz, 1963), for empathy implies penetration of self by another and another by the self. Control is lost and the therapist fears no return. Empathy means that at a level beyond the therapist's control, the patient is influencing him or her, not intellectually but emotionally. This implies then, that the therapist is vulnerable, subject to experiencing any feelings, intense feelings, uncomfortable feelings, almost against his or her will. Thus, an empathic experience adds insult to injury in that the therapist comes to the situation troubled about experiencing his or her own feeling states, let alone someone else's. By defending against the ability to empathize, the therapist aims not to recapture the vulnerability of his or her position in the parent-child relationship.

The therapist's developmental narcissistic experience has indeed influenced how readily he or she can empathize and how, through detachment, he or she can escape from what can be seen as a natural ability. As a matter of fact, the therapist probably has more, not less inherent empathic capacity than most persons, but in order to ensure that the original parent-child pattern is not replicated, the growing child, and now the therapist, builds a veiled wall of involvement, a barrier of emotional detachment. So the problem is, while the therapist has enormous empathic potential since a significant portion of his or her life's childhood "work" was to be tuned-in, there is not much "available" empathy.

When a therapist reaches a point where he or she is not so afraid of emotional closeness, and is losing a bit of narcissism, the empathic experience may occur but might at first be overwhelming. Sometimes a therapist reacts by taking on the feeling as his or hers in a way to overwhelm and, in a sense, negate the patient,just as the therapist in early life may have been negated. Sometimes, and we hope, eventually, a therapist can "sit" with the feeling and live with its pleasantness or with its disequilibrium or precarious state. Sometimes, and we hope ultimately, the therapist will be pleased that he or she is free enough to allow the empathic process its place in the relationship, and is pleased, too, at the emotional contact if not always comfortable with the particular feeling of the moment.

A word is in order about the discomfort of the empathic experience. Too often, empathy is talked of in glowing, lovely terms as if, through this feeling process, therapist and patient go off together in the sunset. Yes, empathy can be a pleasant experience, but far, far, from always. More often, even for a therapist unafraid of experiencing another or of experiencing his or her own or another's feelings, when a patient is full of dread or anxiety or rage, and the therapist feels that feeling, it is not fun. It is decidedly unpleasant. Any therapist could want it to stop. Yes, it may be a sign of real communication, of affectual self-other contact, and indeed, it may be an indispensable quality of a relationship, but those attributes do not make the feeling of the moment necessarily a pleasurable one.

NARCISSISM AS "HELPFULNESS"

As has been indicated throughout this chapter, many persons attracted to the therapy field tend to be those adults who have "served" their parent(s) emotionally. That is, in their development, they have been used in the service of the parental narcissistic needs instead of vice versa. Thus, the kind of selflessness that develops in persons who become therapists is born out of the pathologic hope that by doing perhaps "one more thing" for the parent, the parent will come through. This desire is not based on fantasy alone. Neither is it based alone on the self-interest of making the parents whole in order to identify with them for the sake of maturing, as Searles (1967/1979) would have it. One can be led to believe the parent will come through because of "good" early caretaking, when the mother's needs were met through fusion with the infant, allowing her then to meet the infants needs. Later, however, the time comes when she cannot let the infant move on to a point where infant demands no longer meet her needs and in fact exceed her emotional limits.

If, as a growing child, or as an adult, the person for whom being helpful has become a way of life stops being helpful, guilt comes soaring forth; yet when forever helpful, he or she never thoroughly feels satisfaction and security and eventually feels angry and exploited. Such is the case with the "chronic helper."

Chronic helpfulness (Rouslin, 1961; 1963) is a term used to refer to a behavior pattern where the helping behavior has a demand quality to it. That is, instead of the person having a simple desire to help another, there is a driving, compulsive need to help. The behavior was first recognized in state hospital patients, who, through their helpfulness and the hospital's tacit approval of what was failed to be consciously recognized as pathology, became indispensable to the psychosocial and economic systems of the hospital. In the process, their pathology was reinforced and they became chronic. They became the mainstay of the hospital's work force.

When the pattern was first measured, it was recognized there was a cornerstone of low self-regard and that as soon as a bid for mutuality was made by the helper, the alliance fell apart. The helper would become enormously anxious, then angry, feeling exploited and helpless at the rejection. The way to feel better and in good grace was of course to start all over again. Thus, there was the lack of satisfaction and security and the "chronic" part of the helpfulness. Although the pattern was operationalized, the dynamics were more complex than the original formulation allowed. It became clear, for example, that low self-regard was a function of the more basic lack of self-confirmation, which, developmentally, has its roots in the fusion and symbiotic phases of narcissistic development. That problems in his lack of separate-self-feeling move on a continuum from more (fusion) to less (symbiotic) primitive, accounts for the original observation that the pattern could be found to fall in the framework of any diagnostic category. The expression might be bizarre or highly socialized depending on the depth of ego impairment.

What was observed but not addressed in the original writings was why the chronic helper seeks pseudo-mutual relationships (Light, 1974). It would appear now that this is related to the lack of separate-self-feeling, causing a rigid structure of helper-helpee relationship to be maintained. While the chronic helper does at some point seek what would appear to be a more mutual relationship, it is actually a false move. The choice of person (who too, has some investment in the structure of the relationship) and an unconscious need to be at the mercy of the other while identifying with the person as the one being helped, militate against such a shift. The chronic helper pattern is now seen in a larger context of narcissistic organization where self-feeling and confirmation is sought through the other, with the challenge and hope that the other person will come through being a central aim. Interestingly, what was noted but not investigated in the writings on chronic helpfulness was how familiar such a pattern was in helping professionals. Just as the pattern as originally defined is not so simplistic as it appeared, it is also one not confined only to patients. Probably, in fact, every helping professional has at least a touch of it, and it seems to us, because of the nature of the service, therapists lead the list!

The notion that therapists need their patients is not new. Nowadays, Searles (1979) is perhaps the most cogent formulator of how the therapist's mother-child dynamics are replicated in the therapist-patient relationship. Although he (Searles, 1975/1979) sees "therapeutic strivings" in all human beings, that is, the aim to make the mother whole in order that she may mother, he considers it of paramount importance for the therapist to "examine personal selfless devotion to complementing the ego incompleteness of the mothering person" (p. 393). Otherwise patient and therapist are engaged in a kind of mutual sustenance and resistance that inhibits growth.

So, we have established that therapists and patients are alike under the skin after all. Each, to one degree or another, at one level or another, has an inordinate need to dedicate his or her life to another for not-so-selfless reasons. Actually, the notion that some children are therapists to their parents has been suggested for years (Ferenczi, 1955; Lichtenstein, 1964). Ferenczi speaks about a premature maturity in children—a developmental phenomenon initiated out of physical or psychic trauma or exploitation. These children give a sage-like impression, often looking older and sounding wiser than their years. They tend to minister to others, mother them, help them. As an example, he reports the 'wise baby' dream: The newborn talks to the parents, imparting his wisdom. Such a child early senses the mother's need and meets it, becoming a therapist to the mother and in the process creating a crucial relational bond to be repeated throughout the child's life.

From what adolescents and adults have demonstrated and reported in therapy, it would seem there is always the hope that through the ministrations the mother will become a mother. As we mentioned earlier, this is probably not based on wish alone, but on the fact that early on, some of the child's needs were indeed met, leading him to feel tantalized, to continue to hope for more. Lichtenstein (1964) goes so far as to say that the mother creates needs that she then meets, thereby adding fuel to the expectation (and skepticism) that needs will be met. He says that the mother creates and meets the needs for essentially the wrong reasons, for she only creates an instrument for the satisfaction of her own unconscious needs. The child helper becomes mother to the mother then, not out of healthy desire or concem, but because there is no choice. Often, this is a therapist's heritage.

Sometimes it does not appear that the child is the mother, as in the instance reported by a therapist. It seems one day she noticed how her mother repeatedly told her two-year-old grandson that she was going downstairs—interrupted his play in fact to tell him, an action unconsciously designed to help nourish his need for her and feed his anxiety at her absence. When the child finally went looking for her, it would have appeared she was the concerned, missed mother and he the anxious child needing his mother. On a deeper level, however, he was meeting her needs—a projection of her own desire for a mother who wanted her. Further, he helped her to control "nicely," aiding her in her need to appear the good, loving mother; all the while certainly tightening the symbiotic knot.

Some children develop into rather ostensibly mothering persons. Modell (1975) suggests that there occurs precocious separation when such a mother's unreliability or intrusiveness is perceived. A premature sense of self develops, supported by omnipotent and grandiose fantasies. And these are features we often note in those persons who become therapists. However, as Serales (1967/1979) puts it, "It is our omnipotent self-expectations that more than anything else, pinion us and tend, as well, to stalemate or sever the therapeutic relationship" (p. 73). Surely, the dedication of such a therapist becomes a burden to self and patient, a tedious, unending replay of the therapist's developmental narcissism gone awry.

By this time, you may have concluded that, as Grunberger (1971/1979) says, narcissism has a "bad reputation," and if a therapist holds such a strong narcissistic position, better to forget doing therapy altogether. We suggest no such thing. Rather, we think the very hope for the therapist and the therapist-patient relationship lies in the therapist's ability to turn an essentially pathological stance into a therapeutic one, a "narcissistic liberation" as Grunberger would put it. After all, the ability to merge with the unconscious without either compulsion to do so or compulsion to avoid doing so, is a narcissistic function, a healthy narcissistic function. And do we not aim for such union as a vehicle for growth in our patients and in ourselves? This is what Searles (1973/1979) is talking about when he writes of therapeutic symbiosis, where there is a genuine degree of selflessness on the part of the therapist; a state as we see it where the therapist has no vested interest in how the patient proceeds in treatment and in life, or in how numerous and lengthy and varied those paths might be.

In this chapter, our point has been that the quality of the therapist's narcissism facilitates, if not compels, him or her into a field where ostensibly the task is to help others. In doing treatment, however, it becomes clear there is a hidden agenda, namely, that it is the patient who is to help the therapist, simply by being a patient in need of the therapist's help. The therapy situation, then, becomes an arena for the expression of the therapist's narcissism, a dilemma where the therapist's developmental lacks in mothering result in his or her becoming mother to his or her own needy mother, now the patient. The therapist, in a single operation, becomes the competent, all-giving mother *and* through identification, the mother whom the child (patient) must attend.

With this complex "need to be needed," it is, at times, difficult to tell who is therapist and who is patient, a problem which goes beyond the fact that all patients help their therapist's emotional growth. To some degree, the therapist is on a tightrope, trying to balance conscious and unconscious forces, forces where the rational desire to help competes with its unconscious, irrational motivation. The result is a therapist who should take heed of innermost responses and needs, and who, ultimately, will realize that while helping people can be a worthwhile and satisfying pursuit, it is a far cry from the kind of experience providing the special gratification we may have been searching and hoping for.

Now that we have discussed the scope of the therapist's narcissism, it is time to move on to show how its existence can influence major treatment issues. The first of these, to be addressed in our next chapter, is contracts, a popular subject in today's consumer-oriented society. We ask if therapists are democratic, realistic, or rigid in thinking that a contract for treatment is based on rational motive alone, by either patient or therapist. We suggest and elaborate on two levels of contracts, rational and irrational. Further, we raise the question as to what kind of contract is most useful to the patient, and what dynamic and practical considerations such a contract should take into account. This is designed to clarify what really goes on in the practice of psychotherapy.

REFERENCES

Avery, A. W., D'Augelli, A. R., and Danish, S. J. An empirical investigation of the construct validity of empathic understanding ratings. *Counselling Education Supervision* (1976) **15:**117–183.

Balint, M. *The basic fault* (London: Tavistock Publications, 1968).

Bellak, L. The life of a psychotherapist. *Treatment Monographs on Analytic Psychotherapy* (Fall 1974) **5:**7–10.

Blanck, G., and Blanck, R. *Ego psychology II* (New York: Columbia University Press, 1979).

Bursten, B. The narcissistic course. In M. C. Nelson (Ed.), *The narcissistic condition: A fact of our lives and times.* (New York: Human Sciences Press, 1977).

Bursten, B. Some narcissistic personality types. *International Journal of Psycho-Analysis* (1973) **54:**287–300.

Carkhuff, R. R. *Helping and human relations*, Vols. 1 and 2 (New York: Holt, Rinehart & Winston, Inc., 1969).

Charny, E. J. Psychosomatic manifestations of rapport in psychotherapy. *Psychosomatic Medicine* (1966) **28:**39–47.

Dorpat, T. L. On neutrality. *International Journal of Psychoanalytic Psychotherapy* (1977) **6:**39–64.

Ferenczi, S. Child analysis in the analysis of adults. In S. Ferenczi (Ed.) *Final contributions to the problem of psychoanalysis* (New York: Dover Press, 1955).

Ford, E. S. Being and becoming a psychotherapist: The search for identity. *Psychotherapy: Theory, Research, and Practice* (1963) **17:**472–482.

Freud, S. Notes upon a case of Obsessional Neurosis. In *The complete psychological works of Sigmumd Freud*, Vol. 10 (London: Hogarth Press, 1957). (Originally published, 1909).

Freud, S. On narcissism: An introduction. In *The complete psychological works of Sigmund Freud*, Vol. 14 (London: Hogarth Press, 1957). (Originally published, 1914).

Gomes-Schwartz, B. Effective ingredients in psychotherapy: Prediction of outcome from process variables. *Journal of Consulting and Clinical Psychology* (1978) **46:**1023–1035.

Goz, R. On knowing the therapist "as a person." *International Journal of Psychoanalytic Psychotherapy* (1975) **4:**437–458.

Greben, S. E. Some difficulties and satisfactions inherent in the practice of psychoanalysis. *International Journal of Psycho-Analysis* (1975) **56:**427–434.

Greenson, R. R. Empathy and its vicissitudes. *International Journal of Psycho-Analysis* (1960) **41:**418–424.

Grunberger, B. [*Narcissism*] (J. S. Diamanti, Trans.) (New York: International Universities Press, 1979). (Originally published, 1971)

Havens, L. L. The existential use of the self. *American Journal of Psychiatry* (1974) **131:**1–10.

Jones, E. *The God complex essays in applied psychoanalysis* (London: Hogarth Press, 1951).

Katz, R. L. The effective empathizer. In R. L. Katz (Ed.), *Empathy, its nature and uses* (The Free Press of Glencoe: Collier-Macmillan, Ltd., 1963).

Kernberg, O. *Borderline conditions and pathological narcissism* (New York: Aronson, 1975).

Klein, M. The origins of transference. *International Journal of Psycho-Analysis* (1952) **33:**433–438.

Langs, R. *The bipersonal field.* (New York: Aronson, 1976).

Lax, R. F. Some comments on the narcissistic aspects of self-righteousness: Defensive and structural considerations. *International Journal of Psycho-Analysis* (1975) **56:** 283–292.

Lewin, B. D. Education and the quest for omniscience. *Journal of the American Psychoanalytic Association* (1958) **6:**389–412.

Lewis, J. M. *To be a therapist: The teaching and learning* (New York: Brunner/Mazel, 1978).

Lichtenstein, H. The role of narcissism in the emergence and maintenance of a primary identity. *International Journal of Psycho-Analysis* (1964) **45:**49–56.

Light, N. The "chronic helper" in group therapy. *Perspectives in Psychiatric Care* (1974) **12:**129–134.

Lipp, M. R. What's in it for the therapist? *Hospital and Community Psychiatry* (1978) **29:**40–41.

Mahler, M. S. *On human symbiosis and the vicissitudes of individuation* (New York: International Universities Press, 1968).

Marmor, J. The feeling of superiority—An occupational hazard in the practice of psychiatry. *American Journal of Psychiatry* (1953) **110:**370–376.

Marmor, J. The psychoanalyst as a person. *The American Journal of Psychoanalysis* (1977) **37:**275–284.

Mehlman, R. D. Becoming and being a psychotherapist: The problem of narcissism. *International Journal of Psychoanalytic Psychotherapy* (1974) **3:**125–141.

Miller, A. The drama of the gifted child and the psychoanalyst's narcissistic disturbance. *International Journal of Psycho-Analysis* (1979) **60:**47.

Modell, A. H. A narcissistic defense against affects and the illusion of self sufficiency. *International Journal of Psycho-Analysis* (1975) **56:**275–282.

Paul, N. L. The use of empathy in the resolution of grief. *Perspectives in Biology and Medicine* (1967–68) **11:**153–169.

Rogers, C. R. *On becoming a person* (Boston: Houghton Mifflin, 1961).

Rogers, C. R., and Truax, C. B. The therapeutic conditions antecedent to change: A theoretical view. In C. R. Rogers (Ed.), *The therapeutic relationship and its impact* (Madison: University of Wisconsin Press, 1967).

Rouslin, S. Chronic helpfulness: Maintenance or intervention. *Perspectives in Psychiatric Care* (1963) **1:**25–28.

Rouslin, S. Coping with chronic helpfulness. *Mental Hospitals* (1961) **12:**10–12.

Salzman, L. *The obsessive personality* (New York: Science House, 1968).

Searles, H. F. Concerning therapeutic symbiosis: The patient as symbiotic therapist, the phase of ambivalent symbiosis, and the role of jealousy in the fragmented ego. In H. F. Searles (Ed.), *Countertransference and related subjects* (New York: International Universities Press, 1979). (Originally published, 1973.)

Searles, H. F. The "dedicated physician" in the field of psychotherapy and psychoanalysis. In H. F. Searles (Ed.), *Countertransference and related subjects* (New York: International Universities Press, 1979). (Originally published, 1967.)

Searles, H. F. Feelings of guilt in the psychoanalyst. In H. F. Searles (Ed.), *Countertransference and related subjects* (New York: International Universities Press, 1979). (Originally published, 1966.)

Searles, H. F. The patient as therapist to his analyst. In H. F. Serales (Ed.), *Countertransference and related subjects* (New York: International Universities Press, 1979). (Originally published, 1975.)

Sharaf, M. R., and Levinson, D. J. The quest of omnipotence in professional training. *Psychiatry* (1964) **27**:135–149.

Sullivan, H. S. *The interpersonal theory of psychiatry* (New York: W. W. Norton, 1953).

Winnicott D. W. *The maturational processes and the facilitating environment* (New York: International Universities Press, 1965).

VI

At Issue: Rational and Irrational Contracts

INTRODUCTION

In this chapter we will consider some unusual and relatively unnoticed, yet very powerful aspects of contracts. However, prior to introducing these we want to reaffirm "contracting" as a definite ingredient of the therapeutic process, regardless of the type of psychotherapy. The concept of the therapist-patient agreement, while varying in degree and content, has received some mention in all our discussions thus far, and is a very "alive" topic at the present time.

Montgomery and Montgomery (1975) suggest that contracts can be efficient in that they may avoid wasted time and game-playing for client and therapist. They can provide safeguards for the therapist and insurance for the client. They can define mutual responsibilities and commitments for the patient to try to change and the therapist to attempt to help the patient proceed in the direction of the change desired. Of course the power of a contract in psychotherapy is limited by the difficulties mentioned earlier in this book in regard to defining what can, is, and will be done, as well as certain limitations on forecasting results. But, while admitting to these limitations, Strupp (1975) has affirmed that the client has a right to know what the services are, explicitiy, and it is the therapist who has the obligation to be explicit about these services.

He believes that the nature of the therapeutic process, the aims, and the probable outcomes, all should be specified so that a specific contractual agreement can be negotiated in all these respects. Unfortunately we doubt at the present time that it is possible to deal with such complex issues so clearly. The idea has more difficulties and hidden traps than most people notice, and we have already spent quite a bit of this book pointing out both the need for specificity and how hard it is to do it. The results have often tended toward polarities. Either we are offered an overwhelming vagueness about what psychotherapy is and does, or we get some very concrete attempts to be very concrete, and somehow the whole process appears diluted into "common sense." Neither can be the answer in terms of establishing a useful, working, client-therapist contract.

THE DEVELOPMENT OF THERAPEUTIC CONTRACTS

Perhaps it appears simple upon looking at what appears to be happening. A person is paying for services being received and so is entitled to knowledge about these services. An agreement is reached between the purchaser and the service provider as to the nature of the service, the goals that can be set and reached, the procedures followed, and the delivery date. The expertise of the provider and the characteristics of the purchaser govern the substance of the agreement. The two parties now have a contract, which in therapy is usually verbal, but sometimes written.

Interest in contracts has accelerated in the last fifteen years. Motivating forces include increased consumer participation in determining the type and process of their health care services, and the increased call for the accountability of health care professionals by people in and outside of the professions. More than ever before, patients' rights are inherent in the substance of the treatment contract concept. Yet the contract in psychotherapy is certainly not a new concept, as is illustrated by Freud (1937/1964) with the term "analytic pact" applied to the psychoanalytic procedure. We will describe that pact in more detail later in the chapter. It is of course true that at the time of the analytic pact the setting of treatment conditions and objectives was more private, and less specific. Now it is more collaboratively conceived, and is hopefully aimed at greater clarification and facilitation of psychotherapy.

To do this, and therefore to be considered appropriate, therapy contracts should do the following (Hare-Mustin, Marecek, Kaplan, and Liss-Levenson, 1979): Specify the methods and goals of the therapy, the duration and frequency of the sessions and of the total treatment, cost and payment procedures, cancellation and renegotiation provisions, the extent of each party's responsibility, and the degree of confidentiality. The exact issues covered will vary somewhat according to the orientations and inclinations of individual therapists and clients.

Specifying procedures, goals, indirect effects, qualifications, policies, and practices are all complicated activities for therapists, yet it seems to us that the difficulties involved are beginning to be underplayed in an admirable desire to protect the consumer. We have repeatedly urged that the profession aim for more accurate, prescriptive therapies, but making an overt contract with a client is only part of that effort. And that part—contracting—is no easier than the other parts.

Some present the making of a contract as though it were the major answer to many of psychotherapy's woes. Morrison (1979a) has been particularly vocal in advocating a consumer-oriented approach to psychotherapy. This has as integral parts the clients' evaluations of services they receive, and therapist-client agreements open to modification based upon evaluation by both therapist and client. He suggests strong client involvement in problem definition and a clearly understood therapist-client contract. While we can again agree with the principles suggested, we believe there are severe limitations as to what the therapist and client can be certain about in any contract they make.

Morrison (1979b) wants specified the effectiveness of a particular type of therapy with particular clients under particular circumstances. As we, and others, have said before, we would like that too, but we can only approximate what will happen in most instances. We have painfully illustrated the limitations on our own certitude, and we experience these limitations as being shared by most people in the field. What Morrison and other consumer advocates want we don't contest, but we can't produce it, and we doubt those who claim they can. Beyond that, we feel that such rather exact promises as are desired may currently contain a hidden danger for the consumer. The specific contract may offer a new variation on convoluted therapist narcissism. These therapists may have unconsciously found a way to rationally offer what their irrationality demands they seek.

Hare-Mustin et al. (1979) appear aware of a number of the problems that cannot be neatly resolved through the use of a contract. In particular, making a contract is no guarantee that certain clients will be able to keep it, or in some cases, depending on their ego functioning, even be able to try. Nonetheless, we see the potential value of clear contracts. Yet, we insist on a balanced presentation that includes the realities of the current state of psychotherapeutic practice. We do not think THE CONTRACT ought to take on a significance and life of its own, thereby becoming an end in itself instead of being a possible means to an end. We will continue to support the idea of making contracts for the good of all concerned, but it is erroneous to consider this a simple undertaking, particularly if we now look at an aspect of contracting thus far avoided.

It is our contention that a contract as most therapists and patients think of it goes beyond its rational intention. Actually, Hare-Mustin et al. (1979), in describing and illustrating a patient's right to challenge the competence of the therapist, to disagree, or to criticize the therapist, are implying there is more to a contract than meets the eye, but they do not say there may be two levels of contract operating simultaneously. We believe this is the case, and we call them the "rational contract" and the "irrational contract."

From our own clinical work and that of our colleagues and supervisees we have found that it is something more than the details of a given contract per se that become really problematic in the process of therapy. What becomes clear is that there is a level of contract which is irrational, a level often interfering with carrying out the rational contract. Thus we see in operation two levels of contracts, one rational and one irrational. The levels indeed may have conflicting intentions, thereby sending out mixed messages, placing therapist and patient in a most confusing position.

Conflicting levels make for the kind of therapeutic impasses where neither therapist nor patient knows exactly what went wrong or how it happened, but each feels intense and uncomfortable about the experience. Interestingly, this description can also be applied to the pathological dimensions of the parent-child relationship. The subsequent development of defenses to explain, inattend, or obscure one's inner perception of noxious experience provides the substance for neurosis and psychosis. This is not the aim of the therapeutic experience, at least from the therapist's vantage point, yet it becomes a possibility.

It is with the desire in mind to assure that therapy be a therapeutic experience that we address ourselves in this chapter to the genesis of irrational contracts, suggesting ways in which irrational contracts impede or impinge on rational contracts, rendering rational contracts impotent. To this end we will define rational and irrational contracts and discuss related concepts of "therapeutic alliances" and "working alliances." We will focus our attention on the irrational contract as the more problematic contract because of its insidious negative consequences and its customary low visibility in contrast to the problems of rational contracts. Many of these, such as trying to define psychotherapy, have already been explored.

Through question, commentary, and presentation of clinical data we will now explore how an intricate combination of therapist-need and misconception makes way for the use of irrational contracts. Our aim, as when we discussed the therapist's narcissism, is not to indict the therapist. Rather it is to examine and clarify a process occurring naturally in human experience and inevitably in the therapy experience. By so doing, our desire is to help the therapist increase awareness of the complexity of the patient-therapist experience. With increased perception it is hoped that the therapist's clinical use of self can be understood and refined in such a way as to be truly therapeutic.

Definitions and Related Concepts

Our definition of "rational contract" presumes a conscious intent and plan. It is a verbal or written agreement between therapist and patient which has four components:

1. What the patient wants from the treatment process, for example, changes regarding personality and behavior, intrapsychic and interpersonal problems
2. What the therapist is willing and able to agree to or offer to the treatment process, for example, expected changes regarding personality and behavior, intrapsychic and interpersonal problems
3. Time arrangements, including frequency and length of sessions and duration of treatment
4. Financial arrangements.

Our definition of "irrational contract" is more complicated. For the most part, it is presumed to take place on an unconscious level. Even if the contract terms are conscious when they are recognized by the user, the idea that the contract is irrationally based is rarely recognized without assistance. There are two related types. Type A is that agreement a patient or therapist has with the other which the other has no knowledge of, and therefore has not agreed to. Further, not only is the establisher of the contract unaware of it or its irrationality at the outset, but the one becomes aware of the contract only after the other person breaks it. The contract is held "privately" by either patient or therapist.

The following illustrates what we mean. It is a prototype in kind and complexity and so it is presented in some detail. A supervisee-patient was reporting to his supervisor that a problem he had not experienced in some time was re-emerging. It seems with several patients he felt unusually angry because they were not "appreciating" him. While they "allowed" him to help, he nevertheless felt superfluous. He said he thought the problem was worse because of his dissertation with which he was having a terrible time. On the face of it, the reaction he had to the patients didn't make sense, but when he amplified on what he had been going through, the situation became clear: "I got the proposal done for the last time and sent it out. At first I felt relieved, but then when I went to a party with people from another program they were so disparaging of "my" university I felt horrible. I started to think I looked like hell and about what was wrong with my proposal and how everyone else's was better. I thought they would be happy for me or at least not criticize my program. Then I heard a friend had twins and that was the last straw; I felt even more defeated."

The explanation for what was going on was part and parcel of his narcissistic tie to his mother, which at this point, he was seeing in every relationship, including those with his patients. Although this therapist desperately wanted his doctoral degree, that the desire was his alone was not enough. First, "who was he anyway," since he could not receive standing or respect from his family, even with a degree. So entering into a situation with shaky regard, as he said, "How can what a nobody does count, anyway?" To have it count for himself obviously was not enough, for who was *he*?

In addition to everything else, he had been having unexplainable anxiety. In fact, on his way to the session he kept looking over his shoulder thinking someone was following him. Indeed, figuratively, it was the mother he was leaving behind, but obviously not quite, for he had a menacing feeling that some piece of bad luck would befall him on the way. In other words, separating from the symbiotic tie with his mother, particularly from the struggle to get from her the confirmation he needed, was occurring, loosening a life-long grip. But in the transition to autonomy he thought he would surely be punished for breaking their bond. Here he was, relating this to not feeling appreciated by his patients, when he was "the diligent therapist, working hard and doing what he should despite the terrible pressure of a dissertation." It seems that the terms of the irrational contract in operation were: if he did all he should for the patients, despite personal suffering, the patients were expected, at the very least, to appreciate him, certainly to let him know that somehow he was having an impact on them. Obviously, they neither knew about nor agreed to the terms of the contract, and therefore, did not know they were breaking the rules. (It is useful to note that they could have been unconsciously compliant, which will be discussed in Type B; or they could have negativistically resisted the therapist's demand, neither of which seemed to be taking place. Rather, the therapist's problem was short-lived enough that the patients weathered it without that much trouble.)

The irrational contract established by this therapist had a parataxic basis, as all irrational contracts do. The original contract ran something like this: If he produced well, surely he would be loved and respected by his parents. The hitch, really a doublebind, was that if he produced *for* his parents he felt diminished, and so, unappreciated, which was how he continually felt too in his early years of working with patients. If, on the other hand, he produced for himself, and so, without parental approbation and appreciation, he was on his own, which was how he now felt with his patients. His patients then, were being asked to appreciate him for far more than their therapy. And as he perceived it, they could not or would not, which at least could prevent them from buying into that irrational contract.

Another example of Type A irrational contract comes to mind, this one held by the patient, imposed on the therapist. The gist of it was that if the patient deigned to let the therapist in on her life the therapist was to be thoroughly consistent. Not knowing of the contract and not having agreed to its terms, the therapist made a "mistake" during a group therapy session. She interpreted another patient's behavior in a way different from the way she had interpreted similar behavior of the patient with the contract. Indeed, the behavior was similar, but the two patients' dynamics, needs, and levels in therapy were quite different.

When the event occurred the contract patient was unexplainably enraged, saying only that she felt betrayed and wanted to leave, *had* to leave treatment. During the weeks following her initial response she was able to figure out that she was furious because there existed what amounted to several levels of irrational contracts: If she were to be involved with the therapist, such involvement should not come to her (the patient's) attention. If the therapist happened to have caught on, the therapist should keep the knowledge secret. The therapist, in demonstrating involvement with someone else, was not seen so much as deserting the patient, but as reminding the patient of their involvement, so she could no longer ignore it. Too, since it was so difficult for the patient to let the therapist know her, the therapist was not to become close to any other patient with a tailor-made, "special" interpretation. In addition, for the patient to feel relatively comfortable in putting herself in a position where the therapist would finally be admitted to the patient's inner sanctum, the therapist was to be totally predictable, which obviously she was not.

This very bright patient kept repeating, "How could the same behavior mean two different things?" On an intellectual level she understood the difference a context could make, but on an emotional level an admonition imbedded in her by her mother not to let anyone in on her business caused her not to trust any outsider. As a child, when approached by other children as to what she was doing or where she was going, she told them, "Business is business, so please mind your own." Only her mother was to be confided in and trusted. Now, the therapist at once was seen as the transferential mother in whom the patient put her trust and the outsider who proved not to be trustworthy.

During this time, the patient was also very anxious. She dreamed often of her mother locking her in her mother's room. This content pointed to the patient's fear of punishment lest she let anyone in but her mother. Here, yet another irrational contract dimension emerged, which came down to the patient wanting the therapist exclusively, the way her mother had wanted her.

The therapist neither knew of nor had agreed to any of these levels of contracts, nor should she have. The contracts arose spontaneously and proved to be a most useful indicant of the patient's dynamics and progress. Interestingly, the expression of these particular irrational contracts could have never been predicated, though in retrospect their existence seemed logical in an irrational system. For several years, this well functioning patient had carefully avoided looking at the therapist directly or even calling her by name. She had even said there was no relationship between them. During those years, there had been what now could clearly be identified as a reaction-formation against allowing the recreation of the original symbiotic bond on one level, while on another level there existed a defense against allowing "the outsider" to intrude on the original bond. The protection had now worn thin.

Type B irrational contract is that agreement, quite unspoken, into which therapist and patient have entered in partnership without awareness or acknowledgment on either of their parts. The contract can be initiated by either patient or therapist. To illustrate: A therapist had several sessions with a young man in his first year of college. The fellow could not bring himself to go to classes, even at the urging of parents and friends. He came to treatment reluctantly, quite depressed to the point of having made at least one suicide attempt prior to coming for help. He thought there was no hope for his very disturbed parents to change, there was no hope for his lot in life, or for his feeling to change. He had come to therapy because his parents wanted him to and though he held no hope for it helping, he came anyway.

The therapist had been in the business and in her own treatment for a long time and so had very little hope left that she would get gratification from either her patients or her parents. Too, she was aware of the suicidal risk and felt appropriately anxious about it. What she did not realize was that from the first moment of the first session until the middle of the sixth session, with all her emotional growth and smartness, she had been in partnership with the patient, joined in an irrational contract initiated by the patient. It went something like this: "I am depressed, suicidal, maybe even homicidal. If in any way you reach me I may explode, so stay away. Ask me questions maybe, but don't 'disturb' me. I propose to sit here and control everything that happens here by saying nothing and you are to say nothing, at least nothing of significance." And the therapist agreed. But the therapist's "agreement" was not rational. It went beyond the reasonable, theoretically and clinically based caution one would ordinarily have with such a patient to not intrude, to not push, to not struggle for power. It was an irrationally based agreement. Obviously, it was wise to neither say something inflammatory nor to force a reaction from this time bomb or to have him set goals for treatment which he volunteered was probably useless anyway.

During the sessions, the therapist began to realize she felt intimidated by the patient, feeling anxious when she made even a benign comment ever-vigilant to his response. The anxiety went beyond worry about suicide, homicide, being sued, all the regular worries. Interestingly, it never occurred to her she could be a homicidal victim of his rage. She apparently was so concerned about the immediate situation that concrete realities took a back seat. Although indeed she felt intimidated by the patient and was not sure why, in the sixth session she forced herself to ask him a question about what (qualities) in his parents he thought he was reacting to. The patient had just finished saying he was angry at them for certain concrete things they did or did not do and for their doing nothing about fixing their relationship and "cleaning up the house." The therapist's question did not seem inappropriate in level, time, or placement. Yet he claimed he didn't understand. A look of disdain appeared on his face that the therapist should ask such an obscure question.

The therapist was to become aware that indeed this sensitive, schizoid young man did understand the question. He understood too, that his depressive stance had enormous power to control this therapist and make her quake by turning her into a powerless child subjected to the power of her depressed mother. It was not until this moment that the therapist realized the full extent of her participation in the irrational contract and what its dimensions were.

Although intuitively she realized he understood the question she asked, she rephrased it, not out of need to penetrate or ingratiate, but to give him another chance, lest he change his mind. When he still did not understand, for one second it ran through her mind, "Is a thought disorder interfering? Is his preoccupation with his problems and depression stopping him? Am I really being obtuse?" Simultaneous with these thoughts she found herself saying, without anger or force but with conviction, "I find that awfully hard to believe. You're really a smart guy." His look of surprise and glare of hatred were unmistakable. The therapist had received the message of the patient and of the irrational contract; and receiving messages was not the wont of this young man's parents. Thus the surprise, and the transferential hatred. In addition, however, the therapist would not be intimidated further into joining in partnership in the irrational contract, adding to the surprise and hatred.

It is only natural that because of the existence of irrational contracts in everyday life such contracts will be replicated in the therapist-patient relationship. It becomes academic, therefore, and a bit naive, to think that if goals in a rational contract are set, goals will automatically or easily be adhered to. Acknowledging the existence of irrational contracts helps facilitate the treatment process once it has started, and may hold lessons for therapists as they debate a wide variety of schemes for contractual agreement with their patients. In essence, we are asking therapists to recognize that irrational contracts are made all the time, throughout the course of treatment, not just initially, so they must look out for them. We are asking therapists to go beyond the rational contract, to notice a deeper dimension of relatedness and communication, not because that is "the analytic way" but because it seems the only way to assure that any rational contract can be carried out. More important, such scrutiny assures that the process is not therapy in name only. In essence, such examination is part of the therapist's accountability.

Therapeutic Contracts: The Alliance

In one form or another, contracts have been written about for some time. As early as 1893–95 Breuer and Freud (1964) were writing about the patient as a collaborator in treatment, although the collaboration itself as a process was rather taken for granted. There were hints in Freud's later papers that through his emerging theories of transference and his enlarging on the process of analysis, he was moving in the direction of what might be seen as an early conceptualization of what today might be called a contract. Freud (1937/1964; 1940/1964) coined the term "analytic pact."

The major terms of the pact were simple, and referred mostly to the conduct of the session. During the session, to the extent it was possible, the patient was to say everything that came to mind. On the analyst's side there was one essential rule (aside from the abstinence rule, which both therapist and patient were to follow with each other), namely, to utilize the patient's distortion (transference) of him for therapeutic purposes, for "after-education" as Freud put it. Actually, this was more of a cooperative than collaborative effort in that the thrust seemed to be that the patient defer to the therapist-parent by doing, in at least the session, what the therapist indicated, albeit for the patient's benefit. The therapist indicated what to do to help him provide a corrective emotional and intellectual experience. The context for such an experience was respectful, permissive, and growth-facilitating and not really as authoritarian as it would appear. There was, however, certainly an element of "parental" control over the patient's personal life at times.

While Freud (1916–17/1964) introduced the idea that the therapist in an alliance with the patient became a "new [parental] object" in the process of being seen as the original object, it was Anna Freud (1965) who extended and elaborated on the new object concept as a facilitator of growth beyond the original after-educator and transference-interpreter roles of the therapist. Thus it seems to us, the way was paved for development of the concepts "therapeutic alliance," (Sterba, 1975; Zetzel, 1956, 1966) and "working alliance" (Greenson, 1965; Greenson and Wexier, 1969).

According to Sterba (1975), he coined the term "therapeutic alliance" in 1932, in a paper presented at the International Psychoanalytic Congress in Wiesbaden, although the literature often attributes the term to Zetzel. While at first Zetzel (1956) used the term interchangeably with what Greenson (1965) called the "working alliance," later she distinguished the two (Zetzel, 1966). Greenson (1965) also initially drew no distinction between the two, but he focused on the nonneurotic relationship with the therapist. Frequently the two concepts even today are used interchangeably, which made our task of finding clear definitions difficult. To make matters worse, variations in definition of therapeutic alliance and working alliance are anything but consistent and are often couched in jargon.

As we understand it, the concepts are seen by many as the operations involved in the patient's alliance with the therapist. Each concept presents a difference in emphasis for understanding the therapist-patient relationship, but each seems to focus on the patient end. Zetzel (1966) emphasizes that the alliance is based on positive transference. The current relationship is meaningful and potentially helpful mostly in light of the patient's earliest experiences. On the other hand, Greenson (1965) stresses that the alliance is based on the current, nondistorted relationship and the nonneurotic dimensions of the patient's personality which make this "real" relationship possible. Therefore, both authors attest to the positive value of the relationship with the therapist for the progress of therapy, one from a transferential view and one from a nontransferential view. But interestingly, both exclude negative transference as part of the alliance; rather they see negative transference as separate from the alliance; any irrational aspects of the relationship being seen as the so-called "transference neurosis." To us this separation seems artificial in light of the replication of both good and bad parent images in the one therapist-patient bond.

As Arlow (1975) sees it, "Both Greenson and Zetzel establish an artificial dichotomy between external reality and internal fantasy life. Each one sees the need to breech this dichotomy with a bridge of reassurance and interpretation of the so-called 'real relationship.' Both deemphasize thereby the dynamic interplay of the mutual influence of perception and fantasy, memory and reality, past and present" (p. 72). We agree, and would add some.

A compromise approach to the problem of defining the nature of the alliance between therapist and patient has been suggested by Dickes (1975), although he too does not see the negative transference as in any way part of the alliance. He does, however, use both the therapeutic alliance and working alliance concepts to explain the therapist-patient alliance. He sees the therapeutic alliance as the full-scale therapeutic rapport including all elements facilitating progress in therapy, "factors as the patient's motivation for treatment based on ego-alien symptoms, positive transference, and the rational relationship between therapist and patient" (p. 1). He sees the working alliance as also operating in the relationship, but sees it as more limited in scope than the therapeutic alliance. He thinks the working alliance refers to the healthier interpersonal exchange between therapist and patient and is a reflection of the mature state of many of the ego's functions. Dickes' package is a bit neat and a bit incomplete for us, but we do agree with his idea that the two dimensions of alliance coexist.

The point is, there exists "an alliance" in the therapist-patient relationship promoting emotional development through some kind of interpersonal, emotional process. It is neither Zetzel's therapeutic alliance nor Greenson's working alliance. It is both. They cross and blend and separate from one another, these alliances, and when seen as coexisting in therapeutic work each is an integral part of the therapeutic process. In addition, we add that the disturbed dimension of the patient is also part of the alliance. For example, the healthier dimension of an alliance or the positive transferential dimension of an alliance allows the sicker dimension to manifest itself as an integrated part of that alliance—for many patients the forerunner to integration of the good and the bad dimensions of the parent. In operation, it is as if the rational, reasonable, or positive portion says to the irrational portion, "Right, I feel comfortable here with this person, this therapist, to react any way I feel, so here goes, you son of a bitch!"

Our consideration of the illustrations and the definitions of therapeutic and working alliances leads us to conclude the existence of what we will simply call the "therapist-patient alliance" in psychotherapy. This alliance contains dimensions of both Zetzel's and Greenson's alliances but goes beyond them in a few major ways. The therapist-patient alliance as we see it, is an unconscious, unspoken commitment on the part of both therapist and patient to allow the emotional relationship between these partners to develop in whatever direction the patient points it. This does not mean the patient or therapist has permission to act out against one another or with one another for destructive ends. Nor does it mean the therapist is free (with clear conscience) to burden the patient with his or her emotional needs. It does mean that at some level, undiscussed and even privately unarticulated or unformulated, the therapist provides a "holding environment" (Winnicott, 1960/1974; 1963/1974) for the patient in which the patient "agrees" to "be him or herself" to the degree possible, and in so doing, uses the therapist in a way suitable at any given point in time to the patient's needs and emotional life. The "uses" include various distortion experiences and nondistortion experiences. The uses are bound only by the patient's capacity and the therapist's emotional and social limitations and which uses could be seen as destructive to the patient or as a patient response to the therapist's own need.

Further, the therapist "agrees" not to retaliate against the patient and if it happens, then to examine the precipitant as a force evoked by or arising not simply from the patient but from the therapist's internal life. In short, the therapist and patient unconsciously agree to stick together while the very forces against a positive alliance are operating. The patient vents rage and empathically communicates anxiety to the therapist. At the same time that it could logically be assumed that such goings on would herald the end of an alliance, there is an unconscious agreement the therapist makes and the patient "learns" about. This dimension of the agreement is that the therapist will not be frightened away by the threat and not be demolished by the mutually shared anxiety. To the extent that the therapist can tolerate this incredible disequilibrium the patient will benefit with a beginning awareness and acceptance of psychic imbalance and interpersonal imbalance.

We know only too well from our own experience and that of our colleagues and supervisees that what we describe as the therapist-patient alliance is an ideal to be aimed for and one that must be worked on constantly. It does not just happen. Sometimes it does not happen. And sometimes it does not happen completely enough to salvage a relationship. Of course, then we lose patients, but we like to think it is possible to learn from these experiences. This is what a contract is about. This is what patients' rights and therapist's responsibilities are about. This is what being an "expert" and "participant observer" (Sullivan, 1954) and being accountable are about. No terms drawn up by patient and therapist can promise the sort of therapist-patient alliance we have described, for each relationship is different and sets off different features of our dynamics and the patient's dynamics. But the definition can serve as a guide for the growth of the therapist. And if the therapist benefits from the guidance, the patient will benefit, and to that contract we can agree.

Questions and Misconceptions

The use of contracts altogether and what features (aside from time and financial arrangements) comprise the contract provoke spirited debate among therapists over questions like this: What if the patient or the therapist breaks the terms of the contract? For example, a patient and therapist contracted for twelve sessions to direct their efforts at understanding why the patient chose the man with whom she had recently broken off after a peculiarly satisfying, yet stormy affair. After the third session, the patient was no longer focusing on the relationship or its meaning, at least on a discernible level. In such an instance, should the contract be renegotiated? If so, with every apparent shift in focus on the part of the patient, should the contract be renegotiated? Could such contract rigidity interfere with the unfolding of the meaning the patient seeks and the development of relatedness between patient and therapist? Is it possible that a therapist's need to negotiate or renegotiate is based on a need, in a most acceptable and benevolent way, to control the process, and the patient and the therapist, thereby establishing boundaries: who is where, who is who, and who is in charge; all in the guise of clarifying direction in the patient's interest?

This brings us to another point. The therapist in the example cited earlier was found to be nodding off at times during some of the sessions. If a therapist breaks his or her end of the bargain, in this case, to at least stay awake in order to raise questions and make comments leading to understanding of the patient's choice of partner, should the patient break the contract? If the patient decides to explore the situation by bringing out in the open the therapist's failure, should the therapist simply attribute it to a response to the patient's drifting off the subject? Or should the therapist sever the contract on the grounds that the therapist has been an obvious failure at performing the task? Perhaps by this time you can see how the questions proliferate and how difficult it is to respond with certitude, which is a major burden for rational contracts.

Perhaps too by this time it has become abundantly clear there is more to this contract business than the written or verbalized word. Adding to the confusion, we have noticed in patients and therapists a certain belief in the magic of words. Here, we are not necessarily talking about psychotics in whom we might expect such thinking. We are referring to a kind of approach to words whereby words are taken as the sole communication dimension, whereby what is put into words is taken as the only reflection of one's motivation, or whereby words are used as a basic outline, the details to be filled in differently by patient and therapist.

In writing about the "uses" of interpretation by narcissistic patients, Rosenfeld (1965) says about interpretation what could easily be said about mutually agreed upon rational contracts. While the patient uses intellectual insight to agree with the therapist, the patient puts the insight into his own words in such a way as to deprive the interpretations of life, leaving words bereft of all meaning except that they belong to the patient. So too can a patient or a therapist "use" a rational contract. Each can put the terms of the contract into his or her own system, thereby adding a private dimension to the contract that in Sullivan's terms is not consensually validated.

Akin to the private use of the contract is the capitalizing on ambiguity which is bound to occur no matter how tightly drawn-up the contract terms. Bion (1963) coined the term, "reversed perspective" in writing about distortion or misuse of interpretations. In such instances, the patient and therapist would appear to agree on an interpretation but the patient capitalizes on an ambiguity in the therapist's presentation to give the interpretation a slightly different meaning than intended.

In establishing a rational contract, patient and therapist might appear to agree on terms, but one or the other may capitalize on an ambiguity, frequently something not said rather than something that has been said, in order to turn the treatment into what one or the other wants it to be. Often this distortion does not occur until the therapy process is well under way, when the need for maintaining distance may become paramount. It occurs as a defensive operation to hold the other person at bay. It keeps the person from intruding on one's emotional territory, except in a way one deems acceptable, and fits the other person into one's own system so as *not* to experience the other as separate from the self, and *to* experience the other as being in the service of the self. In the extreme, the feared dynamic would be that the therapist or patient would be so undifferentiated as to be unable to distinguish between the "outside" and "inside" in Searles' (1 963/ 1965) terms, or the "me" from the "not me" in Winnicott's (1960/1974) terms; or to see there was not a proper fit between the self and the other (Balint, 1968), that the other could not yield to be there in the service of the self of the partner. So, "fixing" the contract to fit one's system has a primitive narcissistic basis dynamically, a symbiosis to which every patient and every therapist is susceptible.

Then there are those to whom the words of the rational contract make it irrevocable. The goals and procedures are absolute. To such therapists and patients there is no such thing as unconscious motivation. The stated intention is the only intention. No levels of intention are thought to exist, no conflicting motivations operating. The implication here too is that words have a kind of magic, a kind of structural magic. The existence of the contract assures both therapist and patient that neither person is there for any reasons other than those stated. Such thinking implies that as unconscious motivation emerges, a person cannot have a change of mind without renegotiating the contract. For example, it would seem conceivable that with every shift of intention and surfacing of resistance, more intellectual and emotional effort would be spent on renegotiating to "get the process on a clear track" than would be spent on allowing the process to proceed unimpeded by the therapist's need to keep things straight, to have an exact match between the contract terms and the process experienced. Furthermore, inattention to the therapist's levels of intention and motivation as they emerge promotes proliferation of irrational contracts, and is just plain denial.

We come now directly to discussion of possible misconceptions on the part of the therapist, misconceptions that render rational contracts impotent, misconceptions that are at the heart of irrational contracts in that they combine with irrational need, producing irrational contracts. For much of what we think along these lines we are grateful to Sullivan (1954), who, although not talking about irrational contracts per se, recognized there were assumptions therapists held, assumptions that served to make for difficulties in the psychiatric interview.

Our understanding of assumptions implicit in Sullivan's work and of his ideas on what he thought the psychiatric interview should be has helped us conceptualize misconceptions we think many therapists bring to the therapeutic situation. For the most part, these misconceptions appear to arise from a narcissistic need. They provide a general context in which various irrational reactions find themselves a rationalized base, albeit a misconceived theoretical base.

A frequently noted misconception is that *the verbal character of communication in psychotherapy is emphasized*. Thus, while open communication is often praised as an effective therapeutic tool, in practice, it may be ineffective because it is limited to what is spoken. Yet there is a nonverbal dimension to communication. The nonverbal level may be consonant with the verbal, or, unfortunately, it may communicate a totally different message from the verbal one. Thus, "open communication" as it is generally used, which tends to be in the verbal sense, is not necessarily as open as it would appear or as we might like it to be.

Sullivan (1954) long recognized that nonverbal levels of communication operated in conjunction with the verbal. If there is incongruence between the verbal and nonverbal levels, the discordance will eventually be perceived, and even before it is consciously perceived, it will interfere with the sending and receiving of verbal messages. Communication then, has two levels, as do contracts. The nonverbal level has great significance in determining the quality of and influencing the therapist-patient relationship, just as the irrational level of contract does. The double dose here is that obviously, an irrational contract itself is replete with nonverbal communication. In fact, from a communication standpoint, an irrational contract is a nonverbal pact.

A focus on verbal behavior alone implies that statements have unquestionable meaning. Thus, although "communication is the channel of interchange between patient and therapist" (Wolberg, 1977, p. 44) words mean different things to different people. How often clinicians have noticed that patients of all kinds, from schizophrenics with blatantly psychotic, private usage of public words, to obsessionals with skillful use of words intended to obscure communication, are not saying what we think they are saying. One cannot, therefore, assume that communication is so exclusively verbal or that there is an exact fit in meaning between sender and receiver. In other words, communication must be scrutinized. While we agree with Wolberg (1977) who writes that the therapist "must be able to subject the patient's communication to selective scrutiny" (p. 44), we would extend that scrutiny to the therapist's communication. The implication of this misconception for contracts is that although words are exchanged in the formation and process of a rational contract, that is all they are. This is not to say that rational contracts are hogwash; it is to note their limitations, limitations which may not manifest themselves until the relationship is well under way.

Wouldn't it be a pleasure if a patient's motivation for treatment were not mixed? Too, would it not be less complicated if a therapist's motivation for being a helping professional were not mixed? As Enright (1975) says, "Motivation is a complex variable [only one] facet [of which] is the expressed willingness to be there" (p. 344). *The assumption that patients and therapists do not have mixed motivation* is another misconception bringing trouble to the therapist-patient relationship. Certainly, as Wolberg (1977) indicates, without a patient's motivation to relieve personal suffering it is difficult to treat him or her. Then, says Wolberg, there are "defective motivations" (p. 424), simply "irrational needs" in our language, needs such as projecting hated dimensions of the self onto the therapist, needs beautifully described by Searles (1971/1979) in writing about pathologic symbiosis in the therapist-patient relationship, needs such as idealizing the therapist, therapist and patient needs for perfection, power, and so on, which Wolberg seems to imply will interfere with the outcome of treatment. Although irrational needs make treatment difficult, such difficulties are essential aspects of treatment. We see such motivations as part and parcel of characteristic patterns of living and think of the therapy experience as an uncommon opportunity for patient and therapist to gain understanding of these patterns in themselves.

No matter how tightly drawn a rational contract is, therapist and patient needs will be revealed through irrational contracts operating. In our view, the goal is not to stamp out the needs, these irrational motivations for treatment, so that a rational contract may be designed and the therapy may "begin." Instead, these motivations become part of the therapy process itself. Certainly there are virtues in paying attention to stated motives, virtues to setting a structure, establishing limits or long-range planning or however one might express the structure and establishment of the rational contract. The issue is whether adherence to the patient's stated motive, to the contract derived on the basis of that motive, takes precedence over the patient's initial irrational motive, or an emerging irrational (or unaccounted for) need to experiment with, to resist, to act out, to manipulate and control the therapy and the therapist. Maybe the issue comes down to how much latitude a therapist is able to give a patient, how much respect a therapist has for the patient's need to proceed at the patient's own pace and way, no matter what rational "terms" for goals and process the patient has agreed to. It is, after all, the patient's nickel.

Speaking of it being the patient's life brings us to an allied misconception—that *a patient must be "properly motivated" to derive benefit from therapy*. Blanck and Blanck (1974) point out that many therapists are prejudiced against "unmotivated" patients, yet these patients make up a large segment of the patients in psychotherapy. Dynamically, such patients show enough of a desire for help to talk to a therapist. But, using projection and displacement they display a conscious reluctance to commit themselves to therapy. In fact, our experience indicates that therapists feel terribly uncomfortable with patients who may come because they have to, or with patients who really cannot articulate why they are coming. In either case, the patients would be unable to establish major elements of a rational contract. Obviously, it is easier for the therapist when the patient is clearly "motivated" or has an idea of why he or she is there and can say what is desired from the treatment.

We think therapists react poorly to these patients who can but "present" themselves for treatment. First the therapist feels anxious and perhaps angry about being unwanted, not being "allowed" to help by the patient whose major contribution to the rational contract is to show up. Second, though there may be good, rational reasons for providing a patient with information and obtaining agreement through the rational contract (Hare-Mustin et al., 1979), the therapist's need to define the therapeutic relationship as a mutual, equal endeavor is not so entirely rational as many would choose to believe, nor is it done solely out of patient concern.

The therapist's need for a "motivated" patient is often based on the therapist's need to assure at least some measure of gratification from being a therapist to this patient. In addition, the therapist may have a need for structure in relationships, a discomfort in allowing relationships to proceed in an undefined and un-predetermined way. Too, the therapist may need to control the parameters of the process lest the therapist lose control (which to those therapists worried about such matters would mean the patient would be in control of them).

After practicing for awhile most therapists learn that there may be little gratification derived from patients—any patients—even those eager and grateful for their effort and expertise. Ultimately, a therapist learns not to count on the gratification; if it comes your way, that's a fortunate experience. They also learn that no rational contract can really clarify the therapeutic relationship. Neither can a rational contract prevent all false expectations and disappointment inherent in relationships, any relationships. Certainly the rational contract cannot prevent all those events with "motivated" or " unmotivated" patients.

In short, we think the therapist's motivation for needing a rational contract with clear-cut goals relating to specific problems may be based on both irrational need and rationality. The former too often has gone unrecognized, helping to perpetuate some unfortunate contracts. This becomes startlingly clear when a therapist works with overtly schizophrenic patients who may not really be speaking our language. In the therapy of potentially mature, adult "neurotics" arriving at a mutually agreeable rational contract would seem a reasonable possibility. It seems unreasonable to assume, however, that schizophrenic or severely regressed patients, or compensated psychotic patients with a high potential for ego disorganization would have sufficient ego functions of self-observation and reality testing to negotiate a substantive rational contract. For such patients, patients who live in a world of pathologic symbiosis (Searles, 1971/1979) or defend against pathologic symbiosis by living in an autistic world (Searles, 1970/1979; 1971/1979), the fact that they come to therapy can be seen as motivation enough for treatment to proceed, if the therapist can tolerate the ambiguity, vagueness, and lack of order. It is a distinct possibility that this "unmotivated" psychotic is not terribly different under the skin from the "motivated" patient who comes with a million irrational contracts covered over by a beautifully articulated rational contract. The psychotic may be just clearer about the motivation issue!

We are not advocating discontinuing the use of rational contracts. Nor are we saying there should never be exploration of why a patient veers from the contract, though we do think that much of that exploration could be unconsciously designed by the therapist merely to bring the patient in line or to gain control over the patient in a "benevolent" way. We are suggesting that when a therapist starts with the assumption that a patient's motives are or should be "pure," it is not simply a reflection of the therapist's naivete or trusting nature. Rather, it would seem to be some manifestation of the therapist's need to help at all costs (Searles, 1967/1979); in short, the general irrational contract that "If a patient comes to see me, that patient will let me help." Or, put another way, "If a patient comes to see me, he or she will help me out, be a mother-therapist to me by meeting my need to be helpful."

This brings us to another misconception—that *the needs of the therapist, such as those for personal satisfaction, prestige, and companionship in the relationship with the patient, can be eliminated through the contracting process.* As indicated in previous chapters, therapists have been trying to fool themselves for years in regard to lacking needs. Here we are concerned with the recognition of the effect of those existing needs on the contract. The danger is not so much that the therapist has needs. It is if the therapist does not sufficiently recognize certain needs, needs that may impinge on the patient, burdening the patient to meet them through the therapist's irrational contract which the therapist does not know about, but the patient senses. In that respect, the irrational contract is reminiscent of Winnicott's (1947) description of the parents who cannot accept those self-images reflecting negative attitudes toward their child. The parents try to alter the situation by implicitly or explicitly demanding that the child facilitate a loving parental image instead, but not without cost to the child. The child gets the message that if the child were to be better, then the parents could be better parents, seeing themselves as better people. Or as Saretsky (1980) suggests, "Just as in the case of the pathological mother-child situation, the [therapist's] activity often succeeds in interrupting the patient's presentation of self so as to quiet the [therapist's] own internal objects" (p. 86).

An important misconception (held by therapists and patients alike) about the therapist is that, *as an "expert" the therapist is "a purveyor of exact information"* (Sullivan, 1954, p. 12). While it is understandable that this attitude about the therapist is a generalization applied to all so-called experts in our society, it becomes a significant problem if the therapist needs to believe it: if the therapist needs to assert authority, needs to force-fit clinical data into existing theory, needs to impress upon the patient the true-truth. The irrational contract would then be developed on the assumption that the therapist had all the answers, knew the true-truth, and that indeed there existed absolute answers. In that event, the patient had better listen or at least act in a fashion allowing the therapist to impart wisdom.

While human behavior shows certain phenomena and patterns, and concepts have been identified and developed to explain the phenomena and patterns, in some ways the study of people remains an inexact science. In our estimation that's not so bad. The study of human beings is inexact because there exist multiple variables in infinite variation expressed on many levels. In one sense, the therapist can be a true scientist: when "answers" are found that explain experience the door can remain open to elaboration and revision of the explanations with further receipt and search for data. Not only does such an approach pave the way for therapist and patient to further understand experiences in living, it aids in the constant growth of theory derived from clinical practice.

Just as it is important to have theory-based clinical practice as opposed to a do-your-own-thing practice attitude, it is important for the therapist to remain open enough to allow that theory will be revised under the influence of the living situation. Furthermore, at the very least, such an attitude communicates to patients that indeed, when they can be unafraid or undefended against doing and knowing and feeling, they can be "experts" on their own lives, certainly better able to live and to cope with the problems in living.

Many therapists, including psychoanalytic therapists, pay lipservice to taking note of and working on their countertransference reactions. Although we will discuss countertransference at length in Chapter VIII, here we want to point up a major misconception based on what too often seems a fear of really understanding what countertransference and transference are all about. This highly unconscious misconception seems to be that *parataxic distortion can be ignored without consequence to the therapist-patient relationship in general and to a rational contract in particular*. To put it nicely, "horsefeathers!" Every relationship and therapy process is affected by it, even if the type of therapy does not focus on understanding the distortions.

Sullivan (1954) puts it well when he says, "Parataxic distortion is one way the personality displays before another some of its gravest problems. In other words, parataxic distortion may actually be an obscure attempt to communicate something that really needs to be grasped by the therapist and perhaps finally grasped by the patient. Needless to say, if such distortions go unnoted, if they are not expected, if the possibility of their existence is ignored, some of the most important things about the psychiatric interview may go by default" (p. 27). Although Sullivan seems to be talking about the patient's parataxic distortion, what he says applies as well to the therapist. In short, we are affected by what the patient brings to the therapeutic situation and by what we bring. It may be entirely possible for the therapist not to notice those influences, but it is absurd to think the process remains untouched, unaffected.

That distortion occurs then, is only natural on both sides. It tells us something about the interaction, about what makes each person tick, about areas of response and living that are peaceful and troublesome. Consequently it is not that parataxis occurs which is the issue. It is whether the therapist recognizes it, how he or she uses it or doesn't use it, that is of primary importance. The hope is, in psychoanalytic psychotherapy in any event, that the distortion will be harnessed in a way to promote understanding of patterns of experience and to facilitate the growth of the therapist-patient relationship as an emotional model for other relationships.

Just as parataxis goes on, so too will irrational contracts, for this kind of distortion of experience is central to the needs expressed through irrational contracts. The distortions may be a projection of dimensions of the self or of parents. The occurrence of distortion is as great, if not always of the same quality, in therapists as in patients. And why would it be different?

Transference and countertransference phenomena are "set to go" even prior to the first visit to the therapist (Adatto, 1977). Adatto calls them "preformed transference expectations . . . more often out of awareness [that] surfaces throughout [therapy], beginning with the initial interview" (p. 12). Therapists have a professional obligation to remember that, when they establish a rational contract, and when they and the patients hit snags in fulfilling the contract. It is safe to say that these preformed transference expectations, these distortions of present experience in light of past experience, this interpersonal expression of intrapsychic experience being relived and expressed interpersonally as it was in the past, is the substance of therapy, but it is also the fuel for irrational contracts. Unless irrational contracts are acknowledged and examined by the therapist on his or her own, and by the patient in the treatment situation, we have little hope that either therapist or patient will be able to come to terms with the image of a relationship as each wants or needs it. Unless this can happen, one is ruled by one's parataxic distortions, by one's original symbiotic bond. True individuation and emotional separation become impossible.

Sullivan's work with schizophrenics and Searles' work with and writings about the quality of the therapist-patient bond in the therapy of schizophrenics has forced the field to go beyond old definitions of such concepts as therapeutic alliance and working alliance, with their narrow range of application. We see that as good and have been influenced by this kind of flexibility and receptivity to experiencing and rethinking clinical experience. When existing concepts do not jibe with clinical observation, the object is to study the situation in a way as to make sense out of what is going on, to try to conceptualize in order to help.

Anna Freud (1976), in discussing changes in psychoanalytic practice and experience, writes of how the widening scope of psychoanalysis in treating many conditions for which the original techniques were designed (and certain concepts formulated) caused a terrible strain. Therapists had to confront "significant changes in the therapeutic atmosphere governing the analyst-patient relationship and, thus, unfamiliar problems for which they had not bargained" (p. 258).

In treating patients there are always problems for which therapists do not bargain in the rational contract, so they manifest themselves through the terms of irrational contracts. Just as clinicians such as Sullivan and Searles have abandoned that classical theory and technique which was not useful and have instead formulated new conceptions and techniques, so too let us not hold on to new conceptions such as the (rational) contract as today's therapeutic model, a shibolleth not to be revised or discarded or reconsidered in light of other formulations such as the irrational contract. Conceptions must fit clinical data or they haven't much meaning for our clinical work.

With a backdrop of the irrational dimensions involved in contracts addressed in this chapter, it seems appropriate to move on to discuss the therapist's motive in termination. In the next chapter we explore the therapist's attraction to certain kinds of termination and fears about other kinds. We consider the therapist's attraction to and motive for short-term therapies as a prototype for understanding what happens in premature and acting-out terminations—that is, premature and acting-out on the part of the therapist, not necessarily the patient. We address what the therapist fears about the possibility of there being no termination of the therapist-patient relationship in the therapy process, of the threat and effect of there being a relationship with no boundaries in time. Certainly the therapist's narcissism is still at work, and now that we have seen how it manifests itself through the irrational contract, let us proceed to see how it works its way into termination.

REFERENCES

Adatto, C. P. Transference phenomena in initial interviews. *International Journal of Psychoanalytic Psychotherapy* (1977) **6**:3–13.

Arlow, J. A. Discussion of the paper by Mark Kanzer, 'The therapeutic and working alliances.' *International Journal of Psychoanalytic Psychotherapy* (1975) **4**:69–73.

Balint, M. *The basic fault* (London: Tavistock Publications, 1968).

Bion, W. R. *Elements of psycho-analysis* (New York: Basic Books, 1963).

Blanck, C., and Blanck, R. *Ego psychology: Theory and practice* (New York: Columbia University Press, 1974).

Breuer, J. and Freud, S. Studies on hysteria. In *The complete works of Sigmund Freud*, Vol. 2 (London: Hogarth Press, 1964) (Originally published 1893–95).

Dickes, R. Technical considerations of the therapeutic and working alliances. *International Journal of Psychoanalytic Psychotherapy* (1975) **4**:1–25.

Enright, J. One step forward: Situational techniques for altering motivation for therapy. *Psychotherapy: Theory, Research and Practice* (1975) **12**:344–347.

Freud, A. Changes in psychoanalytic practice and experiences. *International Journal of PsychoAnalysis* (1976) **57**:257–260.

Freud, A. *Normality and pathology in childhood* (New York: International Universities Press, 1965).

Freud, S. Analysis terminable and interminable. In *The comptete psychological works of Sigmund Freud*, Vol. 23 (London: Hogarth Press, 1964) (Originally published, 1937).

Freud, S. Introductory lectures on psychoanalysis. In *The complete psychological works of Sigmund Freud*, Vol. 16 (London: Hogarth Press, 1964) (Originally published, 1916–17).

Freud, S. An outline of psychoanalysis. In *The complete works of Sigmund Freud*, Vol. 23 (London: Hogarth Press, 1964) (Originally published, 1940).

Greenson, R. R. The working alliance and the transference neurosis. *International Journal of Psycho-Analysis* (1965) **34**:155–181.

Greenson, R. R. and Wexler, M. The non-transference relationship in the psychoanalytic situation. *International Journal of Psycho-Analysis* (1969) **50**:27–39.

Hare-Mustin, R. T., Marecek, J., Kaplan, A. G., and Liss-Levinson, N. Rights of clients, responsibilities of therapists. *American Psychologist* (1979) **34**:3–16.

Montgomery, A. G., and Montgomery, D. J. Contractual psychotherapy: Guidelines and strategies for change. *Psychotherapy: Theory, research and practice* (1975) **12**:348–352.

Morrison, J. K. *A consumer approach to community psychology* (Chicago: Nelson-Hall, 1979 (a)).

Morrison, J. K. A consumer-oriented approach to psychotherapy. *Psychotherapy: Theory, research and practice* (1979) **10**:381–384 (b).

Rosenfeld, H. Object relations of the acute schizophrenic patient in the transference situation. In P. Solomon and B. C. Glueck (Eds.), *Recent research on schizophrenia* (Washington, D.C.: American Psychiatric Association, 1964).

Searles, H. F. Autism and the phase of transition to therapeutic symbiosis. In H. F. Searles, (Ed.), *Countertransference and related subjects* (New York: International Universities Press, 1979) (Originally published, 1970).

Searles, H. F. Concerning therapeutic symbiosis: The patient as symbiotic therapist, the phase of ambivalent symbiosis, and the role of jealousy in the fragmented ego. In H. F. Searles (Ed.), *Countertransference and related subjects* (New York: International Universities Press, 1979) (Originally published, 1973).

Searles, H. F. Pathologic symbiosis and autism. In H. F. Searles (Ed.), *Countertransference and related subjects* (New York: International Universities Press, 1979) (Originally published, 1971).

Searles, H. F. Transference psychosis in the psychotherapy of chronic schizophrenia. In H. F. Searles (Ed.), *Collected papers on schizophrenia and related subjects* (New York: International Universities Press, 1965) (Originally published, 1963).

Sterba, R. F. The formative activity of the analyst. In P. L. Giovacchini (Ed.), *Tactics and techniques in psychoanalytic therapy, volume II: Countertransference* (New York: Jason Aronson, Inc., 1975).

Strupp, H. H. On failing one's patient. *Psychotherapy: Theory, research and practice* (1975) **12:**39–41.

Sullivan, H. S. *The psychiatric interview* (New York: W. W. Norton, 1954).

Winnicott, D. W. Hate in the countertransference. *International Journal of Psycho-Analysis* (1947) **30:**102–110.

Winnicott, D. W. Psychiatric disorder in terms of infantile maturational processes. In D. W. Winnicott (Ed.), *The maturational processes and the facilitating environment* (New York: International Universities Press, 1974) (Originally published, 1963).

Winnicott D. W. The theory of the parent-infant relationship. In D. W. Winnicott (Ed.), *The maturational processes and the facilitating environment* (New York: International Universities Press, 1974) (Originally published, 1960).

Wolberg, L. R. *The technique of psychotherapy*, 3rd ed. (New York: Grune & Stratton, 1977).

Zetzel, E. R. The analytic situation. In R. E. Litman (Ed.), *Psychoanalysis in the Americas* (New York: International Universities Press, 1966).

Zetzel, E. R. Current concepts of transference. *International Journal of Psycho-Analysis* (1956) **37:**369–376.

VII

At Issue: Termination—The Therapist's Motive

INTRODUCTION

When contemplating the broad field of the psychotherapies it often seems that little can be agreed upon other than some apparently obvious features. One of these is that psychotherapy has a beginning, a middle, and an end. Thus, in his comprehensive textbook on the techniques of psychotherapy, Wolberg (1977) presents an eclectic outline of psychotherapy which includes a beginning, two middle phases, and an end phase. While there are numerous arguments regarding both the length and the activities of such a sequence, the field tends to agree on the necessity of some sequence. In essence the prevalent view is that once there has been a beginning to therapy, there must be an ending, sooner or later.

In this chapter our interest is in the end of therapy, which involves the process of termination. We are particularly concerned with the therapist's motivations in the termination process. In our explorations we will attempt to show that perhaps a different view of termination than is customary can be the most fruitful for the therapist's endeavors. The "difference" lies in considering the possibility of therapy as an unending process. In essence, then, our premise is that once there has been a beginning, there may never be an ending. The concept of ending of course here refers to a choice by either or both parties to terminate the therapy.

The mental health field is probably the most given to internal polemics of all the professions; or, perhaps it is simply the one we know best. But it often seems that theoretical and clinical differences blossom into disputes with a ferocity that makes neurotic integration in everyday relationships look like a parlor game. So when we chose to write about termination we realized there was a high potential for vigorous misunderstandings with a lot of therapists whose views differ from each other and may differ from ours. With that in mind we want it to be clear that we are discussing possibilities. At least to us they have a sensible appeal, but they are certainly open to debate and to change. In presenting our formulations concerning certain central unconscious dimensions of the therapist's termination motives we suspect that our views may not be the same as many of our colleagues. But, we believe our ideas can shed some needed light on what appears to be an issue many therapists refrain from exploring in depth. Our impression is that there has been a relative neglect of the therapist's motivations for termination, and such a neglect can be harmful to all concerned.

Earlier we made clear our bias in favor of long-term psychoanalytic psychotherapy. We did this with the awareness that there is considerable current emphasis in psychotherapy on short-term treatment, which incorporates a designed, timed termination. Butcher and Koss (1978) categorize short-term psychotherapies into psychodynamic, behavioral, and crisis intervention therapy. Their common characteristics include temporal limitations and limited goals, as well as the importance of the patient-therapist relationship. They appear to be as effective as more lengthy therapies in achieving the stipulated goals, which tend to be symptom relief, restoration of previous functioning, and the preventive measure of the achievement of some insight. We accept the fact that time-limited therapy is a viable treatment option. It also has the appeal of efficiency. We just do not prefer it, and therefore leave most of this type of intervention to others who do like it. However, our option is not merely a matter of doing what we like and so refusing to recognize what may be better for most clients. Short-term therapy techniques are not acceptable to all patients, nor can all benefit from them, with the possibility of deterioration existing here as well. Furthermore, Butcher and Koss state: "The effectiveness of time limitation over unlimited therapy for bringing about change has not been clearly shown in research" (p. 759). In addition, our focus is on the therapist's motivations for termination, and we believe our concerns have less to do with the length of therapy per se and more to do with the depth of the relationship as a possible reflection of a therapist's defensive motive in terminating therapy of any duration. In other words, the termination motives we are discussing might conceivably be a factor in short or long-term therapy, whether it is psychoanalytic, behavioral, or some other type.

On another level, however, a therapist's sustained, consistent motives may certainly determine the type and length of the psychotherapy the therapist chooses to practice. Such a determination is not a negative in itself, but it can become one when the motive is hidden from the therapist's awareness by converting it into an institutionalized *therapeutic* concept which the therapist holds as appropriate for working with all clients. Thus, we are not "against" short-term therapy, or termination either, but we do want to suggest some other possibilities in regard to how the therapist conceives of the termination process. In order to do that we will look at customary indices of termination for psychotherapy which is not of predetermined duration, but which is considered in advance to have a point of termination.

CUSTOMARY TERMINATION CRITERIA

We have learned that it is quite difficult to formulate a list of criteria for termination from consensus by therapists of diverse orientation and experience in treatment situations with shifting psychological, sociological, and economic currents. There is a range of criteria and a host of techniques. For example, Glazer (1978) discusses the problems of terminations that are premature and so not helpful to the patient. Initiated by the patient, they are based on the patient's distortions of the therapeutic relationship so that it is experienced as a masochistic experience from which the patient must extricate himself or herself in order to gain self-esteem.

Wolberg (1977) suggests five conditions under which termination of therapy is indicated. They refer to termination with the therapist of the moment, and include achievement of planned therapeutic goals, ending with some incomplete goals, the reaching of an impasse, uncontrollable countertransference, and reality interventions, as the patient moving to another location. While believing in the necessity of discontinuing therapy at some point, Wolberg does state: "Theoretically, psychotherapy is never ending since emotional growth can go on as long as one lives" (p. 743).

Maholick and Turner (1979) proceed from the philosophical position that life is a series of hellos and goodbyes. Thus, they view the termination of psychotherapy as a recapitulation of the many preceding farewells of living, and as a preparation for being able to deal better with future partings. The necessity of termination appears inherent to their presentation. They focus on termination in group therapy, and assert that the following are times for appropriate termination. First, when the therapy ends according to a contractual termination point. Then, when the patient has gone as far as he or she wishes in gaining awareness and changing patterns of behavior. Other possibilities include developments such as a shift in the patient's working hours or financial reversals. Another time would be when presenting problems have been clarified with some resolution so that former debilitating patterns are unlikely to return. Also, if the person is too destructive to the group, or the group is harmful to the welfare of the patient, then the therapist should instigate termination. Further possibilities include severe regression by the patient so that hospitalization is required, or when the patient consistently refuses to deal with therapy issues, or when the patient and/or the therapist experience no progress in therapy.

Despite these, and other attempts at formulating termination criteria, it would seem that nobody knows for sure what would be the best rationale for termination (Firestein, 1978). What is known is that therapists, however diligent their efforts and good their intentions, remain responsive to their unconscious motivation, both for better and for worse. So, in an effort to understand the therapist's motivations for termination of psychotherapy our aim is to go beyond the apparently rational motivations by exploring levels of unconscious motivation that may influence rational decision-making.

THERAPY OF UNLIMITED DURATION

In reviewing the literature on termination in psychotherapy two recurring themes or attitudes are clear. One is that most therapists see the process of therapy as having a structure of beginning, middle, and end. The other is that psychotherapy without an end (or an end in mind on the part of the therapist) is not considered therapeutic. Indeed, an endless duration of treatment has a bad name. Often it is seen to reflect poorly on the therapist who may "need" the patient or may need to replace significant others in the patient's life (Goldberg, 1975); or need success or perfect results (Firestein, 1978). Too, it is thought to be a measure of the patient's hopeless "dependency" on the therapist (Gourevitch, 1980); or of the patient's need to replace the function of significant others in life with the therapist and "living," with the therapy process (Goldberg, 1975). Rarely is interminable therapy even hinted at in a positive light (Guntrip, 1975), the very term "interminable" having negative connotation. To some, there is a magic number of years for therapy, unless one wants a patient who will be estranged from reality. For still others, such as Klauber (1977), the issue is approached sideways by referring to "slow analysis" rather than "interminable," in what we read as an effort to avoid a negative connotation yet still not coming to grips with therapy of unlimited duration.

Therapy of unlimited duration is to be distinguished from a therapy where lack of termination stems from a defensive need to never terminate, to have a secure future, to always identify oneself as a "therapist" the way some authors (Goldberg, 1975) write of patients who feel alive only as patients. It is instead, therapy where the concept of termination is seen in all its abstract possibilities, including the possibility of its own demise.

In considering a concept of therapy of unlimited duration, termination is not to be confused with separation, for separation occurs throughout the therapeutic process with a strange combination of increasing complexity and simplicity. Termination, on the other hand, although it represents physical separation, does not necessarily mean there is emotional separation. How many persons have physically left patients with whom they are inextricably bound up and from whom they are not emotionally separated? And paradoxically, how many patients or therapists have physically terminated therapy in order to "not leave" the therapist or patient with whom they could not work through and go beyond their relationship (transferential or otherwise) problem? How many have held on to the image of the therapist or the patient, and so to their bond, by terminating?

It is possible that continuing the relationship would provide a chance for the image to shift, the bond to change, for emotional separation to occur, and for the person to move on to another level of relatedness. Which is of course where the problem may well lie for many therapists, personally, in their therapy roles, and in identifying with their patients. Our aim is to consider why, though with the concept of therapy of unlimited duration we do not have a substantive body of research to aid us. This is not exactly surprising since most therapies and therapists consider the therapies to have a limit, even though the duration of many therapies is both vague and not planned in advance. Nonetheless, in general therapies are conceived as either long or short-term, meaning they are not designed or conceptualized as unlimited. Thus, we have had to rely on repeated observations over time, combined with applications of theory, to offer some conjecture as to why many therapists think rather automatically of the fact of termination, and in turn, can limit their conception of psychotherapy itself.

We are not out of touch with the desire of some patients (and therapists) to know when the therapy will end, nor do we recommend the actuality of unlimited therapy for all patients. We are recommending, however, that most therapists consider such a possibility as useful for at least some of their clients, and not just borderline or psychotic patients at that. While we do not doubt that flaws can be found in a concept of unlimited therapy, we believe they pale with the awareness of the alacrity of some therapists to terminate therapy. For example, it appears to us that certain psychoanalytically oriented therapists, in the supposed service of maintaining therapeutic distance and structure, will refuse to allow emotional closeness to develop to infinity and be content without further analysis of their motivation. This is even more of a problem with therapists whose orientation does not generally support careful analysis of their motives.

Although questions arise as to how to terminate in a way that facilitates ongoing achievement (Weigert, 1 952), to conserve rather than abandon the internalized therapist, the internalized relationship, it is without precedent and with much apology for therapists to talk, let alone write, about the possibility of never physically terminating. For many, even entertaining the theoretical possibility in order to expand their theoretical horizons seems a forbidden exercise. Obviously, therapists' attitudes influence termination (Rosensweig and Folman, 1974): when, how, and if. In addition, the "need" for termination can be seen as a time related behavior reflecting cultural and social values as well as personality processes (Getsinger, 1975). Nevertheless, grappling with the issue of termination is seen by some clinicians as a pseudodilemma in psychotherapy (Goldberg, 1975). By that, they usually mean termination is part of any treatment the same way it is part of life. As in life, it begins from the beginning and is in concrete terms, the ultimate goal. In therapy, it is too often seen as synonymous with the process of separation-individuation, and thus it is an expected feature of development.

Termination, says Goldberg (1975), is the goal of treatment to the extent that the therapist must realize that unless collusion with the patient "in guarantying him a future as a patient" (p. 342) is avoided, therapy will never begin. This advice says something about a popular attitude on termination and the underlying concept one holds of a "patient." If a patient is seen in a stereotypic sense as helpless, dependent, subordinate, weak, without emotional, intellectual and interpersonal competencies and resources and potential, *then* maybe it would be possible to think it would indeed be terrible to guarantee a patient a future as a patient. If, however, one does not hold a rather negative view of a patient; and does not agree that a patient role is forever synonymous with the sick role; and does not see the therapist as the omnipotent, omniscient parent and the patient as the inadequate child; and does see the possibility of both patient and therapist developing into experts in assisting the patient with problems in living, *then* it would seem possible to consider that being a patient forever is perhaps not a curse but an opportunity.

THE HERITAGE OF TERMINATION IDEAS

Lest it be concluded that therapy of unlimited duration has only recently come under fire we point out that as far back as Ferenczi and Freud (1937/1964) there was concern about the duration of treatment. Although today some therapists set time limits as an incentive (Hare-Mustin, Marecek, Kaplan, and Liss-Levenson, 1979) Freud initiated the practice (Freud, 1937/1964). He thought perhaps it would hasten progress but he recognized such a move was effective only if there was a fortuitous match between the time set and the time needed.

Freud was impressed with a 1927 Ferenczi paper assuring that analysis was not an endless process to the point that in writing about termination (Freud, 1937/1964) Freud refers to the paper, seeming to assure himself that analysis does indeed end. On the other hand, Freud realized that although termination time was something clinicians had to consider, if only for practical reasons, he also recognized the existence of factors making the duration of analysis interminable. But this was seen as a problem, reflecting limitations of personality and of psychoanalysis. From our reading of him, in today's framework we would take this to refer to therapy with schizophrenics, borderlines, and maybe severe obsessionals; in general, patients unable to come to terms with object loss.

Sullivan's (1954) attitude seemed to be that psychoanalytic work had to be tightened up. He had little patience for free association, thinking it only made getting to know the patient more difficult and protracted the duration of treatment. His concern was to improve the "utilization of the psychotherapeutic minute" (p. 80), maintaining that if the therapist is diligently task-oriented in focusing the patient on the "defined, recurrent difficulty" (p. 80) in significant relationships the patient will ultimately (sooner rather than later) collaborate with the therapist, now respected for his or her expertise. Unless the patient and therapist were so engaged, Sullivan's opinion was that therapy would "very likely be measured in terms of decades" (p. 80), something he seemed to regard with derision.

Interestingly, though Freud and Sullivan do not ostensibly agree on much, they were singularly alike in some respects. Each seemed to see the therapist-patient relationship in a rather rigid set of roles. That is, the patient has an illness and the therapist has the expertise to cure the illness, clean and simple. As to the relationship, it is true that Freud considered the transferential effect of the patient on the therapist and vice versa, and that Sullivan, as his participant observer function implies, saw the therapist not simply as a distant, detached observer but as an active participant and the patient as a collaborator. However, it would seem to us that both men had an overestimated view of the therapist as "expert" and were a bit grandiose about the impact of this expert on the patient and his or her problems. Granted, the therapist has expertise, but there are patient-variables governing receptivity to be considered (Strupp, 1980) when talking about therapist skill influencing the patient or therapy outcome.

Though neither Freud nor Sullivan say so explicitly, it appears that each holds that termination occurs when the therapist's influence on the patient (Freud through the transference and Sullivan, through single-minded focusing on the task at hand) can go no further or is no longer needed. To our mind, this view underestimates the role of the patient in setting and changing the focus and process of the therapy while it places the therapist in an inherent position of power because he or she holds certain special developmental and psychological-psychiatric knowledge. In other words, there seems to be a metacommunication implying superiority over patients in their writings. And this message goes beyond the reasonable expectation that of course the therapist is an expert with knowledge of the field.

Although certainly the writings of both Freud and Sullivan attest to a kind of collaboration in the treatment each seems to imply the following:

1. The therapist knows best what "the problem" is
2. Whether free-association or problem-focused methods are used the therapist, rather than the patient, knows best when the patient has reached his or her psychological and emotional potential or limit
3. There is an implicit reluctance by the therapist to allow for mutuality in the relationship
4. When all is said and done, the therapist is indeed in charge.

We think their writings do not credit the patient with sufficient innate knowledge of the self. Our tendency is to have a more optimistic view of people, figuring they have the intellectual and emotional knowledge though it may be buried and defended against in a variety of ways which early in life served a necessary function for their security and survival. And our task is not to forget that the knowledge is there.

The writings of Freud and Sullivan do not take into consideration that the patient may emotionally separate from the therapist yet remain in treatment. Moreover, once separation is possible, the patient may go beyond the therapist in development of emotional capacity, something we think has implications for the conservative notions about termination we see in our colleagues today. The patient's ultimate ability to move beyond the therapist has its correlate in the child's ability to move away from the parent(s), then to develop on his or her route and in his or her way and depth from that point on. Just as in childhood the child's ability to break away and move on is initially dependent on the mother's ability to allow and encourage the separation as well as to support the blossoming growth, the therapist must be able to facilitate the movement away and tolerate the separation. A therapist in "emotional bondage" with his or her own parent cannot allow the patient's movement away, for there will be no parent-child representative relationship. There will no longer be the opportunity to give what the therapist's parent could not give nor will there be a chance to repeatedly, compulsively, identify with the patient-child who receives the goods for which the therapist still yearns.

The idea that termination "arrives" once there is sufficient healthy internal, emotional separation is not an unpopular notion. However, it strikes us as unsophisticated and unnecessary. Actually, such reasoning often indicates a therapist's defense against dealing with the patient on another level of relatedness, beyond the traditional "helper" role. We think such a prospect frightens therapists. If their investment is in helping (in the neurotic sense), after separation they would feel forced to say goodbye rather than deal with unchartered, undefined, flexible roles where sometimes they would be the traditional helper, sometimes the so-called parent learning from a suddenly grownup child; sometimes one of two siblings having a good time or on a voyage of discovery or despair. In essence, there would be a less constant distinction between therapist and patient, between parent and child. The therapist locked into bringing a parent around however, needs the distinction, for without it how would it be known who should serve whom?

THE THERAPIST'S RETREAT

In times when uncertain economics and the need for instant gratification govern so much of what people do, including the choice of which therapy to practice and which therapy to be involved in as a patient, particular attention must be paid to the irrational reason for the choice. For example, is the current vogue for brevity in treatment a function of economics, of therapist rational need, of patient rational need? Or, is emphasis on brevity also representative of some kind of interpersonal retreat? Kubie (1971) says it is, that such therapist emphasis impedes both clinical and human maturation in the therapist. To that we would add that of course, such an impediment would naturally affect the patient's maturation, since full development of the patient's emotional potential takes place within a relationship requiring the collaborative effort of the participants.

It is symptomatic of a kind of interpersonal-emotional retreat that therapists find so alarming the idea of therapy of unlimited duration. Those who see patients for years and years are sometimes looked upon as strange, greedy, pathology-reinforcing, needy, maybe even slow to catch on, by those who consider long-term therapy to be a year or two. We see the situation differently. Not to consider that the possibility of unlimited therapy duration reflects a possible problem in the therapist's ability to become intimately emotionally involved with the patient (which, while it can happen immediately, is more likely to develop over time), is a mistake.

It seems likely that a major source of the therapist's reluctance to become deeply involved is, on a presenting level, part of the obsessional defense. There are two specific narcissistic features in therapists we will discuss, which, on close scrutiny, could make for problems in their full ability to be "used" by patients and in their ability to consider therapy of unlimited duration.

The first, the *lack of capacity* for pleasure, sounds contrary to the usual notion of narcissism. Certainly in the layman's mind, narcissism is equated with a kind of self-centered hedonism, summoning up fantasies of self-indulgence. But as discussed in Chapter V, the obsessionally defended therapist cannot let go that much, at least not without paying a price, before, during, or after what would be considered the "emotional spree." And at some level, seeing patients for endless time might well be considered self-indulgent. Such a therapist would feel compelled to consider whether the decision was right, just, and logical; he or she builds a case to justify the pleasure. While building a case would legitimize the pleasure, the hard work diminishes and detracts from it, making it almost contrived and "self-conscious." It is as if the therapist says to the parent-patient, "Give me what I want, but don't notice that I asked."

A therapist who avoided getting herself into such a situation was telling her supervisor that she had discharged a patient she had seen for about a year. True, this difficult-to-reach patient had improved in certain respects, but the supervisor was skeptical of the therapist's motive, especially since he hadn't been consulted. When pressed to reveal what his enigmatic grin meant, the supervisor said his fantasy was that the therapist terminated because now that there was more communication between therapist and patient, the therapist was afraid she might enjoy herself too much.

Allied with the lack of capacity for pleasure is the therapist's *fear of commitment*, a second narcissistic feature interfering with the ability to consider therapy of unlimited duration. The fear of commitment is actually a fear of emotional commitment. This means that with unlimited time the problem is likely to come into clearer focus because lack of time boundaries brings with it the threat of a relationship with no boundaries and its unconscious correlate, an ego with no boundaries. Such a state is terrifying for the therapist in that it is a threat to the obsessional defense against having early in life responded to the excessive parental emotional demands, before being emotionally equipped to handle them. At that time, there was no choice, so the demands were met at the expense of the child's own needs. As a result, commitment becomes synonymous with dependency; not the dependency of being held, cared for, and in general having one's needs met, but the dependency of having no choice, no alternative to being at the mercy of another. It is little wonder that many therapists resist long-standing commitment, commitment that is so likely to touch off the dynamics of their original symbiotic bond.

One dimension of the therapist's dynamics may be seen ironically to reflect a problem in what Winnicott (1963/1974a), in talking about child development, has called, "the development of the capacity for concern." He writes, "In favorable circumstances, the mother by continuing to be alive and available is both the mother who receives all the fullness of the baby's id-drives, and also the mother who can be loved as a person and to whom reparation can be made" (p. 82). It is in such a context that a capacity for concern develops in the child.

If a therapist as a child (as described in Chapter V) had been in the service of the parent, how well would such a therapist be prepared for experiencing true concern? Moreover, if the therapist has identified with an "un-alive," "unavailable," mother who could not tolerate or bend to receive her child's id-drives in all their intensity, or could not be loved, or to whom reparation could not be made, how could it be possible for the therapist from such a union to provide an emotional-interpersonal context for the patient's full expression and development? In addition, if it so happens that reparation had been an abiding requirement of the child, as it would with a parent who needs a child in service, there would be a strong inclination to maintain a "professional" relationship with the parent and to feel extraordinary guilt if one showed one's needs for either nurturance or independence instead of taking care of the parent as the good professional should.

What this adds up to is that because of the quality of their original symbiotic bonds, many therapists stay away from or barely allow the emergence of the patient's full pathology or full healthy capacities. They prematurely terminate therapy; they rigidly set termination dates; they hold rigid concepts of how therapy progresses, they discontinue treatment when the patient's motivation seems vague or the eventual goal seems nearly unattainable or too difficult for the patient to reach. Here a lesson could be learned from Winnicott's (1960/1974) patient who said to him, "The only time I felt hope was when you told me that you could see no hope, and you continued with the analysis" (p. 152).

So it happens that because of the therapist's particular brand of narcissism, it is often not possible for him or her to afford certain necessary "provisions," a term and concept suggested by Winnicott (1963/1974b) in an address to the Association of Social Workers in London. Could such a therapist, one who had been in the service of the parent, "accept being in the position of a subjective object in the client's life, [and] at the same time . . . keep both feet on the ground" (p. 229)? Would he or she instead struggle to gain control by straightening out distortions or by interpreting the transference responses so they will stop developing? Would the relationship suffer, as noted in a critique done by Kernberg (1969) regarding Kleinian technique? He says, "The lack of deepening of the analytic relationship as a consequence of interpreting the same constellation of primitive conflicts again and again, from the beginning of the analysis on, has been pointed out as a consequence of premature transference interpretations . . ." (p. 324).

Work with schizophrenic patients provides a good example in caricature about involvement, one which can be generalized in less exaggerated fashion to therapeutic work with all patients. In working with schizophrenic patients, at times it becomes terribly uncomfortable for the therapist to withstand being the patient's subjective object. It is indeed unpleasant in pathologic symbiosis (Searles, 1971/1979) to "become" the dimension of the patient which he or she cannot withstand and so projects it on to the therapist. On the other hand, to feel impotent in making an impact, as in the autistic phase as part of the symbiosis described by Searles (1970/1979), to our mind, fills a therapist both with conscious and unconscious memory of the failure to make an impact on the parent(s) and anxiety at being unable to fulfill the injunction to serve. Thus, it is easier said than done to accept being a subjective object, to be "taken over" by the patient-parent. It is little wonder, therefore, that therapists notoriously don't want to deal with schizophrenic patients, or want to circumvent the pathology in treating them, surely a contradiction in terms.

It is our contention that the therapist-dynamics that make for reluctance in treating schizophrenic persons also can govern the irrational motivation for reluctance to consider that therapy may be unending. Though the involvement may not be characterized by psychotic transferences, over potential decades, the nature of the involvement certainly is not predictable. Time often paves the way for countless possibilities, direction and untold depth. These features are not apt to make for therapist-comfort in sustaining endless contact with patients.

This brings us to another of Winnicott's (1963/1974b) injunctions: "You are not frightened, nor do you become overcome with guilt-feelings when your client goes mad, disintegrates, runs out in the street in a nightdress, attempts suicide and perhaps succeeds" (p. 229). Well, theoretically anyway. In any event, while this therapist attitude is an aim, it is also an ideal. The message seems to be that the therapist must try not to be overwhelmed either by his or her zeal to help, or the anxiety when the help is thwarted and further, to feel neither anxious nor overwhelmed when the "help" brings forth behavior or events that the patient did not at first present.

Unpredictable behavior is disconcerting to many therapists, and the likelihood of its incidence would seem greater in the less structured psychoanalytic psychotherapy. Add to the modality the dimension of unlimited time, and the likelihood of occurrence, as acting out or as developmental progress increases. It does not seem far-fetched that the popularity (with therapists) of short-term structured therapy may well have its "emotional roots" in the therapist's personal need for a structured helping relationship that has little time to get out of hand.

Perhaps one appeal of short-term therapy is that it is a personification of a reaction-formation to wanting limitless power over the parent-patient. Short time, little power. On the other hand, because in short-term therapy the therapist is often very much in charge, the therapist can "reign," but it is legitimized by the structure and not so obvious as in the therapist who wants to serve or be served by the patient forever. Too, it seems that the therapist is very much the "expert," harking back to Freud and Sullivan. Moreover, the relative structure provided by many short-term treatment methods, even stress-producing methods (Sifneos, 1979), allows the therapist in a sense to touch but not to feel.

Although these features may attract therapists to short-term therapy, they also represent hazards in that therapy, representing risks to both patients and therapists. Small (1979), in reviewing literature on brief psychotherapy, noted that while intense transference feelings arise, they cannot be resolved. Furthermore, brief therapy tends toward an "oppressive, dehumanizing pace" (p. 284). Such a context would seem to foster making inadequate or poorly formulated interventions. It would seem to facilitate making a force-fit of clinical data with theory and accompanying intervention. A neat package, but one perhaps at the expense of the development of relatedness. Even use of early interpretation of intense transference responses, as suggested by Malan (1963) and Bellak and Small (1977), would seem more to inhibit or stop the process altogether rather than bring light to it, as we mentioned earlier in another context. Although that might be the object, the question is whether the therapist has irrational motives for containing the interaction. If so, these would be communicated to the patient at an unconscious level, not only affecting the genuineness of the therapist-patient bond, but influencing a patient's potential perception of the bounds of relatedness.

Another of the therapist's major problems underlying an inability to consider a concept of therapy of unlimited duration may well be the lack of the "capacity to be alone," to use Winnicott's (1958/1974) term. The heart of his concept lies in a person's ability to be alone in the presence of another, an experience rooted in the mother-child relationship where the mother is "reliably present" (p. 30) and the presence of each is important to the other. "Ego-relatedness" develops and, according to Winnicott, "may turn out to be the matrix of transference" (p. 33). He maintains that in a context of ego-relatedness id impulses can be used for ego strengthening. The infant can become unintegrated, can flounder, have no orientation, can just be there. In such a context the "infant can discover his own personal life" (p. 34).

In short, there exists a safe environment where someone nonintrusive is present. The parallel to the therapy situation seems obvious. The problem arises when, due to the therapist's original symbiotic bond, the therapist must intrude himself or herself on the patient. For example, if the therapist's reason for being is to "help" he or she might "require" the patient to talk, to produce, to move in this direction or that. Not only does such behavior impinge on the patient in his or her capacity to be alone in the presence of another in order to discover the "personal impulse" (Winnicott, 1958/1974, p. 34), it reflects the *therapist's* inability to be alone in the presence of another.

For such a therapist, to be alone with another becomes synonymous with intrusiveness. The intrusiveness in turn is a reflection of the therapist's experience with the parent who would not yield her needs for her child's, who would not bend with the rhythm of her child, who instead impinged her self system on the child. Now identified with such a parent the therapist in a sense "ego-impinges" on the patient, making it difficult for the patient to be emotionally separate, to ego-relate. Interestingly, it would follow that such a therapist would make his or her literal presence more necessary for the patient than less, resulting in continuance of the bond rather than dissolution. In other words, the paradox may just be that, from a developmental standpoint, the more active the therapist is (supposedly in the patient's best interest to hasten development and termination) the more difficult it is for the patient to tune in to impulses and allow an emerging self to develop. The therapist is in the way.

So conceivably, the more focused the therapist is in order to narrow down the problem and shorten therapy time, the more important the therapist becomes, fostering the need for literal presence while supposedly being interested in subsequent separation and termination. Certainly the transference of powerful intensity that Malan (1963) and Bellak and Small (1977) discuss can be attributed at least in part to this role-behavior of the brief therapist, making the capacity to be alone, as a developmental objective, a very difficult task for the patient.

For the therapist, brief or otherwise, the capacity to be alone can be impaired. On the face of it, seeing patients for endless years would seem to point to the problem. After all, the therapist obviously needs somebody there. However, what is not often thought about is that in the process of limited therapy time, the therapist "requires" someone there, there to be treated actively, there to be served or to serve, depending on how you look at it.

The paradox is that it is in therapy of limited duration, where the therapist has a timetable, the therapist's need of the patient is greater while his or her capacity to be alone is less. It would seem that in therapy of unlimited duration, the therapist is called on to provide an environment which is reliable so far as the therapist's emotional presence is concerned. But such therapy is unpredictable in its interpersonal-emotional events so far as the patient's behavior is concerned. Such an environment may even invite breakdown, but has the germ of healing (Winnicott, 1963/1974b)—if the therapist has the capacity to be alone, to leave the patient alone, for therapy, to add a bit to Winnicott (1963/1974b) is "a process of self-cure that needs your help" (p. 228) but not the imposition of narcissistic needs. Otherwise there will be no cure and no emotional separation, with or without termination.

THE USE OF THE THERAPIST FOR SEPARATION

The use of the therapist occurs through the reconstruction process in psychoanalytic psychotherapy. Burland (1975) suggests that separation-individuation is one developmental phenomenon that may be completed in the process. We were particularly interested in how Burland combined the work of Freud (1909/1957) and Mahler (1968) to present a cogent picture of how memory of affect is defended against and how the symbiotic experience comes to life, eventually with affect, through the therapy experience. While Burland's focus is on the patient in the therapy experience, we think the symbiotic experience comes to life for therapists as well as their patients. As the infant emerges from the symbiotic phase (Mahler, 1968) he or she is increasingly differentiating from the mother. The point is reached where the child consciously recognizes a separateness—a separateness in image later to progress to a separateness in thought and affect. However, at this early time, called the "rapprochement sub-phase" (Mahler, 1968), the child, in part, sees things uncomfortably, for the child is in conflict between longing for the security of symbiosis and the gratification of autonomy, thus the (Burland, 1975) "push-pull behavior which characterizes the mother-child interaction during this subphase" (p. 308). In addition, the mother image is split: the "bad mother" fosters separation; the "good mother," when turned to, supports the child. Burland (1975) puts it well when he says, "The compromise solution to the conflict involves the development of a new kind of a relationship with mother, one that is loving but predicated on a separateness and independence, and one in which therefore the good-mother-bad-mother split is healed" (p. 308).

Although many analytic therapists ordinarily understand the various needs for a patient's symbiotic attachment to them, too often they do not readily see levels or shifts in the symbiotic experience resulting in a dissolution of the more primitive symbiotic experience. For example, Searles (1976) suggests that when the patient and therapist progress to the phase of therapeutic symbiosis the patient's symptoms and transference images have become transitional objects for both patient and therapist. Through therapeutic symbiosis both patient and therapist emerge in a sense more fully individuated. This result, it would seem, rests on the ability of the therapist first to withstand the patient's affect, both as empathic receiver and as recollector of his or her own affect concerning dreadful experiences, maybe even "nonhuman experiences," as Searles would put it. As Weigert (1952) puts it, "The psychoanalyst needs a dynamic equilibrium which allows him to accompany the patient into the hell of anxieties, tensions and conflicts without undue reservations of self-protection, and to recover anew his inner balance each hour, each day" (p. 467). The therapist not only endures, but, it is hoped, as indicated by Searles (1976), that he or she can "learn to be at home with various inner emotional reactions to the patient" (p. 165).

Our experience has been that it is the "inner emotional reactions," therapist reactions to intense patient reactions, that many therapists assiduously avoid, perhaps with "therapeutic neutrality," otherwise called "emotional detachment." The emotional involvement with a patient through the patient's developing symbiotic experience engenders anything but neutrality in the therapist except as a defense.

The patient's living experience with the therapist touches off the therapist's affect-memory of his or her own parental bond. This disturbing dimension of perceptual experience may be defended against with interpretation, with structure. When it is defended against with structure, it is often done so before the fact. That is, intuitively, therapists "know" that the longer they are involved with a patient in a relatively unstructured, time-free experience, the greater the chance for patient and therapist discovery of cognitive and affective memory. (The patient in this sense is truly the therapist to the therapist, as discussed in Chapter V.) Thus, rediscovery being uncomfortable, it is well worth it to the therapist to avoid recapturing the affectual component to his or her symbiotic bond.

To be able to lose the patient through separation-individuation implies that the therapist could resolve his or her own rapprochement crisis. The question is, is this possible for the therapist still caught in the symbiotic struggle? We think not.

To avoid experiencing the separateness, the vulnerability, the loneliness, the mortality, and the mourning process that separation implies (Burland, 1975), we think therapists would rather terminate. With termination there is indeed no lost object; with continuance of therapy after separation, there is a relationship similar to what Burland (1975) describes developmentally as primarily "predicated no longer on fusion [or symbiosis] but on affection, sharing and communication" (p. 323). This is an emotionally and interpersonally collaborative relationship, one much avoided by many therapists.

In trying to formulate our ideas on separation and its relation to termination we noted an interesting paper on the mother-daughter bond (Friedman, 1980) in which we saw certain similarities to the therapist-patient bond as it relates to termination. Ideally, mothers facilitate separation by allowing and encouraging its process, as do therapists. The drive toward independence may be innate, but with some patients it may not surface for many years. With others, a defensive independence may cover an inordinate or a feared dependency which is unconsciously desired. In such instances, true, healthy independence emerges only after the patient's dependency needs are benignly assisted to arise.

While separation leads to independence, in the mother-daughter bond as in the therapist-patient bond, it does not necessarily lead to abandonment of a bond altogether. In other words, in both relationships, separation is not synonymous with termination, as we mentioned earlier in the chapter. As logical as that may sound, it is surprising to note the frequency with which therapists connect the two. There are several reasons. First, just as mothers must grapple with the naturally occurring rejection implicit in the emotional separation of their daughters (and sons), so too do therapists face a kind of rejection when the patient grows into an emotional peer or beyond the therapist, when the patient develops intellectual, interpersonal, and emotional capabilities equivalent to, different from, or beyond the therapist's. Rather than tolerate the rejection and loss of part of the "self" some therapists then automatically misconstrue emotional separation as a signal for termination.

In fact, termination at that point in time does not allow the patient's independence to develop in front of the therapist's eyes, thus preserving for the therapist the original symbiotic bond (with the patient), thereby preventing the transition to therapeutic symbiosis (Searles, 1973/1979). Here it is useful to point out that while we realize that a therapist, just as a parent, is internalized, we also recognize that many therapists rationalize the decision to terminate on that basis and on the basis that the patient is ready to try his or her wings. Although the separation is a definite shift, termination of the relationship need not occur. Instead, it is conceivable that therapy could now take place on another level of relatedness, *if* the therapist can separate and move on in the relationship as well as to other levels of the unconscious. The shift, however, may be difficult, especially for those therapists who feel most comfortable in the classical, more rigidly conceived helping role.

By now it is more than clear that for some time it has been recognized that in development, the phases of fusion and symbiosis prove "crucial in determining the quality of later object relations" (Giovacchini, 1976, p. 345). It is also clear that one of these relations, the therapist's relationship with the patient, should be included.

Autonomy in all relationships depends on a person's ability to have achieved a reasonable outcome from the symbiotic phase. But the importance of the symbiotic phase goes beyond autonomy, for according to Giovacchini (1976), intimacy is predicated on one's capacity to project the valued parts of the self onto another, to then achieve pleasurable fusion through dissolved ego boundaries, leading to higher levels of ego integration for each partner. Thus, intimacy enhances each partner and the relationship, including the therapy relationship. But what of the therapist's ability to achieve intimacy? We think it may well be that some therapists have inordinate difficulties in this area. A problem in achieving intimacy would interfere with the quality of the relationship the therapist could develop with the patient and with the patient's need to use the therapist as an object with which to fuse and from which to separate.

Just as in pathological symbiosis (Giovacchini, 1976), where "the mother uses her child to maintain defensive stability" (p. 433), the bogged-down therapist cannot allow the free movement of the patient. The therapist is not free to fuse and to separate. As discussed at length in Chapter V, the therapist is locked in a symbiotic struggle with the patient-mother where the unconscious aim is to maintain a symbiosis, albeit one of the therapist's revision.

Obviously, the patient caught in such a situation is not free to be autonomous, just as the therapist is not. Moreover, the patient cannot move beyond the therapist emotionally. It is when patients make such a bid we have often observed therapists determine patients are "finished" therapy. This determination, however, seems based more on the therapist's inability to "lose" the patient, to break his or her own symbiotic tie. With the breaking of the bond, the therapist fears the eruption of envy of the patient for achieving that which he or she was unable to achieve. Further, the therapist anticipates enormous anxiety and guilt for "leaving home," leaving the role of parental caretaker behind. Ostensibly, the therapist would no longer think he or she had a role if the patient emotionally separated, so what other choice but to terminate?

The fact of the matter is that were the therapist to continue therapy, he or she would not have the usual role—the child there to serve the parent or the parent there to be served by the child. The therapist ultimately would have to face a nonsymbiotic relationship, one which could move at times toward the defended-against fusion, and one which could move into the unknown territory of mutuality. Both would be seen as enveloping and annihilating in the sense that each state would be in the hands of the patient.

Thus, contrary to popular belief, termination may have more to do with a defensive holding-on to a particular quality bond characterizing a certain level of relationship rather than representing separation at all. In fact, in this regard, termination could even be seen as parental-therapist punishment for the child-patient breaking an early bond; or on another level, child-therapist punishment for the parent-patient going his or her own way, ignoring and preventing child-therapist influence. In any event the outcome of such termination is emotional bondage rather than emotional separation.

Emotional separation for a therapist symbiotically bound to the parent is often distorted by the therapist in the clinical situation as abandonment. When the patient comes into his or her own, it is as if the therapist has lost the needed good object, so well explained by Winnicott to Guntrip (1975) in describing a dimension of their relationship.

From our perspective, the mother-therapist values the child-patient, but if the value is replaced by narcissistic need, then the child-patient's natural, inevitable movement is inhibited. If, however, the patient manages to move despite the therapist's prohibitions (because they are rarely total), the needy therapist will ultimately feel the abandonment and "retaliate" by considering the patient to be at termination time instead of at a separation phase. Unfortunately for both patient and therapist the patient is then unable to make as much use of the therapist as might otherwise be possible.

To allow the patient to make as much use of us as they can is, after all, central to our work (Guntrip, 1975). And to allow patients to move beyond us intellectually, interpersonally and emotionally (as Fairbairn and Winnicott did in their work with Guntrip, described in Guntrip's 1975 paper) while sticking with them is a central aim in our work as therapists and in our lives as human beings. To paraphrase Saretsky (1980), it would be most useful if the therapist's activity did not succeed in "interrupting the patient's presentation of self so as to quiet the [therapist's] own internal objects" (p. 86), as would have been the case in the pathological mother-child relationship.

THE FUTURE

From a research standpoint there are many questions to be asked. We need to be able to design studies that can answer the question of whether therapy of conceptually unlimited duration can prove effective, ineffective, equally effective, more effective than therapy in other time frames. Assuming the development of an appropriate design, which is certainly a complex and formidable undertaking, what can therapy of unlimited duration be shown to do? We are at a more preliminary step to probing this area. Our intent at the moment is to encourage clinicians to approach this concept with sufficient receptivity. While certainly there are questions that remain unasked and/or unanswered about the therapist's motives for termination as seen through the reluctance to consider a concept of therapy of unlimited duration, our hope is that more psychotherapists will be prompted to think about the concept and the questions.

So far in this chapter we tended to support an impression advanced by Edelson (1963) that perhaps therapists express their feelings about termination mainly through writing about the process. There is an implication in this of an avoidance of more direct contact with the feelings. While this is not at all our intent, it is true that in this chapter we have stayed away from the drama of clinical examples in favor of an expository approach to explaining the therapist's possible motives for termination. We have concerned ourselves with the broad factor, the therapist's narcissistic motive, the unresolved symbiotic bond, to at once help examine and explain the therapist's need for termination yet reluctance to separate emotionally, and the therapist's reluctance to consider a concept of therapy of unlimited duration.

At the same time we did state that repeated observations of therapists in action, including ourselves, was a major consideration in our formulations. We would imagine that our feelings about termination are embedded in this exposition, but as we look over the chapter we realize the importance of being more explicit. Our general impression is that therapists think more in terms of beginning and ending than of continuing. We conceive of life more as a number of beginnings leading to relationships, some enduring and some interrupted, temporarily or permanently. Our thrust is on enduring, satisfying relationships, and we believe psychotherapy can be one of these relationships for certain people.

Of course patients terminate with us, with and without our agreement. Each year we have a number of "shoppers" who take a quick look—one to three sessions—and decide we are not for them. There are people who do not progress beyond a certain point, despite our best efforts, and although they may feel "incomplete," (and although we agree with that appraisal) further therapy at the moment does not seem to be of benefit and we would terminate, though subsequent sessions are certainly a possibility. Also, there are people who entered therapy with fairly definite goals, achieved these, and depart feeling satisfied. We explain to these people other possibilities that are available if they decide at some point to continue. We are open-ended about termination, though of course patients do not have to be and often are not. Nonetheless, we are disappointed if patients with the potential to continue choose not to do so.

In line with such an approach it is not unusual for people to be in therapy for a long time (admittedly a relative concept, but as a specific, more than five years) and frequently (more than once a week). The key consideration is the potential of the patient, which is essentially a combination of the patient's willingness and ability to develop through the medium of psychotherapy with one of us. There has to be an appropriate "fit," the possibility of which we believe is enhanced by our commitment to the possibility of unlimited therapy.

At the same time we are aware that a danger in our approach is the possibility of attempting to "convince" certain patients they need to remain in therapy when they do not wish to stay. Thus, there is the opening for misuse of the concept of unlimited therapy by prolonging what the patient truly wishes to stop. Just as it is possible to talk a patient out of therapy for unconscious reasons on the therapist's part, so it is also possible to keep a patient in therapy for the therapist's gratification—under the guise of therapeutic value for the patient. While our belief is that therapy can be thought of as unlimited, and that unlimited therapy can be of value for certain patients, we do not assert that it has to be unlimited or that it should be that way with every patient. Just as we have cited the problems and concerns involved in both premature terminations and the insistence that therapy must have an end point, we caution against the indiscriminate use of the concept of unlimited therapy.

Our major intention in this chapter has been the examination of possible therapist motivations for termination. The focus on motivation appears to bear extension to the larger question of how the internal countertransference reaction sets the therapist's external agenda, be it in establishing contracts, in facilitating the therapy relating process, or in determining termination. The countertransference reaction can be viewed microscopically, on an individual, unit-by-unit, moment-by-moment basis, or it can be classified into a system personified by fantasy. How the therapist uses or abuses particular brands of fantasy will be examined in the next chapter.

REFERENCES

Butcher, J. N., and Koss, M. P. Research on brief and crisis-oriented therapies. In S. L. Garfield and A. E. Bergin (Eds.), *Handbook of psychotherapy and behavior change: An empirical analysis* (New York: Wiley, 1978).

Bellak, L., and Small, L. *Emergency psychotherapy and brief psychotherapy* (New York: Grune & Stratton, 1977).

Burland, J. A. Separation-individuation and reconstruction in psychoanalysis. *International Journal of Psychoanalytic Psychotherapy* (1975) **4:**303–335.

Edelson, M. *The termination of intensive psychotherapy.* (Illinois: Charles C Thomas, 1963).

Firestein, S. K. *Termination in psychoanalysis* (New York: International Universities Press, 1978).

Freud, S. Analysis terminable and interminable. In *The complete psychological works of Sigmund Freud,* Vol. 23 (London: Hogarth Press, 1964) (Originally published, 1937).

Freud, S. Notes upon a case of Obsessional Neurosis. In *The complete psychological works of Sigmund Freud,* Vol. 10 (London: Hogarth Press, 1957) (Originally published, 1909).

Friedman, G. The mother-daughter bond. *Contemporary Psychoanalysis* (1980) **16:**90–97.

Getsinger, S. H. Psychotherapy and the fourth dimension. *Psychotherapy: Theory, research and practice* (1975) **12:**216–225.

Giovacchini, P. L. Symbiosis and intimacy. *International Journal of Psychoanalytic Psychotherapy* (1976) **5:**413–436.

Glazer, M. The analysis of premature termination in the borderline personality. *Journal of Contemporary Psychotherapy* (1978) **10:**3–9.

Goldberg, C. Termination—A meaningful psychodilemma in psychotherapy. *Psychotherapy: Theory, research and practice* (1975) **12:**341–343.

Gourevitch, A. Termination. *Contemporary Psychoanalysis* (1980) **16:**68–81.

Guntrip, H. My experience of analysis with Fairbairn and Winnicott (How complete a result does psychoanalytic therapy achieve?) *International Review of Psycho-Analysis* (1975) **2:**145–156.

Hare-Mustin, R. T., Marecek, J., Kaplan, A.G., and Liss-Levinson, N. Rights of clients, responsibilities of therapists. *American Psychologist* (1979) **34:**3–16.

Kernberg, O. F. A contriution to the ego-psychological critique of the Kleinian school. *The International Review of Psycho-Analysis* (1969) **50:**317–333.

Klauber, J. Analyses that cannot be terminated. *International Journal of Psycho-Analysis* (1977) **58:**473–477.

Kubie, L. S. The retreat from patients: An unanticipated penalty of the full-time system. *Archives of General Psychiatry* (1971) **24:**236–243.

Mahler, M. S. *On human symbiosis and the vicissitudes of individuation* (New York: International Universities Press, 1968).

Maholick, L. T., and Turner, D. W. Termination: That difficult farewell. *American Journal of Psychotherapy* (1979) **33:**583–592.

Malan, D. H. *A study of brief psychotherapy* (London: Tavistock Publications, 1963).

Rosenzweig, S. P., and Folman, R. Patient and therapist variables affecting premature termination in group psychotherapy. *Psychotherapy: Theory, Research and Practice* (1974) **11:**76–79.

Saretsky, T. The analyst's narcissistic vulnerability. *Contemporary Psychoanalysis* (1980) **16:**82–89.

Searles, H. F. Autism and the phase of transition to therapeutic symbiosis. In H. F. Searles (Ed.), *Countertransference and related subjects* (New York: International Universities Press, 1979) (Originally published, 1970).

Searles, H. F. Concerning therapeutic symbiosis: The patient as symbiotic therapist, the phase of ambivalent symbiosis, and the role of jealousy in the fragmented ego. In H. F. Searles (Ed.), *Countertransference and related subjects* (New York: International Universities Press, 1979) (Originally published, 1973).

Searles, H. F. Pathologic symbiosis and autism. In H. F. Searles (Ed.), *Countertransference and related subjects* (International Universities Press, 1979) (Originally published, 1971).

Searles, H. F. Transitional phenomena and therapeutic symbiosis. *International Journal of Psychoanalytic Psychotherapy* (1976) **5:**145–203.

Sifneos, P. E. *Short-term dynamic psychotherapy* (New York: Plenum Publishing Corp., 1979).

Small, L. *The briefer psychotherapies* (New York: Brunner/Mazel, 1979).

Strupp, H. H. Success and failure in time-limited psychotherapy. *Archives of General Psychiatry* (1980) **37:**708–716.

Sullivan, H. S. *The psychiatric interview* (New York: W. W. Norton, 1954).

Weigert, E. Contribution to the problem of terminating psychoanalysis. *The Psychoanalytic Quarterly* (1952) **21:**465–480.

Winnicott, D. W. The capacity to be alone. In D. W. Winnicott (Ed.), *The maturational processes and the facilitating environment* (New York: International Universities Press, 1974) (Originally published, 1958).

Winnicott, D. W. The developing of the capacity for concern. In D. W. Winnicott (Ed.), *The maturational processes and the facilitating environment* (New York: International Universities Press, 1974) (Originally published, 1963). (a)

Winnicott, D. W. Ego distortion in terms of true and false self. In D. W. Winnicott (Ed.), *The maturational processes and the facilitating environment* (New York: International Universities Press, 1974) (Originally published, 1960).

Winnicott, D. W. The mentally ill in your caseload. In D. W. Winnicott (Ed.), *The maturational processes and the facilitating enironment* (New York: International Universities Press, 1974) (Originally published, 1963). (b)

Wolberg, L. *The technique of psychotherapy*, 3rd edition, Parts 1 and 2 (New York: Grune & Stratton, 1977).

VIII

At Issue: The Use and Abuse of the Therapist's Fantasy

INTRODUCTION

We have been writing about aspects of therapists' fantasies whenever we touched upon the seemingly unstructured private imagery expression, through conscious or unconscious thinking operations, of the therapist's inner life. Beginning in Chapter I, with the therapist defining therapy to his or her patients, and in Chapter II, explaining its aims, followed by the rest of the therapist's behaviors explored in subsequent chapters, a fantasy component has been included, whether implied or explicit. Coupled with the actual "transference to the patient" activity by the therapist, we have repeatedly explored a variety of what could be considered "countertransference" responses. These are embedded in fantasy, and reflected by the therapist's fantasies.

We have previously documented the potential impacts of certain therapist behaviors on patient behaviors, and the reverse, thus alluding to the countertransferential types of responses that are likely to occur, especially through the medium of the therapist's narcissism. For example, not only is it possible for the therapist's narcissism to be manifested through fantasy operations that he or she brings to the therapy situation, but fantasy arises or may be triggered by the assault on the therapist's narcissism once therapy begins. Moreover, the therapist's fantasy picture of what therapy should be and how patient and therapist should act governs much of what goes on in the name of establishing rational and irrational contracts, and contributes to the concept of termination.

It appears that we have the interrelated concepts of fantasy and countertransference, with their associated narcissistic elements, all in need of further exploration. Again as with many of the issues in this book, they have been "thought about" by others, but at the same time too much left alone, as though they were really and completely understood, and so, no longer "issues."

If we take fantasy as the first example, purely from the standpoint of normative human behavior it can be seen as a level of thinking. It is a cognitive operation used to process anecdotal and emotional events. Fantasy is a way of making sense out of unconscious and conscious observations, of internal and external events and their relation. It is a vehicle for the expression of a given intellectual aspect of knowledge and its corresponding affect. Clinically, the therapist's fantasy manifests itself through privately thought "stories," or less formalized "images" that occur fleetingly, or, word or picture associations. At times, fantasy may only be inferred from sudden unexplained breaks in expected or rational behavior.

The interest here is not so much in what the therapist should or should not think about, but with the *fact* of therapist fantasy, and how it can be used or abused. In particular the function of the therapist's fantasy and its relation to countertransference. Through elaboration of the concepts of countertransference and fantasy, and through clinical examples and discussion of the concepts as they operate in clinical work, we try to shed some different light on the therapist at work. Throughout the development of this chapter the intent is that some insight may be found in this complex area, both in regard to the ways in which the therapist's fantasy can work for and against the therapist, and for and against the patient.

We begin by considering the value of the availability of fantasy to the therapist and illustrate what can occur when fantasy is held out of reach as opposed to its potential utility for the therapeutic relationship. From here we move to the key role of fantasy in understanding the countertransference responses of the therapist. We briefly outline the definition and development of countertransference to show its current conception. We point out the possible "good" use of countertransference, note its problematic aspects, and suggest the need for an accurate perspective on its presence and possible effects. Then, we explore the applications of countertransference, the consequences, and possible ways of dealing with the problems. This exploration leads to a classification scheme for countertransference responses which is designed to expedite their recognition and concurrent management. Following this we consider the more generalized idea of the function of therapists' fantasies in therapy. The link with countertransference is continued, and the issue of fantasy that therapists "share" by virtue of practicing therapy is illustrated, along with the possible problems engendered. We conclude by suggesting an increased recognition of the role of the therapist's fantasy in the therapeutic process.

THE AVAILABILITY AND POTENTIAL VALUE OF THERAPISTS' FANTASY

While fantasy at some level is always active, not all therapists are aware of their own. That can severely limit their therapeutic efforts. Fantasy as a route to understanding countertransference is then not available to the therapist, thereby eliminating a source of data for the understanding of the patient and the interaction. Unfortunately, it is not uncommon that therapists, without assistance, remain unaware of their fantasies. Here is an example.

A young therapist was with a patient in her hospital room where the patient had insisted on being for her session that day. Much to the therapist's conscious dissatisfaction (for "therapeutic" reasons), the patient, who did not need her thinking loosened further, lay down on the bed next to the therapist's chair. She was tired, she said, and anyway got a kick out of "playing psychoanalysis." At one point, the patient reached over to the therapist, touching a pearl necklace she was wearing. The therapist, in reporting the incident to her own therapist, said she remembered stiffening up and "seeing herself" with the patient's hand on "her pearls." It was not that she feared that the patient would hurt her, for she had been seeing the patient in therapy for a few years and knew pretty much that "direct attack" was not really the way the patient operated. The therapist best described her own reaction as feeling vaguely uncomfortable but definitely detached.

Appropriately, to gain a more comprehensive picture of what had happened, the therapist's therapist asked her what fantasies she had had at the time. The patient-therapist, who herself had been in treatment for a few years, answered indignantly, saying didn't he realize she was working after all, so how could she be having a fantasy! Unimpressed, her therapist said it sometimes happens anyway and asked about when she told him about the event. Unreached, she was appalled that he thought she might be so out of touch as to fantasize. When he changed the term to daydream she did allow that it happened rarely, but yes, once in a while. This therapist was one with tight obsessional defenses that were limiting her contact with her inner self and others. In that respect she was like her schizophrenic patients, in flight beyond where she worried fantasy would take her, although nobody would have usually thought to make the comparison. Ultimately, the therapist became aware just how much she fantasized, and in years to come, just how much of her life was fantasy. And she felt like a freer, more human, more frightened, but better, therapist.

As Searles (1975) has written, "Analysis is effective insofar as it has given . . . ready access to, rather than somehow effaced, the (therapist's) capacity for primitive feelings of jealousy, fear, rage, symbiotic dependency, and other affective states against which [the] patient's schizophrenia typically is serving to defend the patient from experiencing in awareness" (p. 223). Unconsciously, this therapist held such feeling in check by defending against awareness of the fantasy process whereby the feelings would manifest themselves. For if fantasy occurred and was attended to, then the feelings might be recognized and they themselves might emerge directly. To her way of seeing things, thought would no longer be pure; rather, it would be adulterated and perhaps influenced by feeling; and thoughts and feelings would be open to influence by others, including patients, with whom the therapist had heretofore felt safe. She would then be vulnerable, but instead unconsciously chose to protect herself at a cost to the development of the therapeutic relationship.

Fantasy is very much a part of therapists' lives as therapists. Part of their business is to figure out the place their fantasy operations hold in their work with patients. Exactly how the therapist's fantasy operations influence treatment on a moment to moment basis is highly individual and hard to pin down, but our experience has shown that indeed, the therapist's fantasy operations have clinical effects, that there can be clinical use of the therapist's fantasy through direct or indirect means, and that there can be clinical abuse of the therapist's fantasy through direct and indirect means.

In one respect, the therapist's fantasy can be seen as a "striving to define oneself" (Giovacchini, 1977). Too, it can be seen as an isolating state explained by Winnicott (1971) in his discussion of a patient who used unconscious and later conscious fantasy as a device to withdraw from relating. As with Winnicott's patient, and the one we described, it is possible for the therapist to become so engrossed in fantasy as the whole of an experience that he or she does not in fact perceive all that is happening in the experience. In such a state, the thorough absorbtion in fantasy governs how and what will be perceived. Such a state may mean that realistic hope for relating is implicitly abandoned and the fantasy becomes the life. The fantasy is lived, the life not quite observed. And though fantasy may have started out unconsciously as a way to find a place for oneself, a place in the universe (Giovacchini, 1977), the result is a kind of distance. The therapist's "place in the universe" becomes one of aloneness; not existential aloneness, but defensive aloneness built on conflict and anxiety about relating.

Accordingly, in the process of psychotherapy it becomes the therapist's task to examine his or her place in the relationship with the patient. One means for this exploration is looking into the therapist's fantasy operations. To do so requires an understanding of a central contributor to the therapist's fantasy arousal and fantasy content: the countertransference response.

THE COUNTERTRANSFERENCE RESPONSE

Countertransference is an inevitable in psychotherapy as transference is ineludible. Countertransference goes beyond the early classical psychoanalytic narrow model holding that it is a response to the patient's transference (Freud, 1910/1964). Instead, it involves the therapist's emotional response as transference-object, as projection-object of the patient's personality, as non-transference object (Heinman, 1950; Kernberg, 1965; Racker, 1953). Further, countertransference can be thought of as the therapist's total emotional response, though that view needs some delineating.

It has been some time now since countertransference was seen simply as an unwelcome impediment to the therapy process (Glover, 1955) to be edited out rather than understood as a reaction emanating from the interaction of patient and therapist (Epstein and Feiner, 1979a). And it would seem useful that the thinking has progressed. Although Freud (1910/1964) considered countertransference an obstacle to be overcome, he too thought that the unconscious might be used as an instrument (1912/1964). Perhaps it was then that the movernent began toward considering it entirely possible and maybe even necessary that the countertransference response be seen as an integral and useful part of treatment rather than simply pathological responses of the therapist to the patient's transference as Freud (1910/1964) initially conceived it. Theorists such as Winnicott (1947), Heinmann (1950), Racker (1953), and Giovacchini (1972), attest to the growing interest in an expanded view of countertransference in the years that followed.

For many years it had been one of the field's most enduring beliefs that, with effort, countertransference reactions could be and should be eliminated. The idea was comforting for those looking for a "clean," supposedly "scientific," though perhaps sterile approach, but it was neither practical nor as useful as it seemed. While today, in analytic circles a prevailing attitude is that "countertransference is an instrument for research into the patient's unconscious" (Heinmann, 1950, p. 82) some therapists practice the kind of therapy that tends to ignore the reaction, though it would be impossible to stop its occurrence altogether. In a way, countertransference has probably always been a source and a guide for understanding the patient, albeit an unconscious resource. Indeed countertransference can be a source for the therapist's self-understanding, for it is "intimate self knowledge that is the precondition for the intimate relations with others" (Ehrenberg, 1975, p. 330) and that is, after all, what therapy is about.

One noteworthy feature of the current view of countertransference is that it is practical. In the past, clinicians seemed disdainful of their reactions, or, at least indifferent toward their potential value. "Legitimacy" has helped take some of the sting out of countertransference occurrence while preserving the need for its recognition and facilitating its dynamic understanding. Another important element of the view is that free, unbiased examination of countertransference as a natural and expected phenomenon points the way to a more systematic approach for enhanced understanding of the patient's dynamics: the interpersonal expression of intrapsychic experience. Through the interpersonal experience, often it is possible, in Segal's (1977) words, to "become aware of conscious derivatives" (p. 36) of unconscious, intrapersonal experience. Moreover, it is part of being in touch not only with self, but with the other.

The broadened current view of countertransference is quite reasonable and useful. In addition, even if the therapist were to appear to be "rid" of the reaction, often there is no "quick fix" for the reaction the therapist seeks to end. The danger lies not in the occurrence of the countertransference reaction, but, that the reaction may go unrecognized. And worse, when the treatment "technique" is unconsciously or consciously rationalized on the basis of countertransference. Ultimately there are no beneficiaries of such a situation, although for a while either patient or therapist, or both, might feel more comfortable.

While countertransference reactions have the potential of being helpful *because* the therapist responds (Giovacchini, 1972) and therapist and patient potentially can use that response to promote progress, countertransference problems also account for difficulties in treatment. Even so, difficulties with the treatment do not automatically imply uncontrolled countertransference responses destructive to the patient and to the treatment process.

In that regard, at times it seems countertransference responses are valued beyond their inherent worth, and not simply as a contribution to the therapeutic process. As Singer (1980) says, "While appropriate use of countertransference furthers understanding and dissolution of the pathological system . . . this doesn't mean countertransference is worthy of reification. Countertransference is an important phenomenon, not to be ignored or wishfully treated as if it could be eliminated, but to be recognized not only as part of the solution, but as part of the problem" (p. 264). He cautions that becoming enamored of countertransference is "countertransference at its worst" (p. 265); while it is not a "necessary evil" it is a life-sized "inevitable necessity" (p. 264).

Countertransference Applied

There is a notable lack of authoritative (and not so authoritative) agreement as to whether the therapist directly confronts the patient with his or her countertransference laden response (in the form of fantasy or not), or interprets, or silently processes the response, or bases direction on it. There are, however, some characteristics of countertransference important to recognize whether or not a therapist formally acts.

First, we must remember that at some level the patient is probably sensitive to and influenced by the therapist's countertransference no matter what the therapist "does" with it (Lang, 1976; Little, 1957; Searles, 1958; Searles, 1978). Second, that countertransference reactions are automatic and often initially out of awareness (Segal, 1977), except for a few fantasy or behavioral hints. Third, that countertransference reactions are inevitable because, as Searles (1975) puts it, the therapist's "own more primitive modes of experience, and of interpersonal relatedness . . . are subject to being revived in the course of his ongoing adult life experience" (p. 223), including work with patients. Fourth, that countertransference is not simply as Heinmann (1950) would have it, the patient's creation and a function or part of the patient's personality. The therapist makes a contribution and that becomes a resource, a kind of measurement of the interpersonal process at hand. In that sense, both therapist and patient have a hand in determining the nature or quality or quantity or intensity of the response. And fifth, that countertransference is an inner response, an intrapsychic phenomenon reflecting processed interpersonal experience, present or past, touched off, often suddenly, by interpersonal events, and is at times expressed interpersonally.

So, because countertransference is an automatic response to which the patient is sensitive, because it is an inevitable and spontaneous, often primitive response based in the patient, therapist, or both, it is not always easy to "plan" how to use it and the fantasy that may house it. However, some help is provided by Epstein and Feiner (1979b). It certainly is useful to "distinguish between countertransference as an inner experience, to be *digested*, scrutinized, clarified, understood, and subsequently harnessed for therapeutic understanding, and countertransference as directly, impulsively enacted or discharged" (p. 499). There is a difference. Seen as a discovery, countertransference can be used by therapists to assist patients to examine their contribution to the therapist's response.

Too often we have seen therapists who are too certain of the meaning of their responses, so certain of this never-absolute formulation, that they foist it on the patient to the point of absurdity and struggle. If they are indeed right, time will tell and so will the patient if given the freedom. Interpretation is not valuable when used as a hostile device, a device to control or to create distance. Overzealous interpretation creates distance, signalling the patient that the therapist is indeed in charge, that the patient should "go away" to stop making the therapist uncomfortable, or to continue making the therapist comfortable, which is both controlling and distancing in that the patient must be close to the therapist in the way the therapist deems "right."

Too often we have seen "honesty" in the therapist's use of fantasy material as simply a narcissistic exercise, something of which Searles (1975) warns. Also, these honest confrontations or presentations of countertransference response are sometimes devious. Their expression, whether directly expressed or presented as a formulation, may certainly instead be hostile, burdening the patient with that which he or she cannot deal, at least in that particular context at that particular moment. Honesty, says Giovacchini (1972), should be thought of as a tool rather than a general virtue. After all, therapist irrationality, in all of its diversity, can be treated as a discovery rather than used as a weapon.

So then, is seeing countertransference as a helpful occurrence a bit heavy on the side of rationalization? Is it merely seeing a silver lining on a dark horizon? We think not, although that is not to say that much damage cannot be done in the name of "using" one's countertransference response.

There is a fundamental difference between using a countertransference reaction as one indicant of what *might* be going on in a complex field and using it as the complete explanation of what is transpiring. There is a fundamental difference between using a countertransference reaction in an irrational way and in a rational way. Irrational use may not always appear so because it is often disguised to look psychologically presentable, and the reaction itself may have merit. However, even with a gilt-edged theoretical explanation by a therapist forever reacting and "sharing" or "acting out" the response, who can guarantee vindication by a patient grown weary of what could be seen as the "therapist's problems," no matter what the provocation?

Furthermore, some irrational responses look all too rational, or the irrational and rational exist side by side and it is hard to distinguish whether the therapist is acting on the irrational or the rational response. Indeed, an act such as having to prematurely terminate with a patient can have rational and irrational motives. In fact, we are familiar with a case where therapy was finally terminated for highly rational reasons, but the therapist could not terminate while knowing he had irrational motives for wanting to stop. He did not want to stop for the wrong reasons. To complicate matters, in the process of figuring out his countertransference he also came to see that he had irrational motives for continuing, for being afraid to terminate. Here is what happened:

The patient began coming to the sessions full of whatever tranquilizers he could get his hands on. The behavior had been going on for several months, in and out of therapy sessions which were now in their third year. The tranquilizers did anything but calm the patient. Instead, feeling less inhibited, with less felt-anxiety about his considerable rage, he was freer in shutting out the therapist and acting out against the therapist. The patient had no desire to stop "treatment," yet also had no desire to either stop acting out or to analyze what was going on.

The therapist, who had the usual "need" to help, was thwarted in every attempt. An experienced and long-analyzed therapist, he was totally aware of his rage at the patient, not so much for the bulk of the hostile acting out, but for not being allowed entrance. It seemed he could put up with phone calls from unknown colleagues the patient had "somehow" contacted, who advised him of his misjudgment as to how sick his patient was, and in bursts of unsolicited supervision told him he wasn't really doing his job. And he could put up with rumors circulated "somehow" that the patient was to jump off a twelve-story building, which the therapist's building just happened to be. And he could put up with the patient's propositioning a few of the therapist's neighbors, because they were friends and knew about what sometimes happens in therapy from their own treatment experiences. Not that he liked any of it. Not that he ignored it or neglected to take a stand with the patient about all those things. And it occurred to him regularly that other therapists might terminate and that maybe he should. And that, while he put up with the behavior, he might like living better without it. He clearly entertained the idea of terminating but did not want to do so for irrational reasons. He wasn't sure yet.

What he could not deal with was his persistent anxiety, his almost literal fear of the patient at times, and a vague feeling of guilt. In supervision he had copious notes, determined to find out what surely he was doing wrong. In each session it seemed there was nothing he did that could be pointed to as "the culprit." That was the therapist's problem, at least the tip of the iceberg. Here he was doing what was useful, what was therapeutically indicated, and had done relatively the same for the years prior to this period. Yet there continued to be this terrible, seemingly unresolvable acting out by the patient who actively, to be euphemistic, turned a deaf ear to the therapist.

While both he and his supervisor considered it useful not to terminate with the patient precipitously, to try to ride with the situation for awhile, he began to question his persistence, what he came to think must be his masochism, his need to help. It was his sustained anxiety after a time that provided some clues. When he was anxious he noticed he had a recurring fantasy that the patient would knock on his home door, he'd answer, and the patient would take out a huge knife and kill him. At first the therapist thought the content was reflection of the patient's rage and of his own projected rage, both of which it probably was. As time progressed, however, it became clear that being killed had little to do with rage in itself. Rather, it was seen by the therapist as punishment for not doing his job, not being allowed to help.

Indeed, his need to help filled him with enormous guilt at facing the reality that he, even he, couldn't help this time. Even though it was better not to terminate at this point, he could not *allow* himself to terminate. Initially, the search for what he was doing wrong was not for the patient's sake alone, it was for his own sake as well, for the therapist's life was compulsively dedicated to making "mother" whole, and in early life he would have truly suffered immeasurably had he not taken on the task. Now, as then, the task meant security as well as satisfaction, and provided a protection against guilt. The powerful mother was still alive and functioning. On some level, the therapist's persistence was reflective of the hope that the patient, his mother, would let him in. Not the mature hope that Searles (1977/1979) talks about, but the pathological hope that the patient-mother will come around. The fantasy of a reasonably giving mother prevailed far beyond its time for this therapist.

When the therapist was ready to live with the guilt and anxiety of "not doing his job" he could continue to do his job. He then told the patient that he would have to terminate if the patient would not stop acting out without ever trying to analyze it, particularly were he to continue coming "buzzed out" to session after session, and that when the patient wanted *therapy* he would be glad to see him. The patient left immediately, stumbled in front of screeching cars beneath the therapist's window, surviving, but never to return. This represented the death knell of the therapist's fantasy.

In this instance, the rational and irrational existed side by side and at different levels. Early on, were the therapist to have terminated, his response may have seemed rational, but it would not have been. To have terminated would have protected him from coming to grips with his internal state and the process at hand and it just wasn't useful for the patient at that point. When termination looked like it might be the necessary, rational approach, he had difficulty with it for the same reasons he felt anxiety and guilt when continuing with the patient.

In retrospect, whereas initially he stayed with the patient for the right reasons and for the wrong reasons, ultimately, when he terminated, he did so with good reason, but suffered anxiety before, during, and after. The fantasy that was dying was of the chronic helper therapist, the adult-child needing and hoping to fix his mother. The countertransference response inherent in the fantasy roles and the fantasy images, while helpful in understanding what was happening, was terribly distressing.

Did the patient sense the countertransference? It would have been impossible for him not to. In fact, it may have been used by the patient to thwart the therapist. All this seemed to happen when the patient had felt closer to the therapist than he had ever been, and when he could not tolerate the closeness he reduced the efficiency of the therapist by drawing on needs he saw in the therapist before they became so manifestly obvious to the therapist at this particular time.

The Classification of Countertransference

From experiences such as this, several questions may well be raised. Is countertransference always idiosyncratic, that is, is there ever a response to a patient that any therapist is likely to have? Might then it be possible to classify kinds of countertransference? Answers are possible, but complex, as attested to both by the literature on countertransference and our own experiences. Many definitions of the concept exist. Some are similar to others, some bear acknowledged similarity, and some do not. Other definitions are in their own camps, sometimes bringing clarity or adding depth to the concept, sometimes not. It was surely apparent that we had not discovered the concept (that would be a hard fantasy to sustain!) but it was clear each therapist does have a personal sense of discovery when countertransference occurs. What we did discover was that, as in writings on narcissism, the literature on countertransference is at times written in language so private, so convoluted, that it becomes nearly impossible to follow. Furthermore, many authors seem quite unaware (at least they give no evidence of knowing) that anything on the subject has been written before. They set up their own classification systems that might well be incorporated in or subsumed by others, or at least correlated with other classification systems.

Instead of presenting all major viewpoints or the chronology of the shift away from the "pathology only" viewpoints such as the review done (and so well "translated" in some instances) by Epstein and Feiner (1979b), we chose to abstract and distill consistent ideas, putting them together in such a way as to make sense out of the various, seemingly close pieces that are rarely seen in relation to one another. To this end, we introduce a system of classifying countertransference data, categories we think represent the essence of what many authors say. Our intention is not to add still another definition of countertransference but to bring order and classification to those that exist. Where particular existing terminology would seem helpful to include, we include it.

In the old days, countertransference had one meaning. Now that there are more, there is a danger of promulgating meaningless classifications and nitpicking distinctions of what is and what is not countertransference and in what microcategory the data belong. There continue to be "disputes in the literature over whether countertransference should include all of the analyst's emotional reactions in the treatment situation or only those specifically in response to the patient's transference" (Firestein, 1978, p. 230). So, that is one problem. Furthermore, there are disputes as to whether countertransference should include any emotional reaction of the therapist or only those that interfere with treatment. And then, where does positive countertransference fit in? Can positive countertransference become an impediment to treatment, and if so, how is it to be classified?

To drastically limit the scope of countertransference definition is too simplistic and is probably a carryover of the negative connotation countertransference has had. But with all the problems of comprehending its origins and manifestations, we can understand those who would make things simpler by a limited definition; however, we cannot join them. The therapist is both responsive to the patient and comes into the clinical situation with responses "set to go," that is, there are unconscious images of the patient independent of the patient. Either kind of responses may be triggered during the course of therapy, separately or in some kind of combination, and it is useful to distinguish what comes initially from the patient (as projection) and what comes from the therapist in response to the patient; and what comes as a response from the therapist's own inner, irrational attitudes; and what comes as a response to the patient and the therapist's own inner irrational attitudes combined.

All manner of therapist-response is worthy of exploration and understanding and all could be classified as countertransference. Not that this means countertransference should be broadly defined and left at that. To the contrary, we are proposing a schema to both be inclusive of the possible responses, and give them some order.

One way to classify countertransference response is to think of it in terms of it being a "universal" response or a "particular" response. The universal response is simply the response *any* therapist would have to the patient, a response based on what the patient brings to the situation that would call out similar reactions from therapist to therapist.

Here it makes sense to think of such responses as the "homogeneous" aspects of countertransference (Giovacchini, 1972), having something to do with certain psychic mechanisms or operations evoking rather consistent, predictable responses from therapists of diverse personality structure and dynamics. Cohen (1952) would point to the "objective reality" of such circumstances, as would Singer (1980), noting that "countertransference interactions always have . . . 'objective' components" (p. 263); as does Armony's (1975) "syntaxic level" (borrowing from Sullivan's syntaxic mode of experience concept). Winnicott (1947), in a major break with classical definition of the time, speaks of the "objective countertransference" prompted by the patient, a response called out in anyone.

Here too would seem to fit Racker's (1953) "complementary identifications," those therapist reactions felt as one's own; those internal objects or dimensions of the patient that the patient cannot tolerate and so projects onto the therapist, whose objects or dimensions they then "become." (Sometimes there is a projection and they also originate in the therapist; then there would exist both *universal* and *particular responses*.) Searles' (1971/ 1979) concept of pathologic symbiosis referred to many times in this book contains projective dimensions.

Grinberg (1979) describes "projective counter-identification," a term also to be classified as a universal response. There, the therapist's reaction is "independent of his own conflicts and corresponds in a predominant or exclusive way to the intensity and quality of the patient's projective identification" (p. 234). The universal response, then, originates with the patient as opposed to the therapist, and in one way or another is a reflection of or response to the patient's internalized objects and patterns of relating.

On the other side, there is the "particular response," that therapist response which is idiosyncratic. Such a response is peculiar to a particular therapist, with particular personality features and problems called out in response to the patient. They are, in effect, the reactions or features that the therapist (as opposed to the patient) brings to the situation although they may be called out by the patient. Racker's (1953) "concordant identifications," the reliving of the therapist's problems and processes stimulated by the patient, fit in this category. Too, Racker's (1953) "complementary countertransference" reaction would be classified as a particular response in that it is a patient-induced activation of the therapist's pre-existing neurotic elements to the point that the patient comes to stand for the therapist's internalized objects. The reaction, in other words, would not be likely to occur without the conflict that the therapist brings to the situation.

Also in the category of particular response would fall the "subjective countertransference" described by Spotnitz (1979), and the "fantasy world" reaction of Cohen (1952), based on the unresolved neurotic problems of the therapist, and Armony's (1975) "parataxic level," a fantasy-tinged kind of reality he describes, again borrowing from Sullivan.

Probably one of the best examples of the universal and the particular countertransference responses is a bit extreme, but it should clarify the distinction. It seems that nothing in particular had happened during the session to explain the therapist's fantasy, but it occurred to her that she suddenly pictured this particular patient, who was mildly talking to her across the room, as shouting. It was one of those flash impressions, those clear images that sometimes came to her but that she could not link to any conscious observation of the patient or the content or theme at the moment or in the recent past. Nevertheless, the impression was there.

At once the patient proceeded to tell this story. As a child, she was at a friend's house for lunch when with only a moment's warning she threw up on the table, neatly though, right in her own place, next to her friend's mother. Obviously annoyed but appropriately concerned, the mother was solicitous, inquiring as to what was wrong, how she felt, and the like. The patient remembered feeling fine after the event. "It was like a big liquid burp and I had a sense of relief," she said, "not at all sick or anything." In fact, she went on to recall that even at the time, she felt sort of casual about the whole thing. And even back then, it ran through her mind that she hated this child's mother while she coolly watched the mother help clean up the mess, though she made no direct association between the hatred and the vomiting. The therapist responded with what could mildly be termed preoccupation. She worried that the patient was angry at her and would proceed to "show her." She wanted the patient to sit away from her fine rug and maybe even in a wooden desk chair instead of curled up in the big stuffed chair the patient always sat in. And on and on.

It so happens that his therapist was, as a child, a frequent vomiter. Starting out as a sign of what today would be called separation anxiety, the anxiety and vomiting came to be used as an expression of defiance and anger as well as anxiety. The point is that behind the therapist's obsessional focus, this therapist, reminded of herself, was reacting to the patient as a reflection of herself, and did not want further reminders. Surely her response would be a *particular countertransference* response.

The probability is that most therapists would not welcome vomiting in their presence; thus one might expect the unwelcome response to be in the *universal countertansference* category. The distaste would not be an exceptional response, but it would be an expected response. Moreover, the likelihood is strong that the distaste is a reflection of the patient's internalized other's distaste. Such an occurrence is not pleasant, it is a mess, and even the most determined of chronic helpers might feel pushed too far.

Anybody might react with distaste and annoyance. However, had the therapist not come to the situation predisposed to the identification she would not have reacted so automatically and so strongly, and she even may not have been so in touch with the patient in those moments before the patient told the story. Certainly too, the therapist's dynamics would have at least a measure of influence in calling out the patient's content, though obviously the patient comes with it to the therapy situation.

As a final consideration we want to comment on the views of Reich (1951, 1960), who has no truck with countertransference as a useful guide or tool in the therapeutic process, seeing the "problem" as a failure in identifying with and then detaching from the patient, substituting instead one's own feelings for the patient's. Although she sees countertransference as an inevitable event she sees it as an interference from which therapists must refrain, an emotional response that does not belong in therapy, an indulgence if you will. She holds a classical position more classical than Freud's, that countertransference is a pathological, never useful reaction, of which to rid oneself. It is certainly hard to know how a therapist could do that in a vacuum. She seems to infer that if countertransference exists, the therapist will absolutely and unremittingly lose control of his or her impulses, acting them out all over the place, never to stop. Rather, she says, better to stay uninvolved; or involved in a severely limited way; as if that were always possible or useful. She would suggest a black or white situation where countertransference either runs amuck or is eliminated, never to be observed, understood, and utilized in the therapeutic process and for the therapeutic good. Obviously, we disagree, and we think seeing countertransference in the context of a human normative process such as fantasy provides a useful rationale for our opinion.

Fantasy Function

Conceptualizing countertransference as part of the more general fantasy experience broadens its scope. To our mind, countertransference can be seen in a fantasy context because it involves an interaction of affective process states and information processing elements, which certainly is one way of considering fantasy (Singer, 1974). Fantasy starts out in childhood as an attempt to process information, to make sense of experience; and in adulthood it continues to serve that function if in a partially more sophisticated way. In therapy, the therapist's countertransference response may determine the content of the fantasy; it provides the substance for the fantasy. In therapy, the therapist's fantasy can serve to help make sense out of that which the patient cannot articulate, to process incoming and existing interpersonal and intrapersonal information perhaps unconsciously communicated through empathy, or information communicated in an obscure way. On the other hand, because of the therapist's possible distortion of incoming and existing data, especially in the affective sphere, the information processing may go awry so there is little correlation between what the patient has "communicated" and what the therapist has received. Consequently, the therapist's fantasy would rely more on memory and less on incoming data were that the case. Since long term memory has a function in fantasy (Singer, 1974), and certain affects are linked with certain percepts, there is always the likelihood of the muddying of the current situation with past reflections. Therefore, one has reason to expect that countertransference is inevitable.

The susceptibility to fantasy varies from therapist to therapist and may depend on the match between patient and therapist (Armony, 1975). Besides, regardless of cognitive styles of storage and retrieval of thought (Broadbent, 1958), or how the fantasy would be classified, therapists have at their disposal their own material to tap. Content of fantasy may be the inner expression of business at hand, or as Singer (1975) puts it, "the unfinished business of our daily lives and, more broadly, the unfinished business of our hierarchies of motives and broader fantasy structures" (p. 219).

Although some countertransference always occurs its existence does not always make itself known to the therapist, for fantasy in any of its forms may be unconscious. Sometimes, the countertransference is not identified but its fantasy "housing" is conscious; sometimes the countertransference reaction and its manifestation through fantasy are both consciously recognized; sometimes neither the countertransference nor the fantasy is recognized as occurring, as in the therapist first described in this chapter.

The noteworthy thing is that fantasy and its countertransferential content exist, even if unknown to the therapist. Conscious or unconscious, the reactive content can influence the interaction and ultimately be "known" to the patient, if not the therapist. Although it should seem unlikely, sometimes therapists and patients are totally inattentive to their unconscious processes and their behavioral derivatives, as in the therapist-patient described earlier. Such a situation is worth remedying, for it is through conscious attention to images, to associations, to fantasy, to dreams (which can be seen as extensions of wakeful fantasy) that therapists can better understand their reactions, inordinate or otherwise (Angel, 1979). Furthermore, this activity not only helps the therapist directly, it enables the therapeutic work in the unfolding of new dimensions of the patient's personality heretofore not experienced (Eigin, 1979).

The viewpoint of Singer (1975) on fantasy as behavior certainly holds for therapists: "Fantasy or daydreaming is perhaps best viewed simply as a kind of capacity or skill in us that is part of our overall repertory of behavior" (p. 1 1 6). However, although we suggest that the therapist focus attention on his or her fantasy we are not advocating the use of mental imagery techniques for the therapist in private, or with the patient, regarding the therapist's fantasy.

Unlike those who may use mental imagery techniques to "establish positive affects" or for "role rehearsal" or for "advanced planning" (Singer, 1974), we advocate tuning in to inner process as a method for becoming more aware of the complexity of relating. Since fantasies therapists have may be seen as clues to their countertransferential experiences, our focus is on understanding the countertransference through the fantasy, rather than on using the formal enactment of a fantasy as part of the format of therapy as might be expected in certain kinds of therapy such as transactional analysis (Berne, 1964), or gestalt (Perls, 1972), or psychodrama (Moreno, 1947), or in behavior modification techniques (Wolpe, 1969), or in the European use of imagery techniques originally influenced by Jung (1968).

However, some of the results of using fantasy as a tool for understanding the interpersonal process and the intrapersonal selves of the relating therapist and patient are similar to those occurring when mental imagery techniques are used. Attending to imagery and its context of occurrence can assist therapists in using the imagery as a clue as to what is happening inside the self and the patient. Moreover, it can be a clue as to an emotional response, not for control of the imagery or affective reactions as would be done with mental imagery techniques, but more in the original Freudian sense as a representation of emotional "activity" to understand and work with.

Sullivan (1953) and Singer (1974), from different vantage points, point out that through development, particularly when school attendance starts, people are called on to filter out or to ignore or inattend "private" or fantasy experience in order to get on with business. In one way, this can be a problem in that at times of less vigilance, awareness of fantasy can be startling and frightening. In therapists, the problem can be far-reaching because of the many external stimuli (from the patient) touching off private, internal processes in the therapist. The private material is touched off whether or not the therapist is aware of the process or the content, and in any event, the therapist's behavior is affected. The more tuned-in to the process and to the content of inner response, the more he or she is in a position to make sense of the current interpersonal experience.

Central to our view that the state of the therapist's fantasy is important in psychotherapeutic work is the following theoretical position on perception and imagery set forth by Singer (1974). He says that, "Perception and imagery both are part of a general process of representation of experience" (p. 200) involving: (1) anticipation of new situations; (2) filtering of external information; (3) coding incoming material or "reports" from long-term memory and assigning it to retrieval programs; (4) attributing various meanings or causes to experiences as they occur. And to these we add (5) discriminating between old and new information, for this is the dimension where we think therapists may particularly get into trouble, for it is this relation that comes into play in countertransference. It becomes clear that while in daily life primary and secondary processes are necessary for effective thought (Neisser, 1967), in doing therapy, the strength of the therapist lies in an ability to harness his or her "internal information," the inner, primitive life for use in combination with secondary process (Rouslin, 1975). In creative activity, which in many respects psychotherapy is, there must be integrative control of the primary process, a special use of primary process (Suler, 1980). Making sense of interpersonal experience is not the exclusive territory of the psychotherapist, though it is certainly an active responsibility. The task actually begins in childhood, through play (Groos, 1901; Winnicott, 1971). Through play, a child learns tactics and techniques for how to get along in the world. And one cannot talk about play without considering that fantasy helps make sense out of the world, that fantasy provides the roles and experiences to be played. Fantasy, then, can be seen as central to future experience, to future life.

Although the classical psychoanalytic viewpoint holds that the origin of fantasy and play is in the need for a tool for dealing with instinctual drive versus reality demands, another viewpoint (Singer, 1975) suggests that play and fantasy games represent attempted solutions and manifestations of the various developmental orientations or levels of the child. The wish-fulfillment function or catharsis function, stressing a primary process orientation, would seem to us to be only part of the story, as would Singer's view, stressing primarily secondary process orientation. Piaget (1962) however, seems to contain both primary and secondary process orientations. He suggests that fantasy is more than a method of discharging the energy from conflict. It represents an attempt to accommodate to the environment, to understand and to internalize through systematic memory operations the external environment. There are then, implicit (at least by our reading) pre-existing internal processes that somehow need re-orientation, there are external events, and the secondary process is developed to deal with and make sense of the external world. In other words, we believe he implies that fantasy activity is a kind of bridge between primary and secondary processes, representing both states.

According to Singer (1975), "results do not support the notion of a drive-reducing function of fantasy, at least on the basis of projective techniques" (p. 111). He thinks that fantasy has a broader role "as a general response possibility," not simply as a replacement for emotional expressiveness. To us it would seem that projective techniques don't tell the whole story, and too, Singer's viewpoint seems limited, especially when trying to understand countertransference response in terms of fantasy.

From our clinical observation we would conclude that for the therapist fantasy has multiple, related functions:

1. Drive reduction
2. It is a defense against emotional expression while it is representative of unconscious emotional experience
3. It is both a healthy and pathologic way to process or make sense of interpersonal events, particularly the affective dimension of interpersonal events.

It is when fantasy is used primarily for indiscriminate drive reduction, or as a defense against awareness of emotional experience and expression by the therapist, that fantasy becomes a pathologic vehicle for dealing with interpersonal events. It is then that problematic countertransference reactions implicit in the fantasy response impede rather than facilitate relatedness and treatment.

Therapists' Shared Fantasy

In the broad perspective, the "rescue fantasy" feature shared by so many therapists does little to foster therapy. Indeed, unchecked, that kind of "assistance" is but an expression of the therapist's needs (as discussed in Chapter V). Surely there is a place for therapists to progress from seeing patients as extensions of themselves or their internalized parents or the internalized relationship pattern of themselves and their parents. Hardy (1979) assures therapists: "When we advance from our earlier zeal to the cooler stance of the seasoned professional . . . we can let go of our past . . ." (p. 78), at least in terms of unconsciously and compulsively needing to use the rescue fantasy as an expression of our own needs. This kind of countertransference expression can be seen as a lack in the ability to discriminate between old and new experience, what Armony (1975) might call a kind of "parataxic level" fantasy.

As Singer (1975) says, "Most people in the course of the many daydreams they generate are piecing together complex clusters of fantasy that become in effect their view of what 'real' and 'ideal' human relationships are and ought to be. These longstanding fantasies become the basis for our hopes and expectations. To the extent that they are grossly distorted because our own childhood experience was necessarily limited in scope to a particular family in a particular cultural milieu, we experience painful disappointments and social confusion" (p. 200). And if the therapist is like "most people" the trouble goes beyond disappointment and social confusion, impeding the patient's development and so, the therapist is not really being as therapeutic as he or she might like to believe. Neither patient nor therapist can truly fit into a given "model" of helper or helpee, though they try.

Just as there is a "love-hate polarity" in the transference (Arlow and Brenner, 1964) there exists the same polarity in countertransference. Each may stand on its own or be a defense against the other. These features operate in life and in therapy as part of life (Strean, 1979). Therapists who are encumbered by their need to help, by their fantasy as an omnipotent rescuer, actually collude with the patient in his or her wish to have only the good, loving therapist, an all-need-meeting therapist. Such collusion aids and abets the continuance of fantasy-as-reality and reality-as-fantasy in both patient and therapist. Moreover, it interferes with the emergence of hateful fantasies representing dimensions of the therapist and the patient, transferentially (Oremland and Blacker, 1975) and nontransferentially, and countertransferentially. Consequentiy, there is diminished and distorted perception, offering little chance of integration of the good and the bad dimensions of the object and the relationship, an important developmental and therapeutic phenomenon.

Regarding patients, Corwin (1972) has talked about the "narcissistic alliance," a term he attributes to Mehlman. This phenomenon, he says, is seen as an unconscious alliance whereby the patient seeks to gain an unrealistic position through association with the therapist, a kind of magical way of overcoming limitations; a kind of fantasy as to where the patient will end up through the alliance with the therapist. In our opinion, this kind of alliance is ofttimes sought by therapists as well as patients, to the detriment of both. Its very essence spells the eventual demise of an effective therapist-patient relationship, if it can ever begin, for the "fantastic" qualities inherent in the narcissistic alliance are inimical to the qualities we see comprising the therapist-patient alliance as discussed in Chapter VI.

However, it is our observation that narcissistic alliances are often seen as desirable by the mental health caretakers. Here is a case in point. A narcissistic alliance was what the junior professional staff on a psychiatric unit seemed to want, and unfortunately, the senior supervising staff never identified the situation as problematic.

It happened that one night, a patient who heretofore in her week of hospitalization had shown no psychotic symptoms, had a fierce psychotic episode. She just about broke up the unit dayroom and anyone in it. Predictably, patients and staff were terribly upset, in the interest of the patient and themselves. So in the morning, the staff planned a meeting with the patients, ostensibly to offer them an opportunity to talk about their distress at what had happened. Instead, there was a diabolical turn of events, a hidden agenda. Quickly it became clear that the staff apparently had decided beforehand that another patient or patients had somehow gotten hold of some kind of drug which was then given to the patient they never suspected of being psychotic; and the staff wanted to find the culprits.

The "presentation" by the staff (and it can *only* be called that) bristled with not-quite-spoken accusation in the guise of the helpfulness of explaining, repeatedly, why drugs need to be prescribed. In such an emotional context the staff expected the patients to feel free in discussing their observations of what had happened and their reactions to the patient. When the patients did not speak, some were called on by staff who seemed to be putting words in their mouths, almost insuring that no other patients would talk. But the staff relentlessly proceeded while the patients sank deeper into silence. The despairing tone of the silent patients was leavened only by the acrid, ironic inquiry of one patient who put into words what others were thinking: "Are you crazy enough to think that we would tell you doctors what we feel or if we know anything when you got your minds made up anyway?"

In essence, the patients had caught on that the staff wanted to trap somebody, but more than that, that the staff wanted to engage them in a narcissistic alliance whereby the staff would be seen in the omnipotent position in which they felt comfortable. That way, the staff could confirm that indeed, they had not missed the boat with the now clinically psychotic patient and moreover, it was not through their treatment that the patient had become psychotic. Rather, it was the fault of the patients; and it was the need of the staff to maintain their fantasy of themselves as all-knowing, omniscient clinicians at the expense of the patients, that the patients sensed. The staff clung to their idealized concept of "professional" at the expense of objective reality and the patients. The patients would have nothing of the narcissistic alliance needed to help the staff maintain their fantasy, so the staff had a bit of trouble indiscriminately discharging their anxiety by foisting the fantasy on the patients. But only the one patient could articulate their position in any way.

Like frightened captives, the patients weren't very good at expressing their thoughts, or wouldn't take the risk in this mixed message environment even though *their* perception was not faulty. Like frightened captives their immediate innermost frustrations could not be exposed in front of their accusers. And like some frightened captives, they were being blamed for problems they did not create, and asked to join in others that would be created. Yet it did not consciously occur to the staff that the patients may have had no hand in the event, just as it did not unconsciously occur to them that they, the staff, may have had no hand in what happened, nor were they necessarily at fault for not predicting it.

Clearly, this was an example of shared countertransference response where the narcissistic fantasy of omnipotent, omniscient caretaker is used indiscriminately for drive reduction, that is to reduce the anxiety related to a situation being out of control. Further, fantasy was used as a defense against the awareness of the experience and expression of the anxiety; and the attached narcissism of the staff was threatened. What could be seen as the failure of the fantasy was blamed on the patients, the fantasy thereby becoming a highly pathologic vehicle for dealing with interpersonal events.

Patients in such situations are realistically helpless figures, victims who the staff try to use for their own narcissistic purposes. Staff in such situations are ambivalent figures, both helpless victims of their unconscious needs and processes and persons given a chance to create themselves anew. The appropriate use of the fantasy would have involved recognition of the need for it, and the recreation of self-images so threatened as to have to engage in such distortions.

FINAL NOTES

In conclusion, the therapist's fantasy and its countertransferential underpinnings is not something about which to cheer or groan, even after reading our examples. It is. Hopefully, it will be attended to and tended to so that its potential as a "scientific instrument" (Searles, 1975) can be realized, not as a tool for narcissistic gratification or a weapon for narcissistic acting out, but as a vehicle for helping patients. Therapy outcome, while certainly determined by patient characteristics, is also a function of how well equipped the therapist is to deal with the patient's characteristics, transference reactions and all (Strupp, 1980). Even if countertransference were always positive, it is now clear (Strupp, 1980) that empathy, warmth, and unconditional positive regard are not enough. The therapist must contribute more than that.

We have tried in this chapter to demonstrate that the therapist's fantasy operations affect not only the patient but the therapist. These operations affect not only direct clinical practice, but certainly have a place in how the therapist sees his or her practice. This becomes abundantly clear when a therapist enters private practice as the major, if not exclusive, income producing source. Often, the pragmatics of the move take on significance beyond their explicit meaning because there appear to be developmental issues of separation-individuation that come up for review as the therapist enters this new developmental era of professional life.

In the next chapter we will explore the pragmatics and psychodynamics of private practice in its developmental context. In the process, we hope some light will be shed on the anxiety, aggression, guilt, and accountability issues that may face therapists entering private practice (and giving their narcissism a new threat, or hope).

REFERENCES

Angel, E. The resolution of a countertransference through a dream of the analyst. *The Psychoanalytic Review* (1979) **66**:9–18.

Arlow, J. and Brenner, C. *Psychoanalytic concepts and the structural theory* (New York: International Universities Press, 1964).

Armony, N. Countertransference: Obstacle and instrument. *Contemporary Psychoanalysis* (1975) **11**:265–281.

Berne, E. *Games people play* (New York: Grove Press, 1964).

Broadbent, D. E. *Perception and communication* (New York: Pergamon Press, 1958).

Cohen, M. B. Countertransference and anxiety. *Psychiatry* (1952) **15**:231–243.

Corwin, H. A. The scope of therapeutic confrontation from routine to heroic. *International Journal of Psychoanalytic Psychotherapy* (1972) **1**:68–89.

Ehrenberg, D. B. The quest for intimate relatedness. *Contemporary Psychoanalysis* (1975) **11**:320–331.

Eigen, M. Female sexual responsiveness and the therapist's feelings. *The Psychoanalytic Review* (1979) **66**:3–8.

Epstein, L. and Feiner, A. H. (Eds.). *Countertransference: The therapist's contribution to the therapeutic situation* (New York: Jason Aronson, 1979). (a)

Epstein, L., and Feiner, A. H. Countertransference: The therapist's contribution to treatment. *Contemporary Psychoanalysis* (1979) **15**:489–513. (b)

Firestein, S. K. *Termination in psychoanalysis* (New York: International Universities Press, 1978).

Freud, S. The future prospects of psychoanalytic therapy. In *The complete psychological works of Sigmund Freud*, Vol. 11 (London: Hogarth Press, 1964) (Originally published, 1910).

Freud, S. Recommendations for physicians practicing psychoanalysis. In *The complete psychological works of Sigmund Freud* (London: Hogarth Press, 1964) (Originally published, 1912).

Giovacchini, P. L. Alienation: Character neuroses and narcissistic disorders. *International Journal of Psychoanalytic Psychotherapy* (1977) **6**:288–314.

Glover, E. *Technique of psychoanalysis* (New York: International Universities Press, 1955).

Grinberg, L. Countertransference and projective counteridentification. *Contemporary Psychoanalysis* (1979) **15**:226–247.

Groos, K. *The play of man.* (New York: Appleton-Century-Crofts, 1901).

Hardy, A. G. Rescue vs. contract in defining therapist growth. *The Psychoanalytic Review* (1979) **66**:69–78.

Heinmann, P. On countertransference. *International Journal of Psycho-Analysis* (1950) **31**:81–84.

Jung, C. *Man and his symbols* (New York: Dell, 1968).

Kernberg, O. Notes on countertransference. *Journal of the American Psychoanalytic Association* (1965) **13**:38–57.

Langs, R. *The therapeutic interaction*, Vol. 2 (New York: Jason Aronson, 1976).

Little, M. Countertransference and the patient's response to it. *International Journal of Psycho-Analysis* (1951) **33**:32–40.

Moreno, J. *The theater to spontaneity* (Beacon, New York: Beacon House, 1947).

Neisser, V. *Cognitive Psychology* (New York: Appleton-Century-Crofts, 1967).

Perls, F. *In and out of the garbage pail* (New York: Bantam Books, 1972).

Piaget J. *Play, dreams, and imitation in childhood* (New York: W. W. Norton, 1962).

Racker, H. Contribution to the problem of countertransference. *International Journal of Psycho-Analysis* (1953) **34**:313–324.

Reich, A. Further remarks on countertransference. *International Journal of Psycho-Analysis* (1960) **41**:389–395.

Reich, A. On countertransference. *International Journal of Psycho-Analysis* (1951) **32**:25–31.

Rouslin, S. Commentary on the primitive mind of childhood. *Perspectives in Psychiatric Care* (1975) **13**(1):9.

Searles, H. F. Countertransference and theoretical model. In J. G. Gunderson and L. R. Mosher (Eds.), *Psychotherapy of Schizophrenia* (New York: Jason Aronson, 1975).

Searles, H. F. The development of mature hope in the patient-therapist relationship. In *Countertransference and related subjects* (New York: International Universities Press, 1979) (Originally published, 1977).

Searles, H. F. Pathologic symbiosis and autism. In H. F. Searles (Ed.), *Countertransference and related subjects* (New York: International Universities Press, 1979) (Originally published, 1971).

Searles H. F. Psychoanalytic therapy with the borderline adult. In J. Masterson (Ed.), *New perspectives on psychotherapy with the borderline adult* (New York: Brunner/Mazel, 1978).

Searles, H. F. The schizophrenic's vulnerability to the therapist's unconscious processes. *Journal of Nervous and Mental Diseases* (1958) **127**:247–262.

Segal, H. Countertransference. *International Journal of Psychoanalytic Psychotherapy* (1977) **6**:31–37.

Singer, E. The opiate of the analyst. *Contemporary Psychoanalysis* (1980) **16**:258–267.

Singer, J. L. *Imagery and daydream methods in psychotherapy and behavior modification* (New York: Academic Press, 1974).

Singer, J. L. *The inner world of daydreaming* (New York: Harper and Row, 1975).

Spotnitz, H. Narcissistic countertransference. *Contemporary Psychoanalysis* (1979) **15**:545–559.

Strean, H. S. The unánalyzed "positive transference" and the need for reanalysis. *The Psychoanalytic Review* (1979) **66**:493–506.

Strupp, H. H. Success and failure in time-limited psychotherapy. *Archives of General Psychiatry* (1980) **37**:831–841.

Suler, J. K. Primary process thinking and creativity. *Psychological Bulletin* (1980) **88**:144–165.

Sullivan, H. S. *Conceptions of modern psychiatry* (New York: W. W. Norton, 1953).

Winnicott, D. W. Hate in the countertransference. *International Journal of Psycho-Analysis* (1947) **30**:102–110.

Winnicott, D. W. *Playing and reality* (New York: Basic Books, 1971).

Wolpe, J. *The practice of behavior therapy* (New York: Pergamon Press, 1969).

IX

At Issue: The Psychodynamics of Entering Private Practice

INTRODUCTION

Although the concept of private practice in psychotherapy could be addressed as an interdisciplinary or intradisciplinary issue, or as an economic and sociological issue within society, we intend in this chapter to explore entering private practice principally as a psychodynamic issue. The reason for our focus is because we believe the personal, intrapsychic aspects of being a private practitioner are very important, yet have been relatively neglected. Considerable attention has been devoted to the subject of private practice (Geller, 1980; Goldman and Stricker, 1971; Kramer, 1970; Lewin, 1978; Pressman, 1979; Shimberg, 1979), but the emphasis has been on the pragmatics of developing and maintaining a practice. Although we do talk about certain practical matters in entering private practice we do so selectively, using those examples we find best illustrate the psychodynamic experience and so are most often troubling for therapists. Thus, at times, we elaborate on the psychodynamics at work through certain "pragmatics" of private practice.

Upon entering private practice the time seems appropriate, and the need great, to understand the meaning private practice has in the development of the therapist and in the development of a psychotherapy profession itself. Here we are talking about private practice as either *the* major or a major component of one's time and income. It is then, when the therapist is "dependent" on the practice that certain psychological phenomena most clearly manifest themselves. Consequently, since it is then that the emotional impact is so great it would seem very useful to look closely at private practice from a psychodynamic perspective. Doing so helps provide a backdrop for understanding why strong emotion and emotionality are engendered about such practice within the individual and within the mental health professional groups.

The relevance of the broad concept of narcissism and its component concept of symbiosis and the movement toward separation-individuation combine to demonstrate once again how the therapist's narcissism emerges in entering private practice. In making the move into private practice it is our contention that the therapist is called on to both break the personal and the professional symbiotic bonds, and to utilize them for there to be professional developmental growth. As a result, we discern that the move into private practice is usually far from a comfortable one, despite overt longings for the values therapists believe it holds for them. For example, many therapists look forward and work toward the day when they can "be their own persons." With the sense of autonomy, however, may come feelings of aloneness and emptiness that exert emotional pressure on the therapist beyond the mundane task of making a living. Indeed, the state of the therapist's emotional life may well determine how well he or she negotiates entrance into and sustenance of private practice; and how the therapist sets about dealing with the pragmatics or "business" of the practice such as setting and collecting fees, setting up an office, getting insurance, seeking referrals, and doing in general what many therapists don't like to think of as the everyday task of making a business work.

A DEVELOPMENTAL APPROACH

Since separation-individuation is considered a process actually occurring over a lifetime (Mahler, Pine, and Bergman, 1975), at each point of movement toward independence a person's central issues regarding the original central object relationship of early life re-emerge. The psychodynamics involved in entering private practice seem to be manifested on two levels. One has to do with the nature of the historical symbiotic bond, that is, the parent-child bond. The other concerns the nature of the adult professional symbiotic bond, that is, the bond between the therapist and his or her particular "parent" professional group. The developmental bond affects how one perceives (and perhaps even chose) the professional group and bond, and also determines how well a therapist can utilize the professional group bond to aid individuation. In addition, the professional group in itself, just as the parent from developmental symbiosis days, may either wittingly or unwittingly foster a continuance of symbiosis, or assist the therapist in the process of separation-individuation. It is within the context of these levels that we consider the entry of the therapist into private practice. In particular, we will concern ourselves with the therapist's anxiety, aggression, guilt, and accountability.

In one respect, we think of entering private practice as an evolutionary era in adult and professional development. In another, we see it as a time when internalized developmental phenomena emerge to impinge on, inhibit, or facilitate development through this "new" era. Thus, in childhood (Hartmann, 1958) there is a drive toward autonomy independent of conflict; and in the estimation of some (Colarusso and Nemiroff, 1979) it continues into adulthood despite impairments. As Colarusso and Nemiroff write, "To be sure, the degree of psychopathology or health that the individual brings to adulthood influences both the environment he chooses to live in and his response to it; but in either event the continued evolution of psychic structure—that is the life long development of ego, superego and id—are strongly influenced by that environment" (p. 61).

Consequently, our view of entering private practice as a developmental phenomenon is not without precedent, at least in terms of psychoanalytic theory of adult development. Primary autonomy (Hartmann, 1958), that is, the development of certain ego functions independent of core conflict, introduced the notion that there was indeed a "developmental psychology" distinct from yet working simultaneously with conflict-based ego development. We think that such a distinction is not always so clear-cut and may be an artificial distinction for the sake of conceptualization. Nevertheless, there are certainly two soures for ego development and we see each as both independent and affecting the other.

Theorists have been interested in adult development and adult developmental phases for some time now, both with the idea that adult experiences foster psychic growth (Benedek, 1950) and that certain themes emerge throughout the life cycle (Parens, 1975; Rangell, 1953). We have been particularly interested to see in the literature of the last decade (Marcus, 1973; Winestine, 1973) a meaningful focus on how separation-individuation issues arise repeatedly throughout life. Although Sullivan did not speak in the now popular ego psychology terms about the subject of development, he did make a strong point throughout his work that with each developmental era there was anxiety at a kind of psychic disruption, resulting in a renewed opportunity for revision, all the better to put together the pieces again. We see entering private practice as such a growth producing opportunity.

Anxiety and Aggression

Our supervisory and clinical experience and our own entrances into private practice have convinced us that at no other time in professional life is the therapist more vulnerable in so many areas, simultaneously, than when he or she enters private practice. If Kestenberg and Buelte (1977) were writing about the experience they would say in effect that the therapist, like the infant, would be concerned with "holding-oneself-up." Indeed, that is a necessary psychological and behavioral task in entering private practice, for it quickly becomes clear that no one else will. While being your own person (Shimberg, 1979) has rewards, this "aloneness" also generates anxiety that has its genesis in the therapist's early life holding-environment and its later possible replication in the professional holding-environment. Where the therapist's developmental symbiotic experience features parental needs and demands as opposed to the child's needs and demands, therapists seem to have more than considerable anxiety in entering private practice. The lack of empathy of the parent in tuning into the child and adjusting responses accordingly would not have provided the now adult therapist with healthy experience in the capacity to be alone in the presence of another (Winnicott, 1958/1974). This experience after all is predicated on an experience with an empathic, reliable, trustworthy mother. Consequently, the aloneness of private practice truly could be experienced as the absence of a nurturing object or the memory of one. The conscious or unconscious memory of such a person could produce a sense of emptiness instead of sustenance within. It is not unusual that at this time of need, at a kind of personal-professional going-it-alone, a resurgence of unresolved symbiotic-related symptoms can be expected. Also to be expected is that when any physical symptoms abate, the anxiety becomes prominent.

We relate something one of us experienced on first entering private practice: During this particular period there was a repetitive dream reminiscent of the "infinite falling" dream Winnicott (1957/1974) discusses as implying early holding failure which later can be said (Kestenberg and Buelte, 1977) to be linked with failure in "holding-oneself-up." This was the dream scenario: The dreamer was trying to get into a house. The house belonged to her, or so it seemed, but she realized it was a bigger, nicer house than her childhood family house—one more like she would like to own now or to have had then. Anyhow, she could never quite get all the way down the path and into the entrance because somewhere along the way she would trip over milk bottles—some empty, some filled—and then she would wake with alarm to the sound of bottles breaking, the image of milk spilling, and the feeling either of almost falling or almost standing up, a dinstinction which was perplexing.

This seems almost the perfect private practice entry dream, with the ingredients at the childhood yet adult setting; its nurturing symbols implying need and past or internalized failure; its pathway and entrance; its aggression and thwarting of aggression to get down the pathway; its healthy aggression and defensive aggression through dissatisfaction with the old "home" and nurturing; and the reluctance to use the healthy aggression yet the desire to move beyond the family to "enter one's own home."

The problem in entering private practice is not so much that anxiety exists, for it almost certainly will, no matter how healthy the therapist. There is always some pathological symbiotic residual and besides, entry into a new phase of development brings with it some modicum of uncertainty even when the therapist is ready, willing, and able. Rather, the point is that entering private practice brings to the therapist's attention once again the "constant need to be aware of . . . forces in ourselves and . . . work" (Greben, 1975, p. 433) which influence the practical and creative aspects of being a therapist. Therefore, the problem is not *that* one experiences anxiety so much as it is *what one does* with the anxiety.

Perhaps such complexity is what Freud (1937/1964) had in mind when he called psychoanalysis an "impossible profession." As Greben (1975) says about the work of the therapist, "There is unlikely to be a task which could so completely exercise all of our faculties in the intellectual and emotional spheres" (p. 429). The task is always a bit elusive, "somewhere beyond the capacities," and is never perfected, but because of those qualities retains a freshness for the therapist. While we agree with Greben, it is usually only upon later reflection that the anxious, preoccupied, new private practitioner can see the situation so positively.

There is probably no way to circumvent the anxiety of entering private practice for it is anxiety provoking, and the therapist not experiencing it is probably in even deeper trouble than the therapist who does. Also, it is a developmental phenomenon calling on emotional resources from earlier developmental phenomena strained with unconscious anxiety. Although entering private practice usually comes only once in a professional career, the early life dynamics have been around a long time. Therefore, while they come to the fore in entering private practice, it may be only the beginning of their solution. Through the anxiety inherent in this experience the therapist has an opportunity to experience psychic disequilibrium and survive it and learn from it.

The dynamics within the therapist with this newly emerging identity recall the change in the mother-daughter bond Friedman (1980) describes in discussing the newly emerging identity of the daughter. We have often seen these dynamics reflected in "worries" directly expressed or inferred as to how the "mother," as in actual mother, mentor, professional group, insurance company, patient, and/or patient's family, will react to the therapist "acting" like a grown-up. Or, in the therapist's mind is there a new link with "mother?" And is maintaining a link with the past or internalized mother inimical to separation? Such questions are often first dealt with through the back door. For example, we have noticed that when some therapists enter private practice, they suddenly feel a strong professional group affiliation need where one had not before seemed to exist. Or, they suddenly feel the need for peer group communication about practice. These needs are of practical importance and seem to be purely rational and reasonable needs, which they are. But they are more than that.

To our mind, several things are going on at once. Of course there is conflict about separation, so the desire is strongly to do it, but to take the parent along (by means of parental approval and assistance). On the other hand, since symbiosis in a healthy "therapeutic" sense implies differentiation and free movement in and out of the other person's self system (Searles, 1971/1979), it is a necessary and useful part of life.

So the therapist's needs probably represent both problematic, conflict-laden and healthy dimensions of symbiosis. Such needs represent the need for a useful kind of symbiosis with one's own, where the therapist can emerge as his or her own person in a context of a common identity, yet one which allows for differences, allows in effect, for separation in the context of a relationship, much the way we conceptualized therapy of unlimited duration in Chapter VII. Obviously, the more problematic the original symbiotic bond, the more the therapist will "demand" from the professional group that which was not received during development, and in the process recreate the original frustration. Too, such therapists may be more inclined than is the "norm" to unconsciously demand from the patient the curative efforts toward the mother (Searles, 1975/1979) that these therapists may well have put forth with their own mothers. It is as if finally, without "agency" encumbrances in the new symbiotic context, they will fix it so they will get from the professional group, or from the patient, what they feel they have always deserved if not received. This "demand for caring," as we call it, differs from simple acknowledgment that the professional group or colleagues or patient may simply be good for the therapist, such as when Winnicott told Guntrip (1975) that Guntrip was good for him.

The demand quality infers the therapist's inordinate need to feel that he or she is *the* good therapist among all therapists or *the* good person in the patient's life experience. Marmor (1953) would see such an attitude as a possible hazard in being a therapist, a feeling of superiority as we see it designed to once again create the strivings and unequal relatedness of the original symbiotic bond, but this time with the child, now a therapist, in charge. Interestingly, often one's perception as *the* good therapist among all therapists obscures its narcissistic symbiotic base, and if carried off smoothly merely seems like therapeutic enthusiasm (Greenacre, 1966).

Such therapists find it hard too, to understand why either they don't seem to get along with or are shunned by their colleagues. Moreover, they have little awareness that their attitude is predicated on anxiety about separation. Anxiety about separation automatically implies anxiety about the direction in which one's aggression should move, namely, to maintain the symbiotic struggle or to move away from it. Think of the predicament of the therapist entering private practice. The therapist, feeling unemployed and anxious, has to act to some degree as if he or she is neither. The therapist probably wants to set up a prosperous looking office and not appear desperate for patients. The therapist has monetary investments to make in order to both become established and look established: announcements sent out to potential referral sources, a phone installed, an office to rent or be built or be made ready with furnishings. In a concrete sense, money is going out while none is coming in. And small business loans are not always easily forthcoming. Thus money is invested, by and large, in the self and in one's future with there being no actual economic indicators of whether the investment will pay off. How could a therapist not be anxious, especially an obsessionally inclined therapist? In addition, dynamically, the time is indeed a stressful one, for it is a time when the therapist's difficulties with aggression are prone to emerge. Looking at child development may help explain some of what happens to therapists during this period.

It is now generally agreed that one way aggression functions in human development is as a drive toward separation and independence. It is thus seen as a useful and necessary and productive activity. However, in pre-ego psychology days aggression had often been thought of as destructive, and it is still sometimes automatically referred to derisively. Perhaps it is conceived as destructive because "if aggression leading to [separation-]individuation is obstructed in its development, anger, rage, hostility and hate become intricately bound up with it, leading to distortion" (Rouslin, 1975, p. 170). And since everyone has had some thwarting of naturally occurring developmental aggression, the recall automatically can bring with it a resurgence of the rage, hatred, and hostility toward the parent-obstructors.

On the other hand, "healthy developmental aggression is destructive only in the sense that it is the primary force in the gradual dissolution of parent-child fusion and the symbiotic bond" (p. 171). Early on in developmental aggression there is thought to be (Rouslin, 1975) some anger associated with the separation even though it is the child who initiates the separation. Particularly if the mother responds favorably to the infant's cues, the symbiotic bond weakens. "Thus, through the rise of aggression whose end-product will mean separation and individuation, the infant frustrates his own desire for the mother to exist to serve him at the same time that he wants to break away from their union" (Rouslin, 1975, p. 171).

Just as at this point the infant starts the life-long task of managing his or her inner world or reality as it related to the external world or reality, so too the therapist entering private practice finds that how he or she wants or sees the private practice world to be is not necessarily what he or she gets, or the way it is out there in the big cruel world. If the therapist has internalized the kind of symbiotic bond described in Chapter V there will be incredible difficulty in separating from the internalized parental bond. Put pragmatically, the therapist will be unable to deal effectively with the external realities in the world of private practice. Instead, there will be a tendency to expect (a long wait) or demand (an angry, frustrating wait) that the world respond to the newly hung shingle because it is there; certainly a narcissistic stance. Yet this desire is not as uncommon as it might seem in its extreme form.

Often for years, therapists have to consciously fight the desire to do nothing to help keep their practices developing, to fight the desire for the magic nipple that will find them and nourish them. Such aggression that it takes in expecting or silently or vociferously demanding that kind of care-taking we view as "defensive aggression" (Rouslin, 1975). Defensive aggression then, can be seen as a drive toward maintaining the symbiotic bond, though persons manifesting it (particularly the vociferously demanding type) often appear quite independent. This type of aggression takes many forms, the ostensible "aggression" disguising the desire to maintain the symbiotic attachment, yet representing that attachment. For example, while the therapist may want to be on his or her own there may still be a desire to gain approval for the "separation" or receive accolades for the desire and for doing it and maybe even for a job well done, which is the equivalent of *needing* parental approval for leaving them, and a contradiction in emotional terms.

In any event, therapists' problems with their aggression have serious practical ramifications. After the announcements are sent, the lease negotiated, the office set up, and the phone installed, the therapist can neither just wait for, nor demand the first call. The wait may be interminable and the demand may be met with resistance from colleagues or potential patients sensing the unspoken demand and not wanting to be controlled.

Moreover, should therapists get over the hurdle of getting referrals, the problem may manifest itself more directly in working with patients. For instance, in setting and collecting fees the therapist may expect to earn a good deal but fail to charge a decent rate. This may be a reaction formation move, really wanting to overcharge, to be more than adequately nurtured. Or, it may represent a stubborn magical wish to be well cared for without having to ask the parent-patient. Either way it is a reflection of a problematic symbiotic bond.

Unfortunately, policy in hospitals and clinics, where most therapists start out, has contributed to the problem, thereby unwittingly helping maintain the therapist's symbiotic difficulties. Typically, therapists are not involved in fee setting nor in fee collection, which is unfortunate for both therapist and patient. Such an administrative clinical split reinforces the notion that somehow the therapist's salary is not related to the fee charged and collected, and is thus not related to the patient or the patient-therapist relationship. In those agencies that do involve the therapist in the fee area, the therapist may be uncomfortable initially, but both therapist and patient benefit from the integration of clinical and administrative dimensions of treatment because they are related. Thus, through clinically oriented administrative policy there can begin an erosion of the therapist's magical wishes so characteristic of the narcissistic position. In objective reality the other person *is* there, *is* separate. The patient is not simply the vehicle through which the therapist will have needs met automatically, and the patient is not there to be in the therapist's service.

There are also those therapists displaying signs of defensive aggression by becoming overinvolved in fee setting and collection. In other words, what might look like healthy aggression, or the "handling" of the fee situation, may in fact have a controlling or demand quality to it that goes beyond what is reasonable and rational. In such instances therapists may be too rigid about fees, or at least not matter-of-fact. Too, they may get into unending power struggles, nonverbally or verbally, with their patients. It then becomes clear that money is not the issue nearly so much as is the need to retain and relive the symbiotic struggle to get that which is "deserved." In such instances the therapist would sooner be tied to the patient through a negativistic stance or power struggling, thereby "obstructing [the development of] a relationship between two independent people, each of whom does not need a symbiotic partner" (Rouslin, 1975, p. 175), at least not a "therapeutic" one. In such instances the aim of the power struggle is to thwart the desire of the other person. To obstruct is of paramount importance, even at the expense of the more healthy but perhaps less stimulating gratification to be gained by "leaving the relationship alone" to develop without neurotic control. The fee then has become a neurotic vehicle.

Should such a therapist manage to get over the hurdle of fee setting and collection, he or she may then have difficulty in allowing the patient to move at his or her own pace, and direction, and time, issues addressed in earlier chapters. The therapist, in need of recapturing the symbiotic experience or defending against the experience, may consciously or unconsciously expect certain kinds of "progress," in certain ways, and in certain time frames. Probably, these expectations and demands would be rationalized, which would serve to obscure the irrational intent.

It is not that such things never occur in hospital or clinic practice. Rather, in private practice, with no "grants," and because of the therapist's rational, undisputed economic need for the patient, the psychological needs are propelled to the forefront. The therapist, therefore, may be more subject to, and vulnerable to intimidation. One might "demand" a certain fee arrangement because one "needs" a certain patient on the one hand, or one might respond to a patient's irrational pleas for a certain fee arrangement out of gratefulness or for fear of losing the patient. Although it is advised that therapists not compromise themselves over money (Shimberg, 1979), we think it is harder not to compromise oneself over emotional need.

Guilt

A word seems in order about guilt, which we have noticed that therapists sometimes feel when they enter private practice full-time or as a significant portion of their work. On one level, it would seem that the therapists have a social conscience, worrying that they are serving too few for too long for too much money; or that they should be paid simply for their time and knowledge; or that they should somehow pay a price for finally reaching this long sought after goal. In a previous chapter we considered such feelings as occupational difficulties, and explored some of the "guilt aspects," but there is more to be said.

It is not so much that these are irrelevant explanations but these are not sufficient in explaining the guilt a therapist in private practice may feel. We think something Winnicott (1950/1975) described about aggression in emotional development helps make the feeling of guilt more understandable. Apparently, sometime after the child has been able to discriminate between that which is "me" and that which is "not me" a certain amount of the "aggression appears clinically as . . . a feeling of grief and guilt . . ." (p. 206) and that the frustration the child experiences eases the guilt. Since to our mind the frustration is related to mixed feelings about separation-individuation or conflicting, mutually operating drives, it is little wonder the child experiences guilt, particularly about leaving the parent to go on one's own way. It seems clear that for those therapists still bound up with the symbiotic partner who needs them, entering private practice would indeed engender a good deal of guilt at this "unilateral move." The drive toward separation and independence that private practice stands for would indeed run counter to the parental bond and internalized parental drive to maintain the symbiotic bond.

We have noticed that the guilt often is expressed in roundabout ways, as for example, worrying about getting sued, which, theoretically, could happen in any kind of practice setting. An instance comes to mind of a therapist who had been in practice only a few months when he had to change the location of his office. The first one was on a well-lighted, bustling street where he felt fairly comfortable about letting a particular 10–year-old boy wait alone for his father to pick him up after the session. The new office, however, was in a more residential, not so well-lighted, not so bustling street.

On the child's eleventh birthday he had a therapy session, the first in the new office. When the boy was about to leave the therapist became terribly anxious at the thought of his being alone on the dimly lighted quiet street and said maybe he should wait inside, something the child really disliked doing. The child proceeded to lecture the therapist as to how he, the boy, was after all now grown up and could take care of himself. He also stated that after all these years together the therapist should know that, and then the therapist acknowledged that the boy was right and that the therapist was acting a little crazy.

Off went the boy and up went the therapist's anxiety. The anxiety turned to worries that the boy's father, an Orthodox priest, would be furious with the therapist, for whom he had many times expressed dislike; and worries that harm would come to either the child or him, which one he couldn't be sure. Further, he worried that the father would sue the therapist if something happened to the child "out there on the street"; and he worried that his insurance coverage was not adequate. Later, upon reflection after unrelenting rumination, there was also an intermittent but noticeable sense of guilt that the therapist kept associating with having done something in relation to the child's father.

There are many ways this therapist's reaction can be construed. Certainly there are "intervention" risks in psychotherapy practice that one must take and those are never wholly comfortable. In private practice there is no administrative hierarchy or agency to buffer the risk; the buck stops with the therapist. But the way the therapist's reaction is best understood and makes the most sense in its irrational way is that the therapist, in identifying with the child "out there alone in the big bad world" felt anxious that the move toward adulthood would incur the wrath of this "well-connected" father. Though one might think of the situation as classically or purely oedipal competition, we think it seems more likely that it was a separation-individuation issue, whether separation-individuation from mother, father, or both.

The guilt then masked by, yet reflected in the worries about imminent danger and ultimate punishment from the parent's anger, had to do with the therapist's own fears about leaving home, leaving behind a symbiotic union that his internalized parents wanted to keep. We thought it was interesting that the therapist was able to listen to the child when he stood up for himself, a testimony to the therapist's ability to go against what he "felt" to be his better judgment, but what he intellectually realized as irrational when it was pointed out. Too, it was testimony to the strength of the drive toward separation-individuation, even with the simultaneous countervailing pull toward symbiosis. Although it looked like the child was ahead of him in healthy development of aggression, the therapist was well on his way. As Freud might see it, surely in this case, intrapsychic conflict can lead to growth.

Practical Use of Aggression

Besides self-scrutiny and practice review and study, some things therapists do with their aggression when there are no overwhelming problems with it are not so dramatic but are simply in the line of carrying on. Although a therapist may be indisputably competent, the need to "sell" his or her services remains a vital ingredient of a successful practice (Geller, 1980). Most of the time the exposure is indirect, that is, the therapist does not simply advertise or announce his or her expertise and availability. While the exposure may be through teaching, lecturing to professional groups or to community service organizations or other community groups, or participation in mental health professional programs as speaker or consultant, the "selling" has been done through having actively and with enough frequency placed oneself in a position to become known. That way, when others think about seeking a therapist, the familiar therapist will come to mind, for one cannot always "depend" on patients to refer other patients, for many reasons. And after referrals from various places, there is what Shimberg (1979) calls the "care and feeding of referral sources."

Relationship to a Professional Group

The therapist entering private practice needs care and feeding too. When we consider the symbiotic experience of therapists and their professional groups it is with the hope that the bond that exists will be similar to that which Friedman (1980) describes as useful, as permitting "the separation and potential differences to take place against a backdrop of security and acceptance" (p. 92). Unfortunately, as in the parent-child symbiotic bond, too often it seems that the state of the group's "personality organization and needs" is such that the individual "leaving home" is unable to draw on the group as an emotional resource. In other words, the "parent" is not always desirous or able to let the "child" differentiate and separate. Thus, at the time when the direction of the therapist is toward private practice and a sense of "belonging-while-separating" is most needed, the professional group is often remiss in fulfilling this important parental function. This is even more of a problem when the individual therapist is still engaged in the personal symbiotic struggle for getting needs met, as we suspect so many are.

There are many possible reasons for the vacuum. Within all of the mental health disciplines, though the therapist role is included, there continues to be ambivalent reactions to the role and how large a part the therapist role should take in defining either the discipline or the "image" of the discipline. Thus, there are functional, philosophical splits within the professional associations. In turn, this creates widespread uncertainty and threats to existing status and preparation within each professional group about future professional credentials and demands.

For example, the licensing of psychologists is often touted as a way to indicate who the reputable health service providers are, but, depending on the particular state, it may or may not be a "specialty" license. That is, in some states a psychologist is not necessarily a psychotherapist, but anyone who has a doctorate in psychology and has passed the licensing exam. A similar problem exists in psychiatry where any physician licensed by the state to practice medicine can assume the psychiatrist label, and functions. In both instances training in psychotherapy is not a requirement for getting licensed and so being able to offer "therapy" to the public. Social work and nursing are also both confusing in regard to their general classification as opposed to specialization. It is true that there are psychiatric social workers and psychiatric nurses, as there are clinical psychologists and psychiatrists, but the disciplines themselves, even within these specialities, have been reluctant to designate psychotherapy as their primary function.

These questions are raised not to be definitive or to generate heat, but to help shed some small light on the kinds of pressure on the various mental health professional groups which could render them anxious, defensive, vulnerable to threat from within by those seen as "going their own way" while the rest of the family is unsettled, perhaps feeling pressured to perform in a similar way lest they lose their status or sense of professional identification. All this is added to the possible economic and status threat to the professions who are fighting with one another over whose turf psychotherapy is, and who are projecting a confusing image.

It would indeed be hard for the therapist entering private practice to feel identification with a discipline in relative emotionally laden chaos, and to separate from a parent discipline threatened with disintegration or one forever in its formative years. Yet, that is what therapists are called on to do. But, they survive. The drive toward independence is very strong.

The therapist sometimes has to tolerate a good deal of criticism and withstand feelings of envy at the time when he or she most needs an "anchor" because of the incredible turmoil likely to be experienced during the move to private practice. We would like to think that most of the criticism and envy generated is neither personal nor genetically hostile, though we have noted that within our own disciplines of psychology and psychiatric nursing people are not particularly charitable to each other as a rule. We think the responses of criticism and envy may instead be a kind of symbiotic-partner response of "What will happen to me if you go?" Surely a thought is, "How will we, the professional partners, the colleague group, affirm our self-worth and consolidate our self-image and value if there are shifts and role changes and function differences with our own professional group?"

We think of course, all that is possible, but the point is, envy may be a by-product of the threat to the self-concept or self-integrity of the professional group. That is not to say that individuals are never helpful or pleased or supportive of their colleagues entering private practice, but as a whole, particularly in those disciplines in which private practice is the exception rather than the norm, the therapist often goes it alone at a time when it would be useful to have the support and counsel from an unthreatened parent professional group happy to see the new private practice therapist going in an independent, freely chosen direction. Perhaps the time will come when the current disciplines will have a strong enough sense of identity, alone, or as one discipline, that differences in roles and direction can be accommodated and even encouraged. Thus our previous, and to be repeated, suggestion of the eventual development of the profession of psychotherapy.

Accountability

Accountability is an issue addressed in earlier chapters. There we stressed its increasing importance as a factor in the psychotherapy field and the responsibility of all psychotherapists to be aware of this, and to be responsive. Now we want to consider some of the possible impact of accountability on the therapist's personality and behavior in the private practice setting.

With the growth of complex health care systems and the consumer movement, along with the shift from direct, private payment to third party payment for services, as well as the trend toward entry of the federal government into health care and professional regulation (Peplau, 1980), "accountability" has become a byword. Escalating costs and the deteriorating quality of services has moved accountability into the public sphere. But this has certain drawbacks. As Peplau

(1980) says, "The growing clamor for accountability or regulation of the professions is to assure the public that its interests and claims to health care are being served. . . . However, every increase in these externally applied measures will have some impact on the professional, perhaps the erosion of internally generated, within-person, self-regulatory practices" (p. 130).

The implication is that, although deterioration must be checked, when the source to whom the professional is accountable is merely external to the self, to authorities controlling the service or to the public's representative, something vital to the quality of the service is missing. In psychotherapeutic work, first it would seem that what is missing is the personal, face-to-face accountability of therapist to patient. Perhaps an absurd exaggeration is that in terms of accountability, the therapist is accountable to everybody but the patient directly. The patient and therapist each give the assessor information. The insurance company or regulatory agency can then assure the patient that the therapist is doing a decent job. This may turn out to be neither reassuring nor accurate. Besides, this is not a very effective method for people therapists see who have difficulties with interpersonal communication, or with certain kinds of primary process or circumstantial thinking, or who have in general, problems in interpersonal relations. Although we may sound facetious, to our mind, it should be seriously considered as to how such an arrangement could unwittingly reinforce psychic, interpersonal pathology in the very patients therapists are accountable for treating.

Closely related to direct accountability to the patient is "accountability to oneself" (Peplau, 1980, p. 131), without which a therapist would have utmost difficulty being accountable directly to the patient. We agree with Peplau (1980) who says that it is accountability to oneself that is the primary accountability. In private practice, at least now, there are not yet external accountability measures routinely applied. But, they appear to be on the way, especially if the government is going to be heavily involved. Such a move might well serve to erode individual accountability for its own personal, moral sake. Therefore, therapists should be concerned about the specifics of such procedures, for as had been noted (Peplau, 1980), "It is when individual responsibility fails that external surveillance and accountability measures are instituted." It is a matter of conscience to be accountable to oneself: accountable by being honest with oneself about what one knows and does not know: by constant review and monitoring of one's practice, alone or with colleagues; by being vigilant for signs of one's irrational and internal needs as they compare with and influence overt behavior; by using theory-based clinical practice; by being a perennial student of human behavior; by keeping a watchful eye on who the treatment is primarily for, therapist or patient. To us, this is the nub of accountability—what really matters.

Interestingly, one would think that if therapists tend toward being obsessional and that if obsessionals tend to have an overdeveloped superego function, then it would follow that therapists would automatically do all those things so vital to personal accountability as a matter of conscience, or else they would feel eternally guilty. There is a chink in the armor, however. As Barnett (1969) suggests, "Obsessional guilt is not based on severity of conscience, but rather on a defect of conscience'' (p. 54). He holds that it is due to parental blaming operations used to control the child and ''to the arbitrary morality they (the parents) established by defining right and wrong in terms of their own needs, without regard for the needs of the child'' (p. 54). The motive then for good or moral or just behavior is built on fear of ''retaliation and retribution. It is largely a fear of blame, of being held accountable and consequently suffering disapproval and rejection'' (p. 55). Thus, self-esteem is dependent on external (parental) source assessment and approval; it does not increasingly come from within. It is certainly a shame if therapists allow ''external'' accountability to continue to rule their professional lives, thereby unwittingly supporting and legitimizing the symbiotic pathology of their personal lives as well as unwittingly advocating that external accountability replace internal or self-accountability.

It is surely difficult then, for the obsessionally inclined therapist entering private practice, literally alone, but emotionally, symbiotically linked with the vigilant parent to please, to truly be accountable to himself or herself rather than to the parent, to the ''external accountor.'' Ultimately, it is necessary and possible to be accountable to oneself, but it does require as much time as it takes.

SUMMARY

Our aim in this chapter was to show how the therapist's symbiotic stance serves him or her in entering private practice and how it is reflected through the therapist's anxiety, aggression, guilt, and accountability practices. Furthermore, we discussed the symbiosis in relation to the professional group and the results of the need for pathological and healthy symbiotic attachment on the therapist's practice.

Even as the book draws near the end it is clear that the therapist's narcissism is always at work, always to be looked for if therapy is indeed to be therapeutic and if the therapist is to be a good therapist. In the next and final chapter we will talk at greater length about our perceptions of ''the good therapist.''

REFERENCES

Barnett J. On aggression in the obsessional neurosis. *Contemporary Psychoanalysis* (1969) **6**:48–57.

Benedek, T. Climacterium: A developmental phase. *Psychoanalytic Quarterly* (1959) **19**:1–27.

Colarusso, C. A., and Nemiroff, R. A. Some observations and hypotheses about the psychoanalytic theory of adult development. *International Journal of Psycho-Analysis* (1979) **60**:59–71.

Friedman, G. The mother-daughter bond. *Contemporary Psycho-Analysis* (1980) **16**(1): 90–97.

Freud, S. Analysis terminable and interminable. In *The complete psychological works of Sigmund Freud*, Vol. 23 (London: Hogarth Press, 1964) (Originally published, 1937).

Geller, J. C. Starting a private practice of psychotherapy. *Perspectives in Psychiatric Care* (1980) **18**:106–111.

Goldman, G. D., and Stricker, G. (Eds.). *Practical problems of a private psychotherapy practice* (Springfield, IL: Charles C Thomas, 1971).

Greben, S. E. Some difficulties and satisfactions inherent in the practice of psychoanalysis. *International Journal of Psycho-Analysis* (1975) **56:**427–434.

Greenacre, P. Problems of overidealization of the analyst and of analysis: Their manifestations in the transference and countertransference relationship. *Psychoanalytic Study of the Child* (1966) **21:**220–245.

Guntrip, H. My experience of analysis with Fairbairn and Winnicott (How complete a result does psycho-analytic therapy achieve?). *International Review of Psycho-Analysis* (1975) **2:**145–156.

Hartmann, H. *Ego psychology and the problem of adaptation* (New York: International Universities Press, 1958).

Kestenberg, J. S., and Buelte, A. Prevention, infant therapy and the treatment of adults: 1 . Toward understanding mutuality. *International Journal of Psychoanalytic Psychotherapy* (1977) **6:**340–367.

Kramer, E. *A beginning manual for psychotherapists* (New York: Grune & Stratton, 1970).

Lewin, M. H. *Establishing and maintaining a successful professional practice* (Rochester, N.Y.: Professional Development Institute, 1978).

Mahler, M. S., Pine, F., and Bergman, A. *The psychological birth of the human infant* (New York: Basic Books, 1975).

Marcus, I. The experience of separation-individuation . . . through the course of life: Adolescence and maturity, *Journal of the American Psychoanalytic Association* (1973) **21:**155–167.

Marmor, J. The feeling of superiority: An occupational hazard in the practice of psychotherapy. *American Journal of Psychiatry* (1953) **110:**370–376.

Parens, H. Parenthood as a developmental phase. *Journal of the American Psychoanalytic Association* (1975) **23:**154–165.

Peplau, H. E. The psychiatric nurse—Accountable: To whom? For what? *Perspectives in Psychiatric Care* (1980) **18:**128–136.

Pressman, R. M. *Private practice—A handbook for the independent mental health practitioner* (New York: Gardner Press, Inc., 1979).

Rangell, L. The role of the parent in the Oedipus Complex. *Bulletin of the Menninger Clinic* (1953) **19:**9–15.

Rouslin, S. Developmental aggression and its consequences. *Perspectives in Psychiatric Care* (1975) **13:**170–175.

Searles, H. F. Pathologic symbiosis and autism. In H. F. Searles (Ed.). *Countertransference and related subjects* (New York: International Universities Press, 1979) (Originally published, 1971).

Searles, H. F. The patient as therapist to his analyst. In H. F. Searles (Ed.). *Countertransference and related subjects* (New York: International Universities Press, 1979) (Originally published, 1975).

Shimberg, E. *The handbook of private practice in psychology* (New York: Brunner/Mazel, 1979).

Winestine, M. The experience of separation-individuation in infancy and its reverberations through the course of life 1. Infancy and childhood. *Journal of the American Psychoanalytic Association* (1973) **21:**135–154.

Winnicott, D. W. Aggression in relation to emotional development. In D. W. Winnicott (Ed.). *Through paediatrics to psycho-analysis* (London: Hogarth Press, 1975) (Originally published, 1950).

Winnicott, D. W. The capacity to be alone. In D. W. Winnicott (Ed.). *The maturational processes and the facilitating environment* (New York: International Universities Press, 1954) (Originally published, 1958).

Winnicott, D. W. On the contribution of direct child observation to psycho-analysis. In D. W. Winnicott. *The maturational processes and the facilitating environment* (New York: International Universities Press, 1974) (Originally published, 1957).

X

At Issue: The Good Therapist

INTRODUCTION

In the preceding chapters we have attempted to show that there are a number of significant issues in the field of psychotherapy which have been neglected in a variety of ways, some quite overt, others rather insidious. Since issues are matters in dispute, if subject to neglect, they remain as controversies and increase turmoil rather than reaching a needed resolution. This situation exists because in many instances the issues have been treated as though their resolution had indeed been accomplished, although it has not. Or, many therapists have related to these issues as though their resolution was unimportant in regard to actual practice, which is also erroneous. The latter approach defuses the issues through an unrealistic lack of concern. In either case the "issue ignoring" is an unacceptable state of affairs for the field of psychotherapy and requires change.

With the hope of beginning to bring about some change we have concerned ourselves with some of these issues. In particular, we have pointed out that defining psychotherapy, specifying its goals, and evaluating its effects, all remain as issues although they have received noticeable attention. In our opinion what has been accomplished with these issues remains insufficient. At best they have been brought to limited and rather idiosyncratic resolutions. After discussing these issues we moved to the general behavior of the therapist as a variable in the therapeutic situation. From there we moved on to specific therapist behaviors, such as the nature of the therapist's relationships, which are more obvious examples of the role of self-concerns on the therapist's part, and which have received even less pertinent attention than the issues we first discussed. Our basic contention is that a core personality factor of therapists, namely narcissism or self-involvement, is a strong determinant in keeping these issues as "issues." Our aim has been to note the pathological manifestations of such narcissism, and in response to these, propose the development of a healthy self-relations system which has a far greater chance of producing effective psychotherapists.

The result of our explorations in this book has been to lead to this point of tentative proposals for a good therapist.

In the main our discussion up to now has been concerned with the therapist's problems in self-expression and self-satisfaction, particularly the disturbing, disruptive manifestations of narcissism appearing in the therapeutic process as well as in areas indigenous to it, such as the definition of psychotherapy. Now we want to move into an emphasis on the positive aspects of narcissism and link these with the effective practice of psychotherapy. In order to do this we need to elaborate further on the concepts of narcissism, and our idea of the "good" therapist, which is less literal than it may seem.

Our context for conceptualizing the narcissism of the psychotherapist, and the "good" and "bad" therapist, is developmental ego psychology, although these ideas can be conceived within other theoretical systems as well. The fundamental proposition for our point of view is that early in life the infant-child has divided others, and the self, into all "good," or all "bad." This comes about as a movement from the perception of being rather constantly gratified to being more frequently frustrated by significant others, primarily parents. The gratification, and the gratifiers, are the good, while the frustrators, and the frustrations, are the bad. As psychological development proceeds the child learns to integrate good and bad into one conception of a person, and of the self, and to love someone despite the frustrations which may be involved in the relationship with the person. There is a constancy of impression which is based on a unified representation in one person's mind of what another person is. In that sense then, there is no such person as the good therapist, or the bad for that matter, since people usually evolve as being too complex for that type of absolutist categorization. It is true that the possibility that indeed someone is all good or all bad can be conceived, but it is an unlikely happening in more mature individuals. So, our term, the good therapist, is to be understood as a qualified one.

The view of any person as a mixture of attractive and unattractive features is a relatively accepted one in most theories of personality development, regardless of the belief about how such perceptions may have developed. Thus, whatever the psychotherapist's theoretical orientation, it appears clear that the concern for the development of the good therapist is not the pursuit of an idealized image or process, but of an adequate, "good-enough" person. The good therapist then is one who is considered effective by the majority of people with whom he or she relates as a therapist, and one who feels a definite, realistic sense of self-proficiency. There is a consistency of perception by others and by the self that validates this person being a "good" therapist.

While we have given recognition to the fact that therapists are integrated to various degrees, and so a mixture of "good" and "bad" characteristics, up to this point we have probably stressed the "bad." We have also mentioned antidotes for therapists' problems and struggles, but our focus has been that therapists have personal needs which at times go unrecognized and take precedence over what is most fitting for the success of the therapeutic process. We have tracked this unfortunate happening through the variety of events which we have mentioned as integral to the practice of psychotherapy. And, as we have indicated, our strong belief is that a very fundamental cause of the problems is the therapist's narcissism, which in some fashion is assaulted by the therapist being in the therapeutic situation. In turn, the therapist's response to the assault is too often a display of disturbing self-involvement and self-absorption which has the potential of considerable harm for both therapists and patients.

We have given numerous examples of the problems that occur and the resulting damage, as well as suggestions for rectifying these situations. Inherent in our presentation is the idea that narcissism is to be thought of as a normal developmental personality characteristic, present in all individuals. Thus, feelings and perceptions of self-esteem, self-worth, and personal value are essential to a mature, integrated, functioning person. We consider these also to be the material of narcissism, which can be expressed in healthy, and so helpful ways by the therapist. While we are framing the conception in terms of psychoanalytic developmental psychology, this is certainly not necessary for all therapists in order to make use of the idea. We are stressing the needs of the self for appreciation, attention, and gratification. These are the needs of therapists from all disciplines and all orientations.

At this point then, our general proposal is that the "good" therapist will strive to utilize and display "healthy narcissism." Thus, self-relations are thought of as being intertwined with relating to others, while the love of others is considered empty without love of the self. This view of healthy narcissism as an essential and enduring process has been proposed by others, such as Jacobson (1964), and White (1980), though it has not been directly applied to the psychotherapist and his or her practice of therapy.

White has stated: "It may be that the current interest in narcissism is heralding a wider recognition of the developmental need for healthy self relations and is looking toward a new era in therapeutic technique as well as in therapy" (1980, p. 22). In accord with this hopeful probability we are going to propose some possibilities for the satisfactory use of the self on the part of the therapist, in contrast to many of the unsatisfactory behaviors we have scrutinized in previous chapters. While we certainly believe our possibilities can and ought to be realized, it is more prudent to consider them as hypotheses to be tested as to their specific value for therapeutic effectiveness. Also, our proposals are not intended as an exhaustive list of successful therapist behaviors in the therapy situation, but as some important, useful suggestions that touch upon the less acknowledged difficulties encountered by all therapists. We accept as a given an awareness on the part of therapists that it would be helpful to possess such attributes as concern, intelligence, empathy, and the customary list of fairly obvious behaviors that ought to be useful in practicing psychotherapy. Our proposals are a bit different, going after the influential, yet relatively unrecognized components of the therapist's "healthy narcissism."

PROPOSITIONS FOR THERAPISTS

The Profession of Psychotherapy

As an integration of what has been considered thus far in this book we believe certain needs are of paramount importance for all psychotherapists. While we began with the issue of defining psychotherapy, we did not consider ourselves capable of solving that problem solely by highlighting the inadequacies of present explanations, nor by the presentation of our own definition. These are beginning steps, but the resolution of the problems of inadequate definition, unclear goals, and unwarranted behaviors remains as a task for every psychotherapist. In particular, we wonder if there will be a significant response to our call for unity in the establishment of a profession of psychotherapy, which in turn should require the resolution of the other issues we mentioned. Such a conception whereby psychotherapists might indeed have quite similar competency-based identities also has the potential for solving the shortage of adequate mental health personnel and providing more discernible criteria for accountability.

We certainly sympathize with the struggles of the current disciplines to gain recognition as independent mental health service providers. We both come from parent disciplines that indeed have had to "wage war" for such recognition, but we also see such an approach as unlikely to bring about egalitarianism among psychotherapists. In fact, we doubt it can alter many of the biases and prejudicial impressions existing in regard to different groups of psychotherapists. Thus, it is apparent to us that if the most effective changes are to be made and therefore a profession of psychotherapists created, at least two occurrences appear vital. Leadership is necessary, and we believe for it to be the most effective it should come from psychiatrists because they are really the most powerful of the disciplines involved. Then, once agreement has been reached by all the disciplines as to what competencies are necessary to be a psychotherapist, all who wish to be psychotherapists, regardless of discipline, must develop these competencies. An assumption is made here that appropriate avenues will be created for such development. We believe in this approach as a most needed solution to what can be conservatively described as the current "sticky situation."

So far, we regretfully admit, we have been pessimistic about our proposal getting off the ground. It is our impression that unfortunately too many therapists have their heads stuck in their personal sand. For example, some psychiatrists believe that the granting of independent status to other practitioners is about to destroy their livelihood, and/or the mental health of the entire society. And some of these "others" have their own image problems, so much so that they hasten to become "as-if" psychiatrists, knowing the name of every drug they cannot prescribe. While there are hopeful exceptions, the degree of dissension existing around who is, or is not, entitled to practice psychotherapy should mandate a better solution than the field's current state of practice. We believe we have made a clear and simple proposal to start that resolution, and we want the consideration of all psychotherapists as a beginning in making the profession of psychotherapy a viable reality. Perhaps our initial, and recurring pessimism on this issue may have some redeeming ingredients. Although he reports suffering back pain in proximity to having written this, Stern recently stated: "Psychotherapists work best against a backdrop of pessimism. In a world in which each person must redeem his or her own experience or perish as a psychological being, the oppositional character of pessimism remains a vital life sign" (1980, p. 4).

Our concern recognizes the variety of threats to basic narcissistic components such as self-involvement, status, security, and self-righteousness. It involves a conception of considerable change, and therapists are too well reminded of the difficulties in that through their everyday contact with patients. While we believe the need is pressing, we also sense there is value in small beginnings around a charged issue such as establishing a psychotherapy profession. Thus, we are asking for what we believe could be palatable at the moment, and if that occurs, we can go from there to a more detailed proposal. Our hope, at least, seems really to remain, dispelling pessimism. It is probably based on the belief that "good enough" therapists are fairly determined optimists with sufficient healthy narcissism to see definite value for all concerned in our desire for a unified, competency-based profession. All we need is enough of these "good-enoughs," and our plan should have real possibilities.

Psychotherapists and Research

Obviously the issues just promulgated, and propagandized, we see as very important, and as a political and personal mixture. But, that is only the beginning. Another major concern of ours is increasing the integration of research and practice. We have previously pointed out the many ways in which practitioners can and do "shake off" research, operating selectively in terms of their own needs as far as what is incorporated into an already existing belief system about how any psychotherapist is practicing. Again, we note resistance to change and the threat to the narcissistic self, for the possibility certainly exists as to the empirical demonstration of the efficacy of something other than what one is already doing. And, more disturbing, the possibility is there that the inefficacy of any therapist's theories and/or methods may be shown if put to a representative test.

However, our impression is that nothing so simple comes out of the research on psychotherapy. Instead, what it really offers is an opportunity for greater understanding of the complexity of psychotherapy. This understanding can in turn improve the effectiveness of the psychotherapies. Concern with, and comprehension of research about the therapies, present a growth potential for psychotherapists, rather than the specter of nihilism and denigration of therapeutic efforts. Of course change may be involved, but perfection can scarcely be a current claim of the healing professions. Besides, change is the customary essential goal of most psychotherapies. Also, the changes suggested by the research literature, when its limitations are indeed taken into account, are relatively subtle. They support the diversity, and coordinated difficulty, of successful therapeutic interventions. And they pose the possibility of such strategies, but in so doing, what we would term "inevitable complexity" is consistently revealed. We will give a number of illustrations of this.

In a preceding chapter on the effectiveness of therapy we indicated the probability that some patients could indeed deteriorate in response to some psychotherapies. Our impression was that there is definite research support for a "deterioration effect." We stated then that this was by no means a simple problem, but the complexity of this issue has to be further appreciated. Such findings, particularly if construed in a more generalized way than they have actually been found, are very likely to become political concerns. The inclusion of psychotherapy benefits in health plans is dependent on accountability, and on the likelihood that psychotherapy has sufficient value as a treatment procedure for mental disorders. So, an appropriate perspective on what the psychotherapies can do is essential for consumers, therapists, and decision makers for distributing mental health services.

Bergin (1975) has been the major proponent of the idea that psychotherapy can, and does, make some patients worse. But, this assertion has been challenged in the past, and now again, more recently, by Franks and Mays (1980; Mays and Franks, 1980). They argue that there is no evidence of greater deterioration in therapy patients as compared to untreated patients, and that some of the studies Bergin cites in support of his position, actually contradict it. Their main point is that while there is evidence of patient deterioration during the course of therapy, there is no evidence that psychotherapy causes the deterioration. They suggest several alternative hypotheses. One is that certain patients who would have deteriorated without treatment instead are helped, while others who would have been all right are made worse by therapy. Another is that some patients will deteriorate with or without therapy. The first hypothesis is focused on therapist characteristics, while the second deals with patient variables. Neither, they assert, has been adequately tested, and beyond this, the deterioration effect remains an open question as to causality.

Bergin (1980b) continues to disagree with these critics. He asserts that both empirical and clinical evidence currently support the existence of therapy-caused deterioration in patients. This type of disagreement, particularly regarding the same or similar evidence, unfortunately can reinforce a prevalent feeling among practitioners as to the lack of practical utility of research. Here is a case in which the researchers themselves disagree as to the meaning of the results. The practitioners, with less familiarity and sophistication in the research area, see themselves as less able to interpret research results. Thus, when the researchers vary as to interpretation it tends to confirm an already existing prejudice among practitioners against research.

A more practical approach is available through viewing research as illustrative of both the specificity and complexity of psychotherapy. From practice itself the concept of universal solutions ought to be quickly vitiated for most therapists. Research confirms this, highlights problem areas, usually clarifies what ideally should be taken into consideration, and many times offers possible solutions to problems. The speculative results of research regarding psychotherapy are symbolic of the speculative nature of the psychotherapy process. Research and practice are essentially compatible efforts, and struggles.

In this regard, consider the following statement: "During the discovery or exploratory phase, I am interested in finding a phenomenon, gaining some understanding of the most significant conditions that affect it. . . . During this phase I am quite free-wheeling and intuitive—follow hunches, vary procedures, try out wild ideas and take shortcuts" (Miller, 1972, p. 248). These words could easily have been said about the procedures of psychotherapy, but they were not. Instead they were used to describe the discovery phase of research, as distinct from the proof phase. Bergin (1980b) considers most aspects of psychotherapy and behavior change procedures to be somewhere between the two stages, but not at the proof stage. Thus, both practice and research are in process, with evidence of limited generalizability, yet useful in specific instances.

For example, it appears that sexism among therapists, which we have had described to us by clients, is a changing phenomenon, decreased by having been brought to the awareness of most therapists. Thus, if psychotherapists at one time did endorse a "double standard" of mental health, this is significantly decreasing. We reported evidence for this conclusion earlier in the book, and we can add to it at this point. Recently a study by Stearns, Penner, and Kimmel (1980) concluded that there is: "Little evidence that practicing clinicians tend toward sexist recommendations or sex role stereotyping" (p. 549).

At the same time, client sex in combination with other variables, as therapist sex, as well as client and therapist sex roles, may well be significant factors in the therapeutic interaction. But, they do not appear to operate in as overt or massive a manner as was once alleged. In essence, sex-effects appear to be more subtle, more complex, and in need of investigation as interactive factors in contrast to conceptualizing "sexism" as an independent determinant of the therapy process and/or outcome. Also, we have previously indicated that psychotherapy outcome is best understood as an interaction between specific patients, therapists, and theoretical and technique variables, as opposed to a generality of effectiveness or the lack of it. Nonetheless, the general question of whether or not psychotherapy "works" continues to be asked of therapists by consumers, and with many caveats, the answer is affirmative. This answer is based primarily on work with adults, which is one of the numerous reservations to be taken into account, both when answering the question and interpreting the answer. An awareness of the broad generality involved, such as client category, and how that awareness can be useful in therapeutic practice, is basically emphasized by existing research. Tramontana (1980) reviewed the outcome research on psychotherapy effectiveness with adolescents for a ten-year period. Thirty-three studies were considered, but only five were regarded as methodologically sound. The evidence from these, as with adults, favors the value of psychotherapy. But, more pointedly, this review shows the great need for determining specifics, such as certain therapeutic conditions that will result in particular changes for specific types of adolescents, who are a rather neglected group as far as research and specific treatments are concerned.

Thus, Tramontana concludes: "Too much of what is presently done in psychotherapy with adolescents seems to be simply an amalgam of principles, approaches, and techniques borrowed from work with adults and children rather than being derived from systematic investigations of the special treatment needs of adolescent patients" (p. 448).

Since the role of psychotherapy research has been so limited in affecting practice, the possibility exists that Tramontana's comments may be little noticed, but hopefully not. The work on deterioration in therapy has by now sparked concern at the level of practice, as has the allegations of sexism. Our hope is that more therapists will see that their interests can be served in a practical way by the identification of important questions about practice, and that research often does precisely that.

We believe the possibility of narcissistic threats to the practitioner has been developed by previous misconceptions regarding research, some of which were fueled by misleading statements from researchers as well. While these misconceptions seem to have facilitated the past dismissal of research from serious consideration by large numbers of therapists, such does not have to be the case. If research is viewed as we have suggested, the threat is significantly diminished and recognition followed by curiosity leading to action is a more likely possibility. We are focusing primarily on the greater use of empirical research, since therapists have been much more receptive to clinical investigation, such as case studies, and seem to feel relatively comfortable with drawing specific and selective conclusions from such material. But, that is not enough since such investigations lack the possible power of the scientific method. Thus, as empirical research continues, and, as with clinical practice, gains sophistication, we believe the results can provide continual useful opportunities for greater understanding of the therapist's efforts in action. In turn, such understanding can be translated into more effective practice.

THERAPISTS' "INNER SOUNDINGS"

While the narcissistic struggles surrounding the development of a psychotherapeutic profession and the integration of research and practice are issues of major concern, they pale in regard to our belief in the importance of the therapist's use of his or her "inner voices" in operating as an effective psychotherapist. We have indicated in some fashion in every chapter in this book that the therapist's narcissism is the key to how psychotherapy is going to be practiced. Our view is that self-interest needs to be served, yet is best served in the therapeutic endeavor by attending to the needs of the client while attending to the needs of the therapist. The therapist and client require a "good fit" in regard to both their self-images and self-esteem for therapy to be a positive event for both of them. Our particular concern is with the therapist's use of his or her narcissism, though this is certainly an interactive operation involving the patient as well. Our strong belief is that the therapist who makes sound use of healthy narcissism stands the best chance of affecting therapeutic change in the client. This is accomplished by close attendance to the self while listening to the patient. This self-focusing is by no means a new conception, yet many vital aspects of it have been, and continue to be neglected in the training and development of therapists.

Even some of the more blatant examples of therapists' narcissism, such as sexual exploitation of patients, had at first been treated by nonrecognition or dogmatic disallowance. More recently recognition has set in that this can be a problem, but there is still a strong tendency to avoid the complexities involved and assume the therapist can simply solve the problem if it is brought to his or her attention. The magnitude of narcissistic needs symbolized by this problem, and the extent to which they exist in all therapists, is relatively ignored.

We believe there are beginning to be some positive signs of at least increased recognition of the diverse manifestations of therapists' narcissism, though the issue is not addressed directly. We are going to consider these "rumblings of concern" with parts of the therapist's self, and place them within our schema of the uses and abuses of narcissism. Our aim remains the greater development of the self-as-therapist through increased recognition and activation of healthy narcissism in the process of therapy.

Values

Our first area of consideration is a constellation which we will refer to as therapist values, and which include attitudes and beliefs as well. We consider this grouping an important component of the narcissism of the therapist, and we see values as having a motivational loading indicative of individual goals which may or may not be appropriate for the therapy. That is quite crucial because we also believe that the values of the therapist are often brought into the therapeutic situation.

For example, Beutler (1979) presents a strong case for many instances of the therapist's values and beliefs being transmitted to the patient during the therapy situation. This may be positive or negative in its effects, but either way the potential power of value transmission appears to be strong. Personal and religious values of patients frequently change during the course of therapy, and often in the direction of the therapist's value system. The "persuasive component" of therapy can be helpful, yet there is limited knowledge as to the specifics of the relationship between therapeutic improvement and particular values, beliefs, and attitudes.

For example, one of us recently was admonished by a patient because the patient had the impression the therapist believed that "homosexuality is an acceptable life style for a person." The person the patient had in mind was himself, who although living a homosexual life style at the time, felt guilty about it. In fact, he had repeatedly condemned homosexuality as "wrong." The therapist had raised the possibility a few times that sexuality did not have to be looked on in that way. The therapist in fact did not consider homosexuality to be "wrong." At least ostensibly then, the therapist and patient held different values. The therapist also had the sense that acceptance of homosexuality as an equally viable life style to heterosexuality could alleviate the patient's conflicts considerably, yet the therapist did not want to appear to be imposing a personal, and controversial, view upon the patient. Nonetheless, the therapist's values were involved on a number of levels, and an apparent value conflict was part of the therapy.

The therapist viewed the morality as not the main issue, believing instead that the patient's conflicts about homosexuality were really on grounds other than morality, yet the therapist's values were involved. The patient was claiming homosexuality was wrong, while the therapist did not see it that way, so a value question appeared to be obvious. The possibility that the patient would either insist it was a moral issue about which the therapist was wrong, or simply refuse to recognize any other issues, could be felt as a narcissistic injury by the therapist. The patient may disparage both the therapist's personal value, and the value of the therapist's interpretation of the patient's conflict.

If the patient would have opted for health by disavowing homosexuality solely on the grounds that it was "immoral," the therapist probably would have been uncomfortable. What happened instead is that the therapist questioned whether or not there was a "real" value difference here, or was the patient insisting on a difference to remain "stuck." The patient had always claimed it was evil, yet kept doing it, and suffering. The possibility of the value difference being used as a defense was gradually accepted by the patient and therapy proceeded accordingly. Of course there was an imposition of the therapist's values here, but we would see the questioning as appropriate, regardless of how the therapist felt about homosexuality. Nonetheless, the patient did accept the therapist's view that the apparent value difference was a defense, and the implication that what looked like a difference would dissolve.

We would like to think that if there was a real value difference the therapist would make it clear that if the patient wants to give up homosexuality, and will feel better for having done this, the therapist will attempt to aid the patient in accomplishing this, regardless of the therapist's personal view of the goodness or badness of homosexuality. The therapist's discomfort would have come about if the homosexuality was to be stopped purely on moral principles, since the probable conflict regarding sexual orientation would not really have been resolved. In essence, the therapist strives to remain open to the patient's professed goal, though reserving the necessary option to question it even if such behavior appears as a value conflict, and, in this case, even if the patient really believes homosexuality is bad for the world, but the therapist does not.

Of course the possible influence of the values of the therapist has traditionally received some mention in the psychotherapy literature. But, it has been a relatively complacent designation, pointing to the rather obvious as an issue, yet avoiding detailed considerations. In contrast, Beutler suggests it is time for: "Subjecting therapists to detailed evaluation of their inner beliefs which they have heretofore kept carefully protected from external observation" (p. 438).

Therapists' values are involved in a number of pertinent issues inherent to the practice of psychotherapy. One of these is triage, a somewhat unfamiliar term which refers to the effective distribution of resources within a society. In this case the concern is with the provision of *quality* treatment within the society. As proof of the effectiveness of the dynamic psychotherapies for lower class patients with limited economic means has become more convincing (Karon and VandenBos, 1977), the question of who will serve in the capacity of therapists is more pressing. Analysts can no longer excuse themselves from the possibility of a lowered fee on the grounds that such patients are unsuitable for analytic treatment. We have previously mentioned our own struggles with this issue. Saying that the clinics of the nation can do it is hardly an accurate usage of triage, for the evidence favors the presence of higher quality services in the private sector. Furthermore, even when highly trained therapists are available in the public sector, the current trend there is toward cost-containment, usually translated to mean short-term psychotherapy. Community mental health centers are unlikely to be the future source of analytic services, or any other complex therapies, for greater numbers of people. Thus, the provision of quality services on any large scale basis appears to depend on the willingness of therapists to make such a commitment, and becomes a question of personal values.

Burstein (1979) suggests some advantages for therapists, such as learning from treating patients with different backgrounds as well as contributing to theory and technique through doing this work. He suggests, and we concur, that therapists have a responsibility to treat the people who can benefit from the therapists' skills. On this basis it could be a choice between guilt and lowered income, and if therapists are indeed committed to a belief in the widespread right of people to good mental health services, there is no choice. Triage appears most feasible through the direct participation of all qualified therapists. We consider this kind of public concern an example of healthy narcissism, necessary and more realistic than waiting for changes in the mental health delivery system which will ensure a high standard of economic benefit for therapists. We believe the current limited access to the more sophisticated psychotherapies is at variance with our egalitarian ideals, and so requires what may well feel like a sacrifice to many therapists, yet also is a definite "good," and feels that way to us. Our impression is that most therapists will share our belief, though they will have their troubles putting their altruism into practice, as we do.

Another area where therapists' values are being made more visible is in regard to religion. Therapists have a reputation for antipathy to religion, as for example, Heimann's concern about "the invidious return of religion" (1977, p. 313), and a random sampling of psychologists which showed that the number who believed in God was about 40 percent lower than the general population (Ragan, Malony, and Beit-Hallahmi, 1976).

Lovinger (1979) points out that a religious orientation is significant for many patients, and may indeed pose problems for therapists. He considers these problems as involving specific lack of knowledge about religion, or insufficient therapeutic strategies, or personal factors, as feelings about religion. Any or all could be involved, but here we are concerned with the personal elements. These include the therapist's attitude toward religion, which is usually negative, and the therapist's attitude toward value-free therapy, which usually involves at least a stated reluctance to intervene on value-laden issues such as religion. Also, some therapists have a simplistic attitude about religion which interferes with their comprehension of the client's specific religious orientation. In fact all of these personal attitudes can interfere with the process of understanding the patient. It seems to us more appropriate to consider the religious orientation itself as not a therapeutic issue, but instead try to focus on the meaning of religion for the patient. This provides for detailed psychological exploration regardless of their therapist's personal views regarding religion.

Bergin (1980c) urges a different approach. Taking the view that values are an integral part of therapy, with which we could agree, he believes that the dominant value systems among psychotherapists exclude and frequently oppose religious values. He proposes a "theistic realism" as a more viable alternative, with a definite stress on a religious orientation. Included in this are firm moral standards, tolerance, fidelity, loyalty, love, commitment, and a host of other qualities which in the abstract are virtues and therefore essentially "goods."

Such an advocacy of theism has not gone unchallenged. Walls (1980) believes that this kind of approach provides a dangerous opportunity for justifying personal beliefs by cloaking them in "divine authority" rather than having to provide rational substantiation. Thus disguised narcissism could have an irresponsible, or at least irrational, influence on the process of daily living. Bergin (1980d) replies with the reassurance that he is not advocating wholesale spirituality, but only, "those spiritual trends that appear viable" (p. 645).

Ellis (1980) is even more openly opposed to Bergin's suggestions. For example, the views of Ellis on right and wrong, sex, marriage, and the causes of emotional disturbance, definitely disagree with Bergin. Both Ellis and Walls advocate humanism as a more appropriate value position for psychotherapists, as well as for the general population.

The value issue is by no means limited to a formal disagreement about the place of religion in the psychotherapist's conceptions. While Bergin's contentions are contrasted with humanism on the religious issue, he has also been involved in disagreements about the role of ethical relativism in behavior therapy. The value judgments made by behavior therapists have been scrutinized by Kitchener (1980a, 1980b, 1980c), Bergin (1980a), Houts and Krasner (1980), and Ward (1980). The terms they use are ethical relativism, ethical naturalism, critical dualism, and ethical skepticism, but the values of the therapist are the central concern.

Regardless of the emotional and intellectual positions any therapist may have on these particular issues, the dominant consideration is the degree of pervasion of the therapeutic endeavor by value-laden processes. Psychotherapists have to further consider the implications of their value systems for their therapeutic efforts, particularly since their values often are different from many of the values of their clients. Thus, the therapist's task is to acknowledge to the self the actuality of his or her values, to then be aware of their possible impact, and to respect the values of the clients. This is *not* to be equated with the therapist changing personal values to accommodate the client, who is often seeking help for conflicts about values and so is scarcely in a position of certainty about personal values.

The therapist legitimately questions the client's values, but with an awareness of the therapist's own concerns which enables a sorting out of the primarily self-serving from the therapeutic in the exploration process. In our view the therapist is an investigator and an integrator, but not a value salesperson, even if the values in question would be considered "good" by many people. There are some values the therapist does need to promulgate, such as client honesty with the therapist, but these are integral to the procedure of therapy rather than more absolute beliefs, such as the value of marriage for the good life. The therapist aids the client to make clear, relatively conflict-free decisions about how to live, but in our opinion, that is it. We try to understand ourselves and we try to understand the clients, who have a substantial stake in self-understanding.

Thus, for us, the therapist is limited in "teaching" values, with the client and the therapeutic process defining these limits. Of course the therapy is not neutral for the therapist, but it is definitely restricted when it comes to the expression of personal values. Of course that is a substantive value of ours, which we just happen to believe is usually the most appropriate course. There are some degrees of exception, in consideration of the variability of patients' personality structures, but we generally hold by our view and attempt to act accordingly.

Up to now we have been concentrating on the somewhat more abstract aspects of personal concerns of therapists, as values, attitudes, and beliefs, in regard to overall issues. Now we want to concretize the personal to a greater degree, since we believe we have sufficiently established the general necessity of considering the possible significance of the therapists' concerns on many fronts.

Cognitive Operations

We will begin this section by considering the discussion by Heimann (1977) of ways to look at the cognitive processes of the analyst at work. She suggests that therapists have a number of tasks which deserve more attention than they have gotten. Her concern is with psychodynamic psychotherapy, but appears applicable in many of its particulars to all forms of therapy.

The therapist is pictured at the start of therapy as a receptive listener, which involves a fluid attending, a selecting of pertinent material in terms of the therapist's impressions of its importance. At the same time, the therapist is in continual internal dialogue, noting the flow of the psychic movement, and testing these impressions in a variety of ways. Many are remembered for subsequent use, while some need to be forgotten. This listening process is one of creative selection, with the therapist developing a functional model of the patient's life; past, present, and future. While the therapist is actively involved in imaging and imagining, the patient's communications are continual stimuli for the therapist's associations and formulations.

Heimann describes the chief operations of this stage in therapy as, "Mobile attention, . . . running commentary, . . . and trial interpretations," all of which are not overtly expressed. Instead they serve as the groundwork for another, subsequent activity of the therapist, namely action in the form of verbalizations to the patient. The attending process is an intense one, with numerous opportunities for narcissistic intrusions that deflect the accuracy of the therapist's understanding. As Heimann puts it: "Reik spoke of the 'analyst's third ear' (1948). I think he needs more than three."

This special and difficult listening process then is changed into a still more complicated overt participatory dialogue. The therapist's part in this is designed to be a fashioned one, customized to what is "therapeutic." The judgment factor looms large here, and there are certainly possibilities for the therapist to be self-serving at the expense of the patient and under the guise of therapeutic work. We suspect all therapists can notice at least a touch of this kind of narcissism at work, be it only in retrospect. The need is to tune into it just before the time of occurrence and gain a different self-satisfaction by the more effective use of the self.

The dialogue begins with the therapist sorting and organizing the diffuse impressions that have been cognitively, and affectively, recorded within the self of the therapist. A personal internalized discussion is carried out in a search for conceptual clarity, which will result in the translation of these concepts into formal speech. At relatively the same time that these formulations are being made, an assessment of the patient's readiness to receive them also has to occur. The patient's reactions must be anticipated as much as possible since the basic thrust of the therapist's communications is designed to be purposive. Also, it is fruitful to recognize that therapist's responses occur in a variety of ways, many of which are gestures, monosyllabic intonations such as grunts and sighs, incomplete sentences, and other less than "perfect" verbalizations. Yet, all can be meaningful to the patients, even when they are not intended as such. For example, when one of us during a therapy session shifted our position in a chair, the patient lying on the couch at the time stated that the therapist must be bored. The therapist was not, nor did the therapist intend the communication, yet it happened. The reverse is also true. If the timing is missed, the patient does not hear the therapist, and a "misunderstanding" appears to have taken place.

The new role of active participant does entail the probability of some loss of attention to the patient's *immediacy* because the therapist is focusing on his or her carefully crafted interpretation which is about to be presented. There is an inherent narcissistic element to the transformation of the inner processes to outer interactions. Because of this it becomes especially important for the therapist to keep the patient in focus while interpreting. The formation of words from inner images by the therapist during therapy is a creative action deserving more intensive exploration than it has gotten up to now. It is very complex, designed to serve the patient and the self of the therapist, yet it can so insidiously become a selfish narcissistic exercise.

Finally, after the session, the therapist has the opportunity, responsibility, and need to look at his or her own work. Such scrutiny is admittedly selective, and not purely cognitive by any means, being strongly influenced by emotional components. When we ourselves recall what we did in a session, we are struck by what did or did not prove to be effective. For example, one of us was listening to a patient reproach himself for being "confused." The therapist asked, "What is wrong with being confused?" The patient appeared relieved in response to the question, though he remarked that he thought therapy was designed to clarify matters. The therapist nodded, somewhat ambiguously. The next session the patient said: "That was the greatest thing you said, that it was all right for me to be confused." The question asked by the therapist with the intention of probing intense feelings appearing to surround the patient's self-image of confusion, opened up the analysis of the patient's self-esteem/self-degradation feelings, and went beyond that to alter a "given" as far as the patient was concerned and facilitated a "new look" for the patient, and for the therapist. It was a useful verbalization by the therapist, yet had some mysterious components. It is remembered more for its effectiveness than its design. Had the patient not responded as he did, it may well have disappeared from the therapist's self-review of the session.

Self-scrutiny is certainly complicated by the narcissistic need for self justification, as well as a host of other self-absorbing factors. The therapist's motivation has a wide range, from highlighting themes deemed important, through the scientific communication of what may appear to be a considerable discovery about behavior, to greater analysis of the self. And while material may be overlooked, or overemphasized, the very process of self-scrutiny raises still another possibility for distortion. Also, narcissism can be fed by self-accusation if it is accompanied by a promise to do better next time and a belief in the accomplishment of the promise. When this approach is used, then a castigating superego would seem to be at work, which can be still another distortion. In defusing these unwarranted concerns reality testing has to be invoked, not only against errors of omission and self-aggrandizement, but to avoid false errors designed as food for guilt. Therapists can indeed do much of their work correctly, and retrospection should reveal that, as well as genuine mistakes. Healthy narcissism means an appropriate perception of the therapist's work in the session.

Personal Concerns

We have just considered the cognitive/emotional mix in the good therapist, with a direct focus on the therapeutic process. Now we will look at the therapist's professional-personal life style, following up on our discussion of occupational hazards in an earlier chapter. Three authors have addressed some of these concerns recently. The authors are Will (1979), who is a psychiatrist, and Freudenberger and Robbins (1979), who are psychologists. These writers have primarily a psychoanalytic orientation, but their comments are applicable to most, if not all psychotherapists. They cover a variety of therapist variables, some of which we have already delved into sufficiently, so our emphasis now is on selected material which we believe has not yet been emphasized as much as it should be.

Will attests to the fact that the practice of psychotherapy invades aspects of the therapist's personality that are not so well established. As a result he believes that therapists are never free from anxiety in contacts with patients in the therapeutic setting. Therapists accordingly have considerable difficulty in acknowledging their doubts about their own lives and their feelings of inexpertness in dealing with other people. Denial, and its variations and derivatives, are tempting in the hopes of avoiding the anxiety of insecurity around carrying our psychotherapy. Also, the being of a psychotherapist, despite its intimate involvement in the lives of others, is very often a lonely position, and thereby threatening in its reminder of self-vulnerability.

In our opinion many therapists have entered the profession with hopes of dispelling loneliness by constantly working with people. But, due to "work parameters" of psychotherapy, therapists are instead often left with the loneliness of an extreme type of narcissism which imposes an enforced solitary existence of the self. Mijusovic (1979–80) sees loneliness and narcissism as substantially and consistently intertwined, and as inevitable experiences for all persons. Becoming a psychotherapist bears no inherent resolution, and in fact contains a strong potential for exacerbation of the problem. Sometimes everyone in the therapist's life may appear to be a patient, leaving the therapist painfully alone. Patients arrive, stay varying lengths of time, and frequently depart, as we have pointed out in the discussion of the possibility of unlimited termination in a previous chapter. As we indicated there, while separations are not as inevitable as they are often made out to be, they are fairly probable. Furthermore, the degree of therapist self-expression, of being the personal "me," is more distinctly limited. The pervasive influence of being a psychotherapist is such that it is often a major task for any therapist to be a truly social person with a distinct, autonomous identity that contains and expresses love and intimacy outside of the therapeutic situation. Thus, Will states: "I often think that I am seeking something, lost in the now distant past of my childhood, yet persistently drawing my attention. . . . It is as if I doubted my hold on a relationship with another human being. . . . In my work I may continue attempts to solve this puzzling but common problem of many years past" (pp. 574–575).

Freudenberger and Robbins also indicate that narcissism and loneliness are definite possible byproducts of the profession of psychotherapy. They have noticed a high incidence in the field of individuals who are still struggling with early life experiences and longings that their professional work has not resolved or fulfilled. In particular, they describe a common danger of being in the profession, namely therapist "burnout." The prominent symptoms include loneliness and inability to relate to others, as well as psychic depletion. They stress the necessity for psychotherapists to learn ways to "feed" themselves in a constructive manner. In our view this is an affirmation of the essential nature of developing healthy narcissism.

FINAL NOTES

As far as we are concerned this ending could become a beginning for psychotherapists. The role of psychotherapist as it is known today can be conceptualized as containing apparent expectations and covert qualifiers. The expectations are supposedly described openly and available for public inspection, while the qualifiers are essentials which tend to be unspecified and relatively hard for the public to detect. In fact, even within the profession some of these qualifiers, though known, are given limited mention. In general the role title serves to mask the qualifiers.

Sherman (1971–72) has indicated that the role expectations for psychotherapists are almost as masked as the qualifiers. Role behavior is markedly ambiguous, allowing for considerable personal indulgence, yet operating as a source for many threats to the self system of the therapist. Sherman states: "The ability to enact treatment relationships in which actual intimacy and secret gratifications are masked under sincere beliefs of professional behavior constitutes one of the most essential (covert) *qualifiers* of the competent psychotherapist. . . . " (p. 524).

Our interest lies in the closer examination of this therapist behavior that has become masked and so often a large blind spot out of awareness and under limited control. We believe the origins, development, and perpetuation of such masking in psychotherapists is often connected to narcissistic concerns. This can translate into therapist need gratification at the expense of the therapy, which we believe is really not in the therapist's self-interest either. In contrast immediate, rather irrational satisfactions are to be patiently bypassed in favor of the facilitation of healthy narcissism. This means a strong sense of personal and professional identity enveloped in the giving and receiving of affection to and from others, and therefore, to and from the self. Our belief is that far too little attention has been devoted to this type of development in psychotherapists. In response we have attempted in this book to facilitate more exploration of the topic by discussing important issues in the field which are both open to various types of neglect, and have at their core the manifestations of the therapist's narcissism or self-relations.

And what about us? Where do we stand in respect to all this? Well, we believe we have been quite lucid about both the areas that need examination, and about what ought to be carried out in many instances. Nonetheless, it is possible that readers of this book would want to know how we actually operate in more, or different, instances than we have already described. In response to that possibility, we can offer a compromise answer. Our task as the authors has in our opinion required that we be both discerning and discreet, preserving the confidentiality of the patient-therapist relationship and our own sense of what we deemed "appropriate privacy." Yet, at the same time, realizing we are asking others to unmask to themselves, we want to be explicit as to our faith in the value of such a procedure. This involves some concluding specific statements on our part regarding what kind of therapists we believe we have been, are, ought to be, and can be.

Essentially we want to be "good enough" psychotherapists, defined by the criteria we have already indicated. In our opinion the majority of the time we achieve this goal, but it certainly involves a continual working process which shifts its strains and rewards. Undoubtedly we have learned from experience and continue to do so. Much of what we have learned is hopeful, easing the "task" component of our work and increasing its positive flow. But, some of what we have learned is frightening because it makes explicit our limitations and what may have to be done to overcome them, or if they need to be accepted and consequently respected in our practices.

The resurrection of insecurity is one of these kind of concerns. For example, recently a therapist we both know decided to work exclusively in private practice, despite some fears that there would be less economic security. We were discussing how we envisioned this therapist's situation and in so doing began to talk about our reactions to doing this ourselves. We both hold, and have always held or wanted to hold, other "regular" positions, meaning the pay in these situations is to be counted on as always arriving at a particular time and in a set amount, all of which affords the sense of security. Do we pursue this course primarily because these positions satisfy our interests, such as teaching and research, or because they provide a needed measure of security that we feel we will never have if we are exclusively in private practice? Most probably we operate as we do for both reasons, but our point here is that we notice that, despite all our years of practice as psychotherapists, we are still vulnerable to a variety of anxieties which require effort to ensure that they do not interfere with our performance as therapists.

We are not attempting perfection in the sense of aspiring to be able to treat anyone who has a problem and asks for our help as therapists. We are most skilled at a particular type of psychotherapy, broadly designated as psychodynamic, and we have a sense of the fact that within these parameters there is still a question of how appropriate the personal match is between ourselves and possible clients. While we do not believe it happens very often, it is nonetheless a reality that our personal concerns will prevent us from working with some people who may do well with other therapists having the same theoretical orientation as we do. In accepting this fact we believe we also mitigate competing with other therapists, or even with each other. We like to approach our practices with the idea that their success depends on our individual efforts, and we believe we are fairly adept in that regard. In particular we consider our existence as therapists a very serious undertaking which, while containing its share of humor and levity among other things, is never to be taken lightly. We believe we convey our sense of commitment to the therapy to our patients, and in accord with this they respond positively, to their benefit, and to ours.

Our successes and errors have their share of uniqueness and commonness. Thus, in one sense, neither of us is anybody special, yet in another, because we are ourselves, that is very special. We would like to feel that specialness more often. We believe it augurs well for us and for our patients. Sometimes it comes so easily, while at other times it is desperately elusive. Our aim is have it happen without feeling we had to make it happen.

In developing as psychotherapists we have pursued many of the customary and recommended routes. That is, we gained a professional identity through credentials, namely schooling and licensing in our professional disciplines with specialized training in psychotherapy, particularly psychoanalysis. We followed the usual paths of self-knowledge, namely personal therapy and supervision. We also did some unorthodox things as well, so that we did not progress just in linear fashion. In general we were and are impressed with formal learning, as far as it goes. Yet we also believe it generally has too impersonal a cast, including the more focused training. In our schooling the person of the therapist, ourselves, could have remained relatively invisible, and often did. We would change that, and when we are involved in doing teaching and training, we do. Our persons become visible, and we expect the same of our students. We want to know who the people are we train, and we want them to know us. This is not a plea for indiscriminate openness, but for greater freedom of discussion in exploration and training, particularly in regard to the issues discussed in this book.

As we come to the last lines we start agitating about issues we did not cover, and ones we mentioned but could have said more about, and we awaken in the night with the "just right" sentence which does not get written in the morning because we forgot it. The very procedure of writing this book is analogous to the process of working as a psychotherapist, with the blend of creativity and discipline, the compulsiveness, anxiety, and seemingly inescapable miscues, all so characteristic of the profession. These are the behaviors that got most therapists where they are, and keep them going. Finally, we cannot end without mentioning one more key ingredient of "good-enough therapizing." We believe therapists improve through living life fully. Specifics are available upon request, and the possibilities approach "better than good-enough therapy."

REFERENCES

Bergin, A. E. Behavior therapy and ethical relativism: Time for clarity. *Journal of Consulting and Clinical Psychology* (1980) **48:**11–13. (a)

Bergin, A. E. Negative effects revisited: A reply. *Professional Psychology* (1980) **11:**93–100. (b)

Bergin, A. E. Psychotherapy and religious values. *Journal of Consulting and Clinical Psychology* (1980) **48:**95–105. (c)

Bergin, A. E. Psychotherapy can be dangerous. *Psychology Today* (1975) **11:**96–103.

Bergin, A. E. Religious and humanistic values. *Journal of Consulting and Clinical Psychology* (1980) **48:**642–645. (d)

Beutler, L. Values, beliefs, religion and the persuasive influence of psychotherapy. *Psychotherapy: Theory, Research and Practice* (1979) **16:**432–440.

Burstein, A. G. Socialized psychotherapy. *Psychotherapy: Theory, Research and Practice* (1979) **16:**169–180.

Ellis, A. Psychotherapy and atheistic values: A response to A. E. Bergin's "Psychotherapy and religious values." *Journal of Consulting and Clinical Psychology* (1980) **48:**635–639.

Franks, C. M., and Mays, D. T. Negative effects revisited: A rejoinder. *Professional Psychology* (1980) **11:**101–105.

Freudenberger, H. J., and Robbins, A. The hazards of being a psychoanalyst. *The Psychoanalytic Review* (1979) **66:**275–296.

Heimann, P. H. Further observations on the analyst's cognitive process. *Journal of the American Psychoanalytic Association* (1977) **25:**313–333.

Houts, A. C., and Krasner, L. Slicing the ethical Gordian knot: A response to Kitchener. *Journal of Consulting and Clinical Psychology* (1980) **48:**8–10.

Jacobson, E. *The self and the object world* (New York: International Universities Press, 1964).

Karen, B. P., and VandenBos, G. R. Psychotherapeutic technique and the economically poor patient. *Psychotherapy: Theory, Research and Practice* (1977) **14:**169–180.

Kitchener, R. F. Ethical relativism and behavior therapy. *Journal of Consulting and Clinical Consulting and Clinical Psychology* (1980) **48:**14–16. (b)

Kitchener, R. F. Ethical skepticism and behavior therapy: A reply to Ward. *Journal of Consulting and Clinical Psychology* (1980) **48:**649–651. (c)

Lovinger, R. J. Therapeutic strategies with "religious" resistances. *Psychotherapy: Theory, Research and Practice* (1979) **14:**419–427.

Mays, D. T., and Franks, C. M. Getting worse: Psychotherapy or no treatment—The jury should still be out. *Professional Psychology* (1980) **11:**78–92.

Mijuskovic, B. Loneliness and narcissism. *The Psychoanalytic Review* (1979–80) **66:**479492.

Miller, N. E. Comments on strategy and tactics of research. In A. E. Bergin and H. H. Strupp (Eds.), *Changing frontiers in the science of psychotherapy* (Chicago: Aldine-Atherton, 1972).

Ragan, C. P., Malony, H. N., and Beit-Hallahmi, B. *Psychologists and religion: Professional factors related to personal religiosity.* Paper presented at the meeting of the American Psychological Association, Washington, D.C. (September, 1976).

Sherman, M. H. Role titles, vocations, and psychotherapy. *The Psychoanalytic Review* (1971-72) **58:**511–527.

Stearns, B. C., Penner, L. A., and Kimmel, E. Sexism among psychotherapists: A case not yet proven. *Journal of Consulting and Clinical Psychology* (1980) **48:**548–550.

Stern, E. M. Aching backs and silver linings. *VOICES* (1980) **16:**2–6.

Tramontana, M. G. Critical review of research on psychotherapy outcome with adolescents: 1967–1977. *Psychological Bulletin* (1980) **88:**429–450.

Walls, G. B. Values and psychotherapy: A comment on "Psychotherapy and religious values." *Journal of Consulting and Clinical Psychology* (1980) **48:**640–641.

Ward, L. C. Behavior therapy and ethics: A response to Kitchener. *Journal of Consulting and Clinical Psychology* (1980) **48:**646–648.

White, M. T. Self relations, object relations, and pathological narcissism. *The Psychoanalytic Review* (1980) **67:**4–24.

Will, O. A., Jr. Comments on the professional life of the psychotherapist. *Contemporary Psychoanalysis* (1979) **15:**560–576.

INDEX

C

G

H

I

T

U

V

W

Y

Z